W9-CLG-925

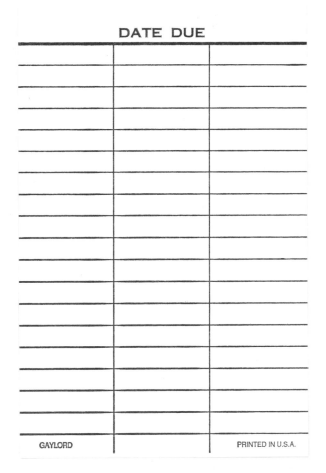

DATE DUE

GAYLORD

PRINTED IN U.S.A.

The University Edition of

SOCIAL
ORIGINS OF
EDUCATIONAL
SYSTEMS

Margaret S Archer

Theodore Lownik Library
Illinois Benedictine College
Lisle, Illinois 60532

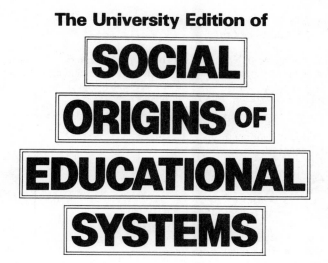

SAGE Publications
London   Beverly Hills   New Delhi

LC
191
.A6742
1984

Copyright © 1984 by
SAGE Publications Ltd

All rights reserved. No part of this book may be reproduced or utilized in any
form or by any means, electronic or mechanical, including photocopying,
recording, or by any information storage and retrieval system, without
permission in writing from the Publishers.

SAGE Publications Ltd
28 Banner Street
London EC1Y 8QE

SAGE Publications Inc
275 South Beverly Drive
Beverly Hills, California 90212

SAGE Publications India Pvt Ltd
C-236 Defence Colony
New Delhi 110 024

British Library Cataloguing in Publication Data
    Archer, Margaret Scotford
        Social origins of educational systems: university edition
        1. Educational sociology
        I. Title
        370.19   LC191

        ISBN 0-8039-9765-5
        ISBN 0-8039-9766-3 Pbk

Library of Congress Catalog Card Number 83-051281

First Printing

Printed in Great Britain by J. W. Arrowsmith Ltd, Bristol

CONTENTS

PART II
EDUCATIONAL SYSTEMS IN ACTION

PREFACE

In abridging the *Social Origins of Educational Systems* I have tried to produce a text which will be useful to students. Doubtless when this version appears, reduced from 800 to 200 pages, some critics will ask why it could not have been a quarter of its size in the first place. Had it been, others would have undoubtedly criticized it for containing undocumented generalizations, unsubstantiated arguments and unjustified theoretical assertions. And the latter would have been right. The original book was not an instance of the proverbial Chinese apology for sending a long letter because one did not have the time to write a short one. The present text is no substitute for the original, hence the constant back-references for theoretical explication and empirical expansion. It is a readers' digest, produced for students working under time limits. Some, it is hoped, may later explore the unabridged version. Even if they do not, this text will have succeeded if it convinces them that the Sociology of Education remains fundamentally incomplete unless it addresses the *educational system* itself.

Margaret S. Archer
Deddington
September 1983

1 INTRODUCTION: THINKING AND THEORIZING ABOUT EDUCATIONAL SYSTEMS

The questions dealt with in this book are macroscopic ones: how do state educational systems develop and how do they change? The nature of these questions means that our approach to them must be both historical and comparative. If sociology is to supplement the work of the educational historian and the comparative educationalist it must develop theories which span their findings. This is what the present study attempts to do — to account for the characteristics and contours of national educational systems and their subsequent processes of change.

Thus, the first question here is, why does education have the particular structure, relations to society and internal properties which characterize it at any given time? The basic answer to it is held to be very simple: education has the characteristics it does have because of the goals pursued by those who control it. The second question asks, why do these characteristics change? The basic answer given here is equally simple: change occurs because new goals are pursued by those who have the power to modify education's previous structural form, definition of instruction and relationship to society. As we shall see, these answers are of a deceptive simplicity. They are insisted upon now, at the beginning, because however complex our final formulations turn out to be, education is fundamentally about what people have wanted of it and have been able to do to it.

The real answers are more complicated but they supplement rather than contradict the above: the theories developed to account for the emergence of educational systems and their subsequent change are theories about the educational activities of people. This very basic point is underlined for two reasons. First, because although fundamental, much of the literature in fact contradicts it and embodies implicit beliefs in hidden hands, evolutionary mechanisms, infrastructural determinism, and spontaneous adjustments to social change. There, education is still seen metaphysically, as adapting to social requirements

1

and responding to the demands of society not of individuals. Secondly, and for the present purposes just as important, our theories will be *about* the educational activities of people, even though they will not explain educational development strictly in terms of people alone.

The basic answers are too simple because they beg more questions than they solve. To say that education derives its characteristic features from the aims of those who control it, immediately raises problems concerning the identification of controlling groups, the bases and processes upon which control rests, the methods and channels through which it is exerted, the extensiveness of control, the reactions of others to this control, and their educational consequences. Similarly, where change is concerned, it is not explained until an account has been given of why educational goals change, who does the changing, and how they impose the changes they seek. To confront these problems is to recognize that their solution depends upon analyzing complex forms of social interaction, for the nature of education is rarely, if ever, the practical realization of an ideal form of instruction as envisaged by a particular group. Instead, most of the time most of the forms that education takes are the political products of power struggles. They bear the marks of concession to allies and compromise with opponents. **Thus to understand the nature of education at any time we need to know not only who won the struggle for control, but also how: not merely who lost, but also how badly they lost out.**

Again, the basic answers are deceptively simple because they convey the impression that education and educational change can be explained by reference to group goals and balances of power alone. It is a false impression because there are other factors which constrain both the goal formation and the goal attainment of even the most powerful group — that is, the group most free to impose its definition of instruction and to mould the structure of education to its purposes. The point is that no group, even for that matter the whole of society acting in accord, has a blank sheet of paper on which to design national education. At the very least, it is restricted by certain universal logical constraints — concepts of education are of necessity limited by the contemporary state of knowledge and their implementation by the existing availability of skills and resources.

Realistically, educational action is also affected by a variable set of cultural and structural factors which make up its environment. Educational systems, rarities before the eighteenth century, emerged within complex social structures and cultures and this context conditioned the conception and conduct of action of those seeking educational development. Among other things, the social distribution of resources and values and the patterning of vested interests in the existing form of education were crucially important factors. Once a given form of education exists it exerts an influence on future educational change. Alternative educational plans are, to some extent, reactions to it (they represent the desire to change inputs, transform processes, or alter the end products); attempts to change it are affected by the degree to which it monopolizes educational skills and resources; and change means dismantling, transforming, or in some way grappling with it.

These considerations introduce important refinements to the basic answers and at the same time indicate the theoretical problems to be solved in answering the original questions properly. **A macro-sociology of education thus involves the examination of two things and the relations between them. On the one hand, complex kinds of social interaction the result of which is the emergence of particular forms of education, in this case the state system; on the other, complex types of social and educational structures which shape the context in which interaction and change occur.** The sociologist's task is thus to conceptualize and theorize about the relationship between these two elements. The aim is therefore to provide an explanation of how social interaction produced specific kinds of state educational systems in different countries and how, from within these contexts, subsequent interaction succeeded in introducing further change.

It is a complicated task because it involves separating the factors which impinge upon education from the wider social structure and network of social relationships in which it is embedded. This means that we have to differentiate continuously between those things in society which influence education and those which may be ignored because they do not seriously affect it at any given time. It also follows that the factors which are included are themselves treated as unproblematic — for instance, in incorporating the educational consequences of economic organization we do not try to explain the nature of the economy, but treat it as given. This procedure is unavoidable, for there is no such thing as an educational theory (which explains education by things educational), there are only sociological theories of educational development and change. Equally, there is no such thing as a unified sociological theory which can be applied to education, while simultaneously explaining the nature of and relationships between every other relevant element.

However, we are proposing to go about this task in a particular way and to develop a particular type of sociological theory to deal with the two major questions. It will be clear by now that both a pure action approach and a purely structural approach have been rejected in favour of a macro-sociological perspective which blends the two. Action theory is held to be incomplete because it has to take the social context of action for granted, and structural theories are considered equally inadequate if they make no reference to social interaction, but instead perpetuate an empty form of determinism. Nevertheless, rejection of these two types of theories does not involve abandoning all their core premises. Indeed, the notion that relations between education and other social institutions condition social interaction and in turn influence educational change is crucially important. But, equally essential to explaining the origins of educational systems and the processes of educational change is the independent contribution made by social interaction. In other words, it is argued that an adequate sociology of education must incorporate statements about the structural conditioning of educational interaction and about the influence of independent action on educational change. Weber's analysis, which gave equal emphasis to the limitations that social structures impose on interaction and to the opportunity for innovatory action presented by the instability of such structures, is the prototype of this theoretical approach.

The macro-sociological perspective[1]

Any development of this Weberian tradition means confronting the major problem of sociological theory, namely how to link structure and agency. The path followed here is the broad swathe cut by macro-sociology: an eclectic category embracing neo-marxists, general functionalists, systems theorists and proponents of exchange theory.[2] Their common denominator is the endorsement of methodological collectivism in contra-distinction to both holism and methodological individualism.[3] The generic method they employ for establishing the link between structure and agency can be divided into seven main stages.

(i) Connections between parts of the social structure are analyzed before proceeding to investigate inter-group relations — as opposed to the preliminary examination of the actors' perspectives and the subsequent study of social organization (the characteristic procedure of individualists, whatever their persuasion). This reflects the conviction that 'the properties of social structures and systems must be taken as given when analyzing the processes of action and interaction,[4] because of the conditional influence exerted by the former on the latter.

(ii) In analyzing the relationship between parts of society it is assumed that certain elements are more prone to change than others at any given time. It is where 'strains' develop in the social structure that the loci of potential change are pinpointed by macro-sociologists, though this mechanism is variously re-ferred to as 'functional incompatabilities' in the Mertonian tradition or as 'structural contradictions' in neo-marxism. Strains themselves are emergent or relational properties. They are the unintended consequences of two sets of institutional operations, developed to meet different goal requirements, then turning out to be non-complementary. This is neither to argue that change will occur there (for contradictions are only condi-tional influences) nor to exclude the possibility of its appearance elsewhere (for conditioning is not determinism). Moreover, to hold that 'strains' influence the locus of change does not involve reification because these emergent factors have no effect unless mediated through the activities of people.

(iii) However, a basic mediatory mechanism is posited through which harmonious or conflicting institutional relationships are transmitted to actors by shaping the situations in which they find themselves. It consists of structural relations of contra-diction or complementarity distributing frustrating or reward-ing experiences to the situations which actors have to confront because of the institutional positions they hold. Where contra-diction characterizes relations between social institutions, then strains are experienced as exigencies by groups associated with the impeded operations. In other words, operational obstructions translate into practical problems which frustrate those upon whose day-to-day activities they impinge.

On the other hand, where operational complementarity prevails, this is transmitted to the relevant action situations as a series of rewarding experiences. It means that for the actors involved, the tasks they undertake by virtue of their positions will (*ceteris paribus*) be easy to accomplish: the contexts in which they work will be problem-free. For example, the complementarity which characterized the operations of the reformed public schools and the reformed civil service in the latter half of the nineteenth century meant that those responsible for the recruitment of administrators were dealing with the 'right kind' of applicant from the 'right kind' of background and possessing the 'right kind' of skills.

(iv) In turn, it is argued that rewarding or frustrating experiences condition different action patterns; groups having experienced exigencies seeking to eradicate them (thus pursuing institutional change), those having experienced benefits seeking to retain them (thus defending institutional stability). The 'neutral' category, which has been left aside, specifies the likely non-participants in any struggle over the institutional relations in question. By this route, macro-sociologists view the points of strain within the social structure as representing the loci of demands for institutional change, whereas complementarity conditions maintenance pressures. Here the spectre of reification makes a brief reappearance. After all, it might be argued, frustration forces no one to do anything about it and rewards are not universally received with gratitude, yet is not the opposite assumed here? This is not the case as will be seen under point (v).

(v) Individuals' interpretations of their situations are important in macro-sociology: it is simply that there are things about these (disagreeable and rewarding) situations which encourage certain interpretations of them. Such 'predispositions' consist in the fact that opportunity costs are associated with different situational interpretations. These costs constitute the final link between the shaping of actors' situations and their subsequent action patterns. Groups opposing the source of rewarding experiences risk harming their own operations (damaging the operations through which their goals can be achieved); groups supporting the source of frustrating experiences invite further impediment to their own operations. There is, therefore, a structured distribution of costs and benefits for given interpretations. It is wholly objective. These force no one, they simply set a price on acting against one's self-declared interests and a premium on following them. Some groups will sometimes be willing to pay this price — to assert the existence of a conditional influence is not to deny this, it is only to assume that much of the time most groups will not tolerate too great a disparity between their values and their self-declared interests. (Sometimes groups may not be fully aware of the relations between the two — in which case they pay the price uncomprehendingly.) Overall, however, this predispositional influence accounts for the coincidence between observable trends in group support or opposition and the complementarity or contradiction prevailing between institutional operations. To posit this involves nothing more sinister than the Weberian assumption that there is a rough congruence between interests and values. (vi) However, structural conditioning and the predispositions it generates are only one side of the equation: the other is made up of independent influences upon action.[5] This recognition of the importance of action (uninfluenced by structural conditioning) is quite explicit in the analytical cycle employed by the macro-sociologists under discussion. Each of them distinguishes three broad analytic phases consisting of (a) a given structure (a complex set of relations between parts), which conditions but does *not* determine (b), social interaction. Here, (b) also arises in part from action orientations unconditioned by social organization, and in turn leads to (c), structural elaboration or modification — that is, to a change in the relations between parts. The cycle is then repeated.[6] Transition from state (a) to (c) is not direct, precisely because structural conditioning is not the sole determinant of interaction patterns. Only holism conceptualizes a movement straight from (a) to (c), without mediation.

What methodological individualists claim is that action alone, (b), constitutes the necessary and sufficient conditions for the explanation of (c). To them (a) can be eradicated. Macro-sociologists do not deny that social interaction is the ultimate source of complex phenomena (which include both unintended and emergent consequences): they simply maintain that because at present we are unable to unravel this causal chain, we must acknowledge that we cannot deduce the latter from the former and thus must consider individual actions to be necessary but not sufficient conditions. Therefore, to account for the occurrence of structural change (c), interactional analysis (b), is essential, but inadequate unless undertaken in conjunction with (a), the study of structural conditioning.

(vii) To work in terms of three-part cycles composed of (a) Structural Conditioning, (b) Social Interaction and (c) Structural Elaboration is to accord *time* a central place in sociological theory.[7] Time is incorporated as a theoretical variable rather than simply as a medium in which events take place. For the occurrence of events, like the progressive structuring of an educational system, necessitates our theorizing about the temporal relations between structure and action. What is crucial is that the macro-sociological perspective maintains that structure and action operate over different time periods — an assertion which is based on two simple propositions: that structure logically predates the action(s) which transform it; and that structural elaboration logically post-dates those actions. These temporal interrelationships are represented in Figure 1.

FIGURE 1
Temporal phases of the morphogenetic cycle

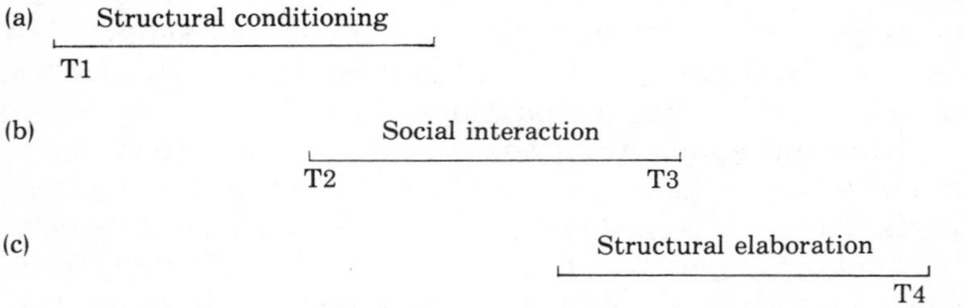

(a)   Structural conditioning
     └─────────────────────────────┘
         T1

(b)   Social interaction
              └─────────────────────────────┘
              T2   T3

(c)   Structural elaboration
                          └─────────────────────────────┘
                                                      T4

First, as far as (a), structural conditioning, is concerned, it is argued that the initial structural distribution of a property at T1 (i.e., the aggregate consequence of prior interaction) influences the time taken to eradicate it, for all structures manifest temporal resistance and do so generically through conditioning the context of action. Most often their conditional influence consists in dividing the population (not necessarily exhaustively) into social groups working for the maintenance versus the change of a given property, because the property itself (e.g., distribution of wealth, enfranchisement, educational control) distributes different objective vested interests to them at T2. In other words, it takes time to change *any* structural property and, no matter how short, that period represents one of constraint for some groups, notably those whose goals lead them to attempt to change it.

Secondly, (b) social interaction, when initiated at T2, then takes place in a context which is not of its own making. Here it appears impossible to follow the methodological individualist[8] and assert that any structural property influential *after* T2 is attributable to contemporary actors (not wanting or not knowing how to change it), because knowledge about it, attitudes towards it, vested interests in retaining it and objective capacities for changing it have already been distributed and determined by T2. On the other hand, between T2 and T3 human agency exerts two independent influences, one temporal, the other directional. It can speed up, delay or prevent the elimination of prior structural influences and also agents can affect the nature and substance of elaboration at T4. (Voluntarism has an important place in this perspective but it is ever trammelled by past structural and cultural constraints and by the current politics of the possible.)

Finally, if action is effective then the transformation produced at T4 is not merely the eradication of a prior structural property and its replacement by a new one, it is (c), the structural elaboration, of a host of new social possibilities. Some of these will have gradually come into play between T2 and T4 and this form of analysis can thus explain the timing of the new structures which emerge. Simultaneously, however, structural elaboration re-starts a new cycle, for it introduces a new set of conditional influences upon interaction which are constraining as well as facilitating. T4 is thus the new T1, and the next cycle must be approached afresh analytically, conceptually and theoretically.

Although in fact all three lines in Figure 1 are continuous, the analytical element consists in breaking up the flows into intervals determined by the problems in hand: given any problem and accompanying periodization, the projection of the three lines backwards and forwards would connect up with the anterior and posterior cycles. This represents the bedrock of an understanding of systemic properties, of *structuring* over time, which enables explanations of specific forms of structural elaboration to be advanced.

FIGURE 2
Summary diagram

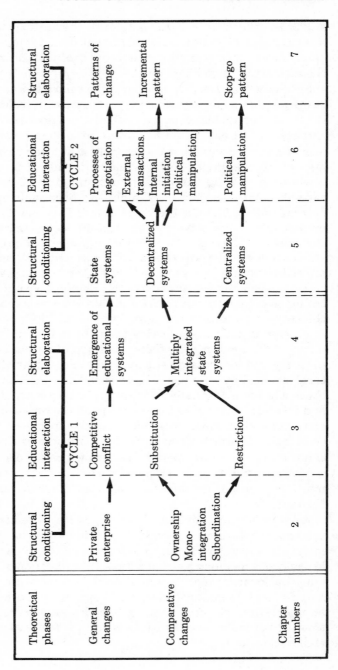

Macro-sociology and educational systems

The organization of this study takes its shape from the theoretical approach adopted. Thus, the book is divided into two parts which deal with two consecutive sequences, two contiguous cycles in the history of educational change. Each part covers the three phases of the (a), (b), (c) sequence just outlined: structural conditioning, social interaction, structural elaboration. Hence, unlike general or unified sociological theory, this type of explanation relates to specific structures and is not atemporal. As the nature of the subject-matter — the structure of education — changes over time, so too must the theoretical framework which deals with it. In the comparative analysis which follows, it is not simple chronology which enforces shifts in the constitution of explanatory statements: it is new forms of educational development which require new kinds of explanations and these may occur at different dates in different countries.

The two parts of the book deal with different stages in the structuring of education. Part I is devoted to the emergence of state educational systems in England and France. Part II is concerned with their influence upon subsequent educational interaction and change. This division between the two parts reflects our conviction that the emergence of state systems represented a crucial break, because of the change in structural relations between education and other social institutions which accompanied it. **The development of state education spelled its connection to the political centre and to a plurality of other institutions in terms of the services it provided.** These two changes are universal (they characterize educational systems which may be strikingly different in other respects), and, it is argued, they profoundly affect the subsequent social processes which produce stability and change in education. Such processes become quite different from the types of interaction which brought about the key break and led to the emergence of state systems in the first place.

However, it should be noted that to accentuate this break in no way necessitates a belief that educational institutions are converging, either during or after the emergence of state systems. The importance of this break, for analytical purposes, lies in the changed processes involved, in their outcomes (whose convergence or divergence will depend *inter alia* on differences in the systems established and in other parts of the respective social structures, which may themselves be either convergent or divergent).

The two parts are continuous since they represent two analytical cycles of (a) structural conditioning, (b) social inter-action, and (c) structural elaboration. (Cycles are analytic in the sense that the historical sequence is in fact continuous.) In Part I, the complex forms of group interaction, partly condi-tioned by the fact that education is owned and monopolized by a restricted section of the population, are analyzed and their unintended consequences — the emergence of state educational systems — are examined. Part II opens with the elaborated structures, these new systems of education, which now repre-sent the new conditional influences upon interaction. Modern educational change is thus interpreted as the joint consequence of such effects in conjunction with other and independent sources of social interaction.

Of course, there are historical cycles which preceded the one leading to the emergence of state systems, which constitutes our starting point. In other words, we open up with the results of *prior* interaction. Here, for the purposes of analysis, such phenomena have been treated as elemental — that is, no attempt is made to account for how the structure we take as our starting point has developed from previous interaction between groups and individuals in the context of antecedent structures even further back in history. The decision to do this was governed by the need to avoid ultimate regress to histori-cally distant and sociologically complex inter-relationships. Quite simply, one has to break into the historical sequence at some point. Thus, we start by examining that cycle which is considered to have most bearing on the phenomenon that we seek to explain, but accept that its own origins figure as elements of 'givenness' in our theories.[9]

However, this means that the theory presented here is tied to the contextual features of that cycle (which it does not itself explain) and it *must not* be detached from them in any unwarranted attempt to increase the historical scope of explana-tion. There are two key properties of the cycle immediately preceding the interaction which generated state educational systems and our theorizing is therefore predicated on the existence of both. On the one hand, it assumes the presence of a differentiated institutional order at the systemic level (to which different groups were associated), and on the other hand, an analagous situation at the level of social integration[10] — the relative autonomy of differentiated interest groups. This means that the theory advanced here is not applicable to earlier social formations, such as historic empires or the ancient Eastern civilizations, which displayed relatively low levels of institutional differentiation (monolithic social structures) and of social autonomy (elite superimposition and mass subordination).[11]

A final decision remains, namely about the most appropriate phase with which to begin each cycle. Here we have started with 'structure'. Part I opens with that structure which conditioned educational interaction immediately prior to the development of state systems, namely one where educational ownership was the basis of educational control. For there is obviously a need, in any study devoted to change, to describe the entity and relationships which undergo modification. Chapter 3 then moves on to examine the specific form of interaction which was conditioned by this state of affairs and which in turn became responsible for the introduction of large-scale change in education — that is, the process of competitive conflict. In Chapter 4, the emergence of state systems is then derived directly from this process of interaction: whether the new systems were centralized or decentralized in structure is held to result from the precise form taken by competitive conflict. This then completes the first cycle.

The start of the next cycle begins in Chapter 5 which discusses the ways in which these new state systems now condition subsequent interaction in a different way — leading to a universal transition from competitive conflict to negotiated change as the principal process of interaction. Chapters 6 and 7 then concentrate on variations on this type of interaction as engendered by centralized and decentralized systems respectively. Chapter 8 deals with the last phase of the modern cycle, where the new processes of interaction are linked to distinctive patterns of change in the two kinds of system. Once this has been accomplished it completes discussion of the second cycle and constitutes the end of the present study; but in reality, of course, it only signals the beginning of further changes and an indefinite number of succeeding cycles.

Figure 2 provides a summary diagram of the theoretical, comparative and historical ground covered throughout the book.

Caveats, case studies and challenges

It is important to be clear from the start about the scope of
the explanation which follows. This study attempts to delineate
the conditions necessary for the emergence of state educational
systems. But it seeks to account for the autonomous emergence
of this macroscopic change as the result of group interaction
in countries where it cannot be attributed to external intervention, via conquest, colonization or territorial redistribution.
This is not to argue that foreign influence, example or
experience were unimportant, only that national education
developed in response to internal pressures not external imposition. Foreign influence has to be assimilated by and mediated
through national groups, but foreign intervention imposes a
given form of education (like the extension of the Napoleonic
system to other countries by military means and the experience
undergone in most colonial territories). Obviously, this concern
with the autonomous development of educational systems
reduces the applicability of the theory to a particular group of
countries and probably even to a minority of cases when world
educational development is considered. Nevertheless, a theory
which limits itself to endogenous processes of educational
change is important, both in its own right, and also because
it helps to account for the nature of instruction imposed abroad.
The origins of the particular system which is exported must
first be understood in order to account for educational change
in conquered or colonized countries. In itself, our kind of theory
will not fully account for educational development in such countries, but it is indispensable to a full account. The additional
problems surrounding retention, rejection or adaptation of externally imposed educational systems warrant a study in their
own right, but cannot be entered into here.

England and France are used as our case studies throughout
the book, partly because they are both countries whose educational systems emerged autonomously and partly because of
two major differences between them. On the one hand, it
is generally agreed that their present systems of education
are very different and that they have undergone dissimilar
forms of historical development. On the other hand, even
more indubitable is the diversity of their political, economic and cultural histories. Thus, the range of variation which
the theory confronts is deliberately maximized. [12]

Perhaps it is worth anticipating the objection that this task is wrongly conceived, because it does not compare like with like in either social or educational terms. For instance, it might be argued that some of the factors which are known to be important in educational change (e.g., mode or level of economic production, nature of social stratification, or type of political organization) differ greatly in the two countries to be examined. Because such factors are not controlled (they are not present or absent, or the same for both), the social contexts themselves are very different. It might then be objected that any educational changes observed later on simply reflect these initial variations. Such an argument would be unanswerable were the problem in hand the examination, for example, of economic influences upon educational development. It is not; on the contrary, the aim is precisely to see whether general sociological propositions about educational change can be advanced in the presence of such variations. The existence of socio-economic differences cannot therefore be used as a basis from which to prejudge the outcome of this theoretical undertaking. If it is possible to develop general theories about education, then they must be ones which embrace cross-cultural differences. There appear to be no grounds in the history of science for deciding in advance that particular phenomena are so intractable as to defy explanation.

PART I
THE
DEVELOPMENT OF
STATE EDUCATIONAL
SYSTEMS

2 STRUCTURE: EDUCATION AS PRIVATE ENTERPRISE

An explanation of the emergence of state educational systems involves the history of education, but not of its entire span, and it entails comparative education, but not an encyclopaedic coverage. The problem is large, but none the less delimited. If what is to be explained is this fundamental structural change in education, then although it was predated by a long sequence of developments, only one of these is of prime concern here, namely that type of formal education which gave way in each country to the state system.

Since the term 'educational system' has generally been used indiscriminately, referring to anything from primitive initiation rites onwards, to define it clearly serves three distinct purposes: identifying what is to be explained, dating when each nation acquired a system, and locating the time from which analysis must back-track in search of explanation. This sociological task, therefore, is not one of comparing like with like in substantive terms (the socio-economic differences between England and France, when each generated an educational system, were monumental). Nor is it one whose historical concern is with the same chronological period (almost a century separates the emergence of their respective systems). On the contrary, the aim is precisely to discover whether general sociological propositions about formal educational change can be advanced in the presence of such circumstantial variations.

The definition adopted is one which follows the everyday meanings of the words 'state educational system', and it should be stressed that very dissimilar types of education can conform to it. Hence **a state educational system** is considered to be **a nation-wide and differentiated collection of institutions devoted to formal education, whose overall control and supervision is at least partly governmental, and whose component parts and processes are related to one another.** Both the political and the systemic aspects are stressed in this definition which insists that they must be present together before education can be deemed to constitute a state system, for the appearance of either characteristic alone is not uncommon. Many European courts controlled elitist or military academies without having any further involvement in the education of the nation: many European churches ran integrated networks, leading from catechization to ordination, quite independently of the political centre.

Having defined a state system helps to distinguish it from earlier forms of education but it does not fully identify the type of instruction which gave way to it. The problem is that the struggle for reform which ultimately generated state systems also lasted for varying periods of time in different countries, and during this time education often underwent gradual transformation. Hence, we cannot simply examine the form it took immediately preceding, or some fixed number of years before, the date at which the state system was consolidated. However, the origins of these struggles themselves provide a guide to those prior forms of education which eventually gave way to state systems. Thus the struggles of historical actors indicate what to examine (that which they sought to change) and when to investigate it (immediately before they began pursuing educational change).

For explanatory purposes it is necessary, therefore, to back-track to the antecedent educational and socio-cultural contexts within which interaction for change first developed. Without this it is impossible to account for the interaction itself or for its consequences — since the very situations that people were trying to change would thus be omitted. Obviously, these contexts must be investigated independently, for the sociological task is not just to record how they were viewed by contemporary actors. It is also to conceptualize how this broader context structured the actual situation in which each group found itself vis-à-vis education, how it helped them to view it in a particular way, and led them to seek its change. The actors themselves, of course, may have been unaware of all the factors which moulded the situations in which they found themselves and of how these shaped their own action patterns.

The prior forms of education identified in this manner may be quite dissimilar. Nevertheless, these substantive differences, however great, do not preclude the existence of formal similarities between them: and it is possible to theorize about the latter despite variations in the former. Thus it is formal similarities (in the relations between education and the social structure) which figure in the propositions put forward about common influences upon interaction patterns. Substantive variations are not dismissed as without influence upon action, it is merely that their effects co-exist with patterns conditioned by shared structural factors.

In the two countries examined, one common feature characterized the form of education preceding the development of state systems — a feature also found in such disparate cases as Romanov Russia, Pietist Denmark and Tokugawa Japan. In all of them, **those who controlled education also owned it, in the sense of providing its physical facilities and supplying its teaching personnel.** Education was private enterprise, and control derived directly from ownership. In turn, ownership was concentrated in a very restricted part of any population, but this educationally dominant group also came from different sections of different societies. Each had a virtual monopoly of the educational resources upon which its control rested and all were concerned to protect their position of domination in instruction.

It is beyond the scope of the present study to explain why education was owned by the various churches throughout Europe, prior to the emergence of state systems. The ideational pre-eminence of the religious institution in the neo-medieval period provides no straightforward answer, since in Japan it was the feudal political elite which occupied the position of domination. Equally, the question of why religious domination proved so enduring in Europe falls outside our purview since answers to both questions would require a detailed analysis of institutional activities and elite goals during earlier centuries and prior cycles of change. The fact of religious ownership has to be taken as given in these two cases, for it is not this itself but rather the consequences of education as private (religious) enterprise for subsequent educational change which are of concern.

Private ownership, mono-integration and subordination

Whenever **educational control was rooted in private ownership this resulted in the same generic relationship between education and the rest of society. The fact that one particular group** virtually monopolized formal instruction meant that education was firmly linked only to a single part of the total social structure, namely that institution with which the dominant group was associated (in whose role structure they held positions as ordained clergymen or priests, with whose operations they were occupied, and whose goals they sought to attain). The link consisted of the flow of physical, human and financial resources from the ownership sphere to education and the counter-flow of educational services, appropriate to the dominating sector. Where churches constituted the ownership groups, these services consisted in religious socialization and a supply of ecclesiastical recruits. Such interdependence between two social institutions does not imply that it was equally advantageous to both, nor that their 'interchange' was freely determined, nor that it contributed to the persistence of the two parts concerned or that of the wider social system.

The term 'mono-integration' will be used to denote this common structural characteristic. It thus refers to one of the possible relationships which could be maintained between education and all other parts of society at a particular stage of institutional differentiation. Logically, education could be interdependent with all others, with some, or with none at all: mono-integration is used when it is related to only one. It is not, therefore, a property of any institution as such but of relations *between* institutions: it constitutes an emergent property which conditions subsequent processes of educational interaction and change. For when education is mono-integrated, two major implications follow — one for education itself and the other for the rest of society (with the exception of the lone institution to which it is linked through ownership).

(a) Effects on education

Interdependence between two social institutions is a relationship based on interchange. The biography of these exchanges is also the history of emerging power differentials between these institutional sectors, unless their mutual transactions remain reciprocal.[1] As Blau has argued, one party may be or become the subordinate of the other because of its dependence on it for the supply of resources or services.[2] When A receives resources from B, this represents some loss of autonomy for A, unless it is capable of full reciprocation — such being the price A 'pays' for continued supplies from B. The more dependent A is on the supplies B provides, the greater the services A has to render to B in order to secure them, and the bigger the loss of A's autonomy to determine the nature of its internal activities and to pursue the goals arrived at in that sphere. Instead, A's institutional operations are defined externally by the party which constrains its services.

The sub-category of integrative relationships where these severe imbalances do occur will be termed 'subordination'. It is defined as the case in which **one social institution has low autonomy for the internal determination of its operations because of its dependence on the other.** Again, it should be noted that subordination is a property of the relations between institutions and not a characteristic of any one part of society. What is significant here, however, is that **as a mono-integrated institution, education was always the subordinate partner** in the relationship because of its total dependence on the flow of resources from the other institution. Education has high material and physical resource requirements for its operations and these make it vulnerable to the source of supply, which is unitary where education is mono-integrated. Historically, there appears to be a built-in, short-run asymmetry between the dependence of educational operations on resources and the reliance of those supplying them on educational services. Quite simply, the operations of another institution can do without new educational outputs longer than education can function without resources. This fundamental source of imbalance in the relationship between education and its suppliers was translated into differences in power and reflected in lack of educational autonomy. Thus, had those working within the educational field attempted to take any initiative (such as the autonomous redefinition of intakes, processes or outputs), they could swiftly have been checked by withdrawal of pay, closure of buildings or their own redeployment, as well as by a multiplicity of less tangible religious sanctions. Hence, it is not simply that the dominant group's ownership of educational resources gave them control over instruction, but that the dependence of education precluded it from ever threatening this non-reciprocal relationship, in the absence of alternative suppliers of resources.

The most important consequence to result from the subordinate status of education in the periods considered is that **educational change could not be initiated endogenously.** In other words, the activities of teachers, pupils, academics and others engaged in instruction could not be an important source of educational innovation and change because of their stringent control by the dominant group. This is not to imply a lack of desire for change on the part of such groups — it is not necessary to assume this when arguing that constraints existed to prevent the realization of any such aims.

Change could not be initiated endogenously because **subordination never involves lower autonomy than when it occurs in a relationship of mono-integration.** Dependence on a single supplier of resources makes education extremely vulnerable and highly responsive to control by the ownership group. The latter, which invests in instruction only because it requires some particular kind of educational output which it perceives as essential to its (religious, political, etc.) operations, does all it can to get value for its money. The dominant group defines education in relation to its goals and monitors it closely to ensure that it serves these purposes. Close control means weak boundaries between education and the institution with which the dominant group is associated. It is reflected in a low level of differentiation between the two institutions.

Typically, this means that there is no distinctively educational role structure, but instead an overlapping of roles between both institutions. Those working in the educational field in no sense constituted a relatively autonomous professional body but instead could be manipulated by external sanctions, depending on the nature of the ownership group. Typically, too, there were no distinctively educational processes, for the content of instruction, the definition and the management of knowledge, as well as teaching methods, were conflated with the values and norms of the dominant group. Hence the inter-related 'Bun and Bu', the military and literary skills of Tokugawa Japan; hence the equation between theology and knowledge in much of Europe, and the use of catechization and disputation as methods of teaching and learning. Correspondingly, educated persons acquired a set of skills the limited relevance of which encouraged their employment in the dominant group's institutional sphere.

Taken together, these consequences of subordination and mono-integration — extremely low educational autonomy and little internal definition of goals — have further implications for the explanation of educational change. They mean that such explanations will focus on social interaction outside the educational field and among groups of actors who are not employed or engaged in it. Unlike the present day, when any explanation of change would be incomplete if it neglected the independent contribution of professional groups of teachers and organized groups of students, large-scale educational transformation in this earlier period can be examined in terms of exogenous influences without loss of explanatory power.

(b) Effects on other social institutions
The consequences of mono-integration and subordination for other social institutions mean that all save one are not directly served by education. Nevertheless, this does not imply that the remaining institutional spheres find themselves in an identical situation vis-à-vis the education available. Instead, the nature of their own institutional operations mediates the impact of education upon them (as defined by the dominant group) and determines their degree of compatibility with it. Potentially, there are three major categories into which other institutions can fall in these respects, although each one need not be represented wherever and whenever education is found in a mono-integrated and subordinate relationship.

(i) Neutral institutions
First, then, there may be some institutional spheres which although not directly served by education are unimpeded by it. This is not to say that they would not have been more efficient, better adjusted, etc., were available educational outputs of relevance to them. It is simply that the existence of structurally induced strains or impediments is dependent upon the *actual* obstruction of operations, not ideal operative efficiency. Such an institution is neither helped nor hindered by the form of education that the dominant group provides. For example, it neither receives pre-trained, pre-socialized graduates nor does it miss them and find itself confronting a recruitment crisis in terms of lack of suitable people with appropriate skills and values.

Of course, it is not possible to determine analytically which social institutions are most likely to be represented in this neutral category. This varies with the nature of the given institution at any time, and the compatibility of education (as designed by the dominant group) with its operations. Basically, this is how neutrality is identified — by comparing the objective goodness of fit between educational outputs and institutional operations in a particular period. (Only occasionally does one find supplementary evidence, like the townsmen and artisans of eighteenth-century Russia petitioning the tsar for a reprieve from scholarization because book learning was irrelevant to their activities: their only objection to the prevailing form of education was that they were forced to undergo it.)[3] Nor is it possible to specify how large this category is cross-culturally, although it will be seen later that it shrinks over time. All that is being stressed at the moment is the *logical* possibility of educational neutrality towards a particular sphere.

The functionalist argument, that mutual normative support between social institutions is the prerequisite of societal integration, becomes a matter for empirical determination here. Cases in which such normative support is demonstrably present can be assimilated to the second category, outlined below, and cases where normative undermining clearly does occur (if, for instance, instruction disseminated egalitarianism while stratification was on hierarchical principles) then belong in category (iii).

In other words, the structural relations between these institutions and education are neither ones of strain nor of complementarity. Because of this, there are no structural factors which predispose these sectors to be loci of support for or of opposition to the prevailing form of education. This, however, clearly does not prevent actors associated with these institutions from participating in educational conflict, either in pursuit of change or in defence of the status quo. It is simply to argue that such interaction on their part is not structurally conditioned by the relationships discussed, which are ones of neutrality.

(ii) Adventitious beneficiaries

The second category of institutions consists of those which derive adventitious benefits from existing education. They do so exclusively because their own operations happen to be facilitated by the educational outputs offered, but determined elsewhere. Again it is impossible to decide analytically which sectors of society will fall into this category — for the receipt of adventitious benefits usually depends upon an accidental compatibility between the definition of instruction and operational requirements, because no interchange has taken place to ensure that educational services are forthcoming. For example, legal systems based upon Roman law were quite well served by the classical education, conducted by the more important Catholic teaching orders in Europe.

Sometimes, though not necessarily, this coincidence is explained by interdependencies between the adventitious beneficiary (C) and the institution (B) with which education (A) is integrated, particularly if there are imbalances of exchange in favour of C in relation to B. Then C may negotiate with B for a certain type of educational service from A. Thus, for example, in eighteenth-century England, the erastian political elite (C), upon which the established church (B) was legally dependent, meant that the latter defined educational inputs, processes and outputs to provide some political services (socialization, legitimation and recruitment to the governmental bureaucracy).

Institutions in this category will tend to be loci of 'support' for the prevailing form of education and hence for its controllers. They will be areas from which support is forthcoming because they gain something desirable for nothing and seek to maintain the situation which gives them this 'bonus'. Again this is only a conditional influence and in any case such pressures are tenuous as complementarity can be reduced over time: since compatibility is generally fortuitous, this goodness of fit between the activities of two institutions can slip if either of their operations undergoes independent change. If this process occurs, there will be a tendency for the institution involved to move out of the category of adventitious beneficiaries — either to become neutral or to enter the third category.

(iii) Obstructed institutions
This third category consists of those institutions which are neither integrated with education nor served by it, but whose operations are clearly obstructed by educational outputs because they are incompatible with them. The precise nature of the obstruction can vary. It may be that those associated with a given institution require instruction but for some reason are denied access, that the values and skills disseminated are

irrelevant or harmful to their activities, or that the graduates who are produced are deficient in either quantitative or qualitative terms. Sometimes an institutional sphere will be impeded in several different ways simultaneously, as was the case with the expanding industrial economy in early nineteenth-century England. The entrepreneurial elite had limited access to secondary and higher education due to social and religious discrimination, the Test Acts erecting a barrier to graduation; the classical nature of secondary instruction was irrelevant to capitalist development while the catechistic nature of popular elementary instruction was an inadequate form of economic socialization for workers which did not teach sufficient respect for private property.[4] In sum, those leaving elementary school did not have the right values, those leaving secondary school did not have the right skills and those leaving higher education had neither the right skills nor the right values.

There is no reason, of course, why there should be only a single institution in this category (or either of the preceding ones) at any given time. Indeed, historically it seems more common to find several different spheres simultaneously suffering from obstructions of varying degrees of severity. However, their members need not be allies but can have interests in complete opposition to one another as will be seen in the cases of both England and France. Also, different institutions are found occupying this category in different countries. In England, for example, it was the developing industrial economy and associated system of class stratification; in France the post-revolutionary polity and governmental bureaucracy. What these social institutions have in common is a structured predisposition to be loci of opposition to the respective forms of education available in those societies. However, before examining supportive and oppositional activities stemming from these different loci it is first necessary to examine the influence that mono-integration and subordination exert upon processes of educational change.

(c) Effects on processes of educational change
It is here that the subordinate status of education reveals its significance. In particular, it means that those in category (iii) who seek radical educational change, in proportion to the impediments they experience from current instruction, cannot

negotiate directly with the profession. Extremely low professional autonomy precludes any endogenous modifications to offset strains between education and the social structure. Thus, the effect of subordination for those seeking change is that **instead of direct transactions taking place with education, these have to be conducted indirectly with the party which has subordinated it. Not only is the ownership group the real source of obstruction because it has moulded education to serve its operations alone, but only by interacting with it can the definition of instruction be altered, for the educational sphere is only responsive to its subordinator — in the context of monointegration.**

Moreover, these structural relations strongly influence the process responsible for large-scale educational transformation during this phase: in essence they discourage voluntary negotiation and instead condition a process of competitive conflict. There are three considerations which lead up to this proposition. To begin with, because ownership and control are exclusive to it, the dominant ownership group defines instruction to suit its own ends. Whatever impediments the relevant inputs, processes, and outputs constitute for other sections of society, they represent the form and content of education that its owners want. (This is not tantamount to saying that such education optimally meets their requirements; only that they *think* it serves them best.) If this is a serious impediment to others, it means that other groups require a very different kind of instruction. In other words those suffering the greatest obstruction therefore need the greatest changes in education in order to remove them.

Next, the magnitude of the changes required to relieve existing strains precludes their resolution by certain processes. Since the ownership group already has exactly the kind of education it considers indispensable, any radical shift in the definition of instruction would be contrary to its declared interests. That these interests are both conscious and extremely strong cannot be doubted, considering the resources that have voluntarily been laid out to meet them. Thus, major educational change would represent an equally major shift away from its ideal — a move which if fully accomplished would place the ownership group itself in category (iii)! Change of this magnitude is therefore the last thing that will be freely conceded; but if it does not occur, severe obstruction continues for other institutions. The net result is that those concerned to introduce the most far-reaching educational changes are least able to do so by peaceful negotiation with the controlling ownership group.

Hence, negotiation is the preserve of those who do not require anything very different from education. Since transactions must be conducted with the ownership group in control, the latter will cease trading at the point where the benefits it receives would be bought at the price of damaging itself educationally. If the modifications in instruction which can be transacted before this point is reached are considered satisfactory, then small changes are clearly all that was wanted anyway. Thus, mutual compatibility between the educational requirements of the dominant group and those who can deal with it, sets stringent limits on the amount of change that can result from such a process. If greater modifications are sought, negotiation breaks down and the other party must seek change through a different process — and one which is not based on the assumption of continuity in control.

Finally, then, when negotiation is precluded, strains are only resolved by one party overcoming the other and thus removing the source of obstruction, which otherwise continues with all its negative consequences. Thus, large-scale change only occurs if the existing structural relations are destroyed and replaced by new ones. Any major changes in the form and content of instruction observed during this period are therefore expected to follow from equally fundamental changes in educational control — through the dominant ownership group being damaged or destroyed. For inputs, processes and outputs will only be modified to service the operations of other institutional spheres when the old relationships have been dismantled — via competitive conflict not peaceful negotiation.

(d) Structural relations
conditioning educational interaction

Since it is an underlying assumption of this study that structural influences only exert their effects through people, a complete discussion of the importance attaching to mono-integration and subordination involves an examination of how such factors condition interaction. First, the fact that education is a mono-integrated institution creates a distinction between the ownership group and all others. Its implication is that there is only one group in society which is *assured* of educational services, whereas all the rest are not. Since, as has been seen, this situation does not mean that no other groups actually receive such services, this distinction is based on differential capacity to control and not upon differential rates of benefit. The existence of mono-integration thus dichotomizes the population vis-à-vis education.

In conjunction with subordination it structures two quasi-groups in society. On the one hand there is a single educationally dominant group, consisting of all those associated with the ownership sphere, who collectively possess the capacity to determine the nature of educational outputs. Since this domination is based on the supply of resources to education, then their abundance, availability and distribution in society provide a key to the security of the ownership group's control over education. Maximum security coincides with monopolization of such resources, although this does not guarantee it since coercion can be brought to bear by dominated groups.

On the other hand, there remains the aggregate of all others who lack control because they are without property in educational terms. Obviously, however, some of these educationally dominated groups will themselves be dominant in other parts of society, because the ownership group only embraces the elite of one particular institution. Perhaps less obviously, some of the educationally dominated may constitute the overall socio-political elite, for during this period there is no theoretical or empirical reason whatsoever to suppose that the educational ownership group occupies or shares this position. In other words, it is unlikely that the dichotomy between educationally dominant and dominated corresponds to the more general social division between elites and masses.

However, there are powerful reasons which make it extremely unlikely that the two quasi-groups, defined by possession or lack of educational control, will 'convert' into opposing interest groups. That only one group has the capacity to control educational processes does not necessarily entail opposition between it and the rest of society. For this would be to assume that all groups at all times have an interest in, and see advantages deriving from, the control of education — and historically this has simply not been the case. Yet it would appear mistaken to assume that the relationships which develop between members of the two quasi-groups simply vary unsystematically with empirical conditions. It was shown earlier that the relation between the kind of education supplied in a society and the type of operations conducted in different institutional spheres led to variations in the objective fit between them — thus producing strains as well as complementarities. It is suggested that these are directly associated with systematic variations in patterns of interaction. However, such objective relationships only exert an influence on interaction because of the ways in which they structure action situations for different groups.

Incompatibilities and complementarities are transmitted to different social roles in different parts of the social structure. For those occupying such positions they will be experienced as frustrating or rewarding situations. Although rewards do not compel support nor does frustration dictate antagonism to its source (for structural factors do not force anyone to do anything), they do render certain actions and interpretations distinctly advantageous, and others correspondingly disadvantageous. This is because of a structured distribution of different opportunity costs and benefits for different courses of action to those having different objective relations with education.

(i) In the 'neutral' category are those whose activities are neither impeded nor reinforced by the existing definition of instruction. Thus, the groups associated with them are not structurally predisposed either to support or to oppose the dominant educational group — since the roles they occupy and the tasks they have to accomplish in them are unaffected by the prevailing form of education. If such influences were deterministic and if all institutions fell into this category, then the educationally dominant group would remain totally unopposed (and unsupported, too), as groups associated with other spheres would remain educationally inactive. However, their members may none the less engage in educational action, but if they do so it will be for reasons independent of educational conditioning. It is groups associated with institutions in the other two categories which are expected to play the most important part in educational interaction.

(ii) Where institutions derive adventitious benefits from education, structural influences predispose groups associated with them to support the prevailing type of education and thus to buttress the position of those dominating it. Actors engaged in different aspects of institutional operations receive a variety of rewards. Although the nature of these may vary considerably (from diffuse legitimation to direct instrumentality) most adventitious beneficiaries will, for instance, find the tasks of recruitment and replacement to be problem-free. Recruitment is facilitated by the availability of suitable candidates with appropriate values and training is shortened by the prior acquisition of relevant skills.

Nevertheless, the values endorsed by such a group, or simply their ignorance, can lead either to an underestimation of the objective advantages derived from this type of education, or to a repudiation of them despite their contribution being correctly perceived. However, groups associated with these institutions are in a different situation from those in the neutral category, for here endorsement of educational values opposed to those of the dominant group carries opportunity costs. Oppositional activities risk harming the operations of the institutions with which these groups are associated by depriving them of the current 'cost-free' service received. Thus, even if the advantageous character of available education has passed unperceived, it may well become evident at precisely the point when the dominant group is most threatened and other operations begin to suffer through attrition of adventitious benefits. Thus, for example, the English Tory Party's rather half-hearted support of Anglican educational domination in the first part of the nineteenth century (until the 1860s), increased throughout the remainder of the century — the benefits of religious instruction for social integration and popular quietism were fully acknowledged just as educational control gradually began to pass out of the hands of the traditional religious ownership group. The general proposition that adventitious beneficiaries have a high probability of playing a supportive role in educational interaction involves only the assumption that most of the time most groups display some congruence between their interests and their values — that the majority of their members does not bite the hand that feeds it.

(iii) From the point of view of structural influences, groups associated with institutions whose operations are hindered by the education available find themselves in situations which are the reverse of those just discussed. Although it is quite possible for some of their members to be convinced by the legitimatory arguments advanced by the dominant group (and the very form taken by education may induce mental limitations about the services thought to be available from any kind of instruction), such attitudes are maintained at a price and it is this cost which places these groups in a completely different position from those already discussed. Members of obstructed institutions suffer inconvenience and frustration in their role situations: to support the dominant group is to incur the penalty of continuing hindrance. If the obstruction is severe, such support automatically threatens operational goal attainment. Sometimes this can be circumvented by the development, for instance, of in-service training, but only at the expense of additional time, effort and money. On other occasions this is quite impossible, especially where personnel and resources are inadequate, or where these alone are insufficient to remove the frustrations undergone by group members. The English entre-preneurs could develop factory-based training and informal systems of recruitment but they could not remove the stigma attached to 'trade' (reinforced by dominant educational values) nor the embargo it placed on certain life chances and styles for the middle classes themselves.

It is argued that groups in this category will be prone to engage in oppositional activities because of the structured opportunity costs involved in *not* doing so. As in the previous discussion of supportive groups, the only psychological assump-tion made here is that, on the whole, groups do not tolerate large discrepancies between their declared interests and the values they endorse. This assumption is not predicated on 'universal enlightenment': in making it and drawing conclusions from it, one is not implying that every group member unerringly detects the source of his frustrations, that every actor is, in other words, a good sociologist. (Of course, in many cases the correct diagnosis is difficult to avoid, e.g., why do new recruits not have the appropriate skills? Where did they learn inappropriate values?) However, initially at least, the oppositional group is likely to be much smaller than the total institutional member-ship and it may well remain so. But for assertion to develop it is not necessary for all members in the same obstructed posi-tion to perceive the reasons for it and actively to combat it — any more than class conflict requires the active support and participation of all class members. Instead it is merely being argued that some members will identify and seek to overcome the source of the frustrations and contradictions they experience. In turn this will lead to a different patterning of educational activities among this group compared with that displayed by members of other groups whose operations are unobstructed. To maintain otherwise would involve a much more dubious psychological assumption: namely, that the existence of objective obstructions makes no difference to people's actions and that the objective costs attaching to certain interpretations have no effect upon people's attitudes.

(e) Determinants of educational interaction

What has been discussed so far is not simply group conflict or antagonism, for the groups involved are representatives of different institutions. However, in examining the conditioning of supportive and oppositional pressures, the structural relations of education have been artificially isolated from the wider social structure and culture in which they occur. Yet the latter will critically influence interaction to the extent that people hold roles in more than one or two institutions and share values that are not narrowly educational. Here the crucial element is the extent to which such factors reinforce or counteract the structural influences conditioning the formation of the supportive or oppositional groups just discussed.

In structural terms the extra-institutional involvements on the part of both oppositional and supportive groups may modify their commitment to educational change (or stasis) as well as the resources they can mobilize to these ends. Here we are on Dahrendorf's[5] familiar ground, where cross-cutting ties minimize conflict and overlapping ones reinforce it — without, however, endorsing his implicit assumption that the former prevail over the latter. The degree of system integration, the superimposition or segregation of elites, the extent of vertical stratification and horizontal differentiation — all affect the nature of social ties and their impact upon educational interaction. Precisely the same is true of the cultural dimension, for the social distribution of values plays a vital role in the emergence of oppositional or supportive activities. In exact parallel it is the degree of vertical and horizontal overlap in the cultural domain which fosters or neutralizes educational conflict. What is of ultimate importance, of course, for educational interaction is the conjunction between the distribution of values and of resources in society.

Finally, a full account of the conflict surrounding education must incorporate the contribution of independent factors, for it has constantly been stressed that structural factors only condition action, they do not determine it. Analysis of interaction must thus make full allowance for the (unconditioned) choice of particular goals; the avoidance of, or affinity for, given allies, the development and appeal of new ideas, etc. Factors like group antagonism, as opposed to structured opposition, can sometimes be as important as the conditioning influences. Because of this, the educational change which results must be viewed as the joint product of both these sources of interaction. Figure 3 thus summarizes the combination of influences on educational interaction which have been discussed in this chapter and which give it a distinctive character in the period prior to the emergence of state systems of education.

The macro-sociology of education and general theories of society

Figure 3 highlights how this analysis of educational change involves a particular angle of vision. It focuses on educational institutions and seeks to conceptualize how other parts of society impinge upon them. Education is thus moved to the centre of the stage and other aspects of structure, culture, and interaction are only considered in relation to it. They are incorporated as variables which help to account for educational change but are not themselves examined or explained. In other words, a theory about education in society is being advanced, not a general social theory. Nevertheless, the relationship between the two should perhaps be spelt out in concluding this chapter.

By analogy, our exercise has much in common with turning a globe until one is looking at a particular country, for optically it has the same implications — distortion of the size or relative importance of the focal point, blurring off of surrounding areas and, above all, neglect of things hidden from view. Thus it remains quite possible that a broader web of social relations, spun in other parts of the social structure, in fact envelops educational interaction. Hence the patterns of educational conflict examined here may map on to wider patterns of social conflict; the uniformities detected here may reflect regularities in the larger social structure; and the explanations advanced here may

FIGURE 3

The structural conditioning of educational interaction

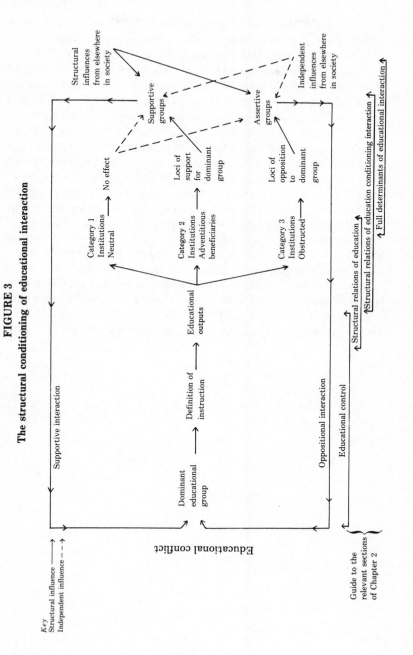

be subsumed under more general laws. As a specialist theory which is strictly about educational change it may thus be consistent with one or more general social theories.

However, Figure 3 indicates that the approach adopted is an open one; if group interaction is heavily structured in other parts of society, then this enters our analysis (though is not explained by it) at the point where it intersects the educational field. This approach allows any such factor freely to filter in, but is neutral in the sense that it excludes none in advance, nor does it give preferential treatment to any particular type of factor. Therefore, while it is compatible in principle with larger scale theories of society, it remains to be seen whether in practice any of these theories *are* capable of subsuming the educational propositions advanced here. Indeed, one way of viewing this type of specialized analysis is as a testing ground for theories which lay claim to a higher level of generality. Macro-sociological work does not itself presuppose a total system of sociological theory,[6] hence the onus is on those who feel that they do command such a theory to demonstrate that it holds the key which can unlock these subsidiary educational problems, as part of its general explanatory power.[7]

3 INTERACTION: COMPETITION FOR EDUCATIONAL CONTROL

The previous chapter concentrated upon structural relationships, and how these condition which groups will be involved in educational interaction and which processes of interaction will lead to large-scale changes in education. However, to understand interaction itself means grasping how structural factors like institutional contradictions and complementarities actually shape the situations which actors confront and why people respond to them in particular ways. Explaining educational change thus entails theorizing about its joint determinants — structure and agency — at their point of intersection.

This chapter presents **a theory dealing with the struggle for educational control before the development of state systems.** The preoccupation with struggle, rather than with peaceable forms of negotiation, does not mean that competitive conflict is held to be the universal motor of educational change. On the contrary, the justification for examining this phase of educational interaction in terms of conflict-analysis is itself a structural one: that there are good reasons for thinking it to be the most important mechanism of change in the period when the ownership and control of education were synonymous. Once these factors themselves change, so do the processes of change, and so must our theories about change.

Domination

When education is a mono-integrated and subordinate institution we have seen that its control and the power to define instruction rests in the hands of its owners, who are termed the educationally dominant group.[1] This was chosen as a neutral concept to designate the educational powers once enjoyed by a particular social group, which differentiated it from all other members of that society. 'Domination', following Max Weber, is defined as the opportunity to have a command concerning education obeyed by a given group of persons.[2] As such, it may be quite distinct from other forms of social dominance: those with educational control may or may not be the ruling class, the political elite, or the most wealthy group in society. When compared cross-culturally, dominant groups can be very dissimilar and may originate from different parts of their respective social structures.

It was argued in the last chapter that prolonged educational stability (which refers to the structural relations between education and other social institutions remaining unchanged and the definition of instruction showing a high degree of continuity), corresponds to the lasting domination of a particular group. This stability may endure either because the dominant group remains unchallenged or because it successfully overcomes threats to its control. Such challenges have been called 'assertion' and defined as the sum of efforts made by another group(s), which does not have the opportunity to issue educational commands, to overthrow the existing form of domination.

It is therefore by investigating the main prerequisites of successful domination and assertion that one can account for educational stability and change at the macro-sociological level. This involves specifying two sets of characteristics, those necessary for a group to be able to subordinate education (through rendering its operations dependent on the resources supplied), and those necessary for another group to be able to change this structural relationship.

Domination ultimately rests on a group owning and supplying those resources which are indispensable for instruction, namely plant and personnel (plus associated costs: upkeep of school buildings, preparation of texts, payment of teachers and provision of auxiliary services like administration and training). However, because domination has been achieved by a particular group which owned and mobilized these supplies at some earlier point in history, this by no means implies that its control is secure and can be maintained over time. For other social groups may possess surplus resources which could be diverted towards the foundation of schools and converted into a trained teaching body. Indeed, the dominant group may have gained control initially, simply because no other party was interested in investing in education at that time — as appears to have been the case with the church in medieval Europe. Where this is so, enduring domination and lack of large-scale change merely reflect the absence of opposition. The prerequisites of educational domination become more complex once one is concerned with the maintenance of control and the continuity of a given definition of instruction in the face of opposition.

For the dominant group to retain its position of exclusive control it must continue to be the only supplier of the resources upon which educational operations depend. Yet, since it is impossible for any one group fully to monopolize the resources itself (if only because of the human component), the dominant group has to preserve its *monopoly* of supplying educational resources by preventing others from converting financial and human assets into schools and teachers. On the one hand, an *ideology* legitimating this monopoly can be used by the dominant group to defend the exclusivity of its control by convincing others that they lack the right, the ability or the experience to engage in educational activities, or that the type of instruction already provided is the best, the proper, or the only form possible. On the other hand, a series of *constraints* can be employed to prevent alternative groups from supplying the facilities for imparting instruction. These may vary from the symbolic to the coercive, depending largely upon the nature of the dominant group itself. Use of either is conditional on members of the dominant group wishing to maintain control and the structural relations on which it is based. It is not necessary to assume that this desire is universal when seeking to specify the conditions for the maintenance of domination, for without it the prerequisites simply will not be developed.

All three factors — monopolization of educational facilities, protective constraints and legitimatory ideology — are together considered to represent the necessary but not the sufficient conditions for maintenance of domination. Without constraints the monopoly is vulnerable, without an ideology recruiting positive support rather than enforced compliance, it is even more so. However, neither may develop until monopoly ownership is challenged, but at that point it is best buttressed if the three elements are mutually reinforcing.

Turning to the countries considered, both dominant groups were concerned to defend their control of instruction but showed varying degrees of success in developing the three prerequisites for its maintenance. In France, the Catholic Church and its multiplicity of teaching Orders early acquired a monopoly of educational facilities, for the Reformation served to underline that religious orthodoxy must be taught not assumed.[3] In the following two centuries a patchy but country-wide network of confessional schools developed. Ownership was ecclesiastical: either religious Orders opened schools or local priests held classes on church premises. Teaching was closely controlled by the church and was generally undertaken by the clergy or by a Catholic lay teacher certified by the regional bishop. Post-elementary education was the preserve of the religious Orders and various types of *collèges* were owned, operated and staffed by Jesuits, Barnabites, Doctrinarians, Oratorians, etc., although the scholastic Jesuit model prevailed there, as in the universities. Instruction was 'characterized by a concentration on Catholic doctrine and literary classicism; the former led to religious conformity, the latter to the intellectual homogeneity of the ruling elite'.[4]

This substantial monopoly was reinforced by an ideology based on traditional legitimation. Appeal was made to the supreme moral authority of the apostolic church, whose priests had the exclusive right to pronounce on ethical matters. Since every academic subject and issue was held to have moral implications, the clergy was presented as the only body which could properly teach. Thus the educational ideology was fundamentally religious, but included strong elements of social elitism and political conservatism, which broadened its appeal beyond the strictly theological.[5] Symbolic constraints were also available within the church, which did not restrict itself to the use of the pulpit for disseminating its ideology. Religious sanctions were imposed on parents to ensure the catechization of children, on pupils in the boarding-schools to induce doctrinal orthodoxy, and on recalcitrant communities harbouring schismatics who might be tempted to enter the educational market to perpetuate heresies. Thus the strong monopoly was protected by the use of religious constraints originating within the controlling group, along with those deriving from education itself, i.e., discrimination and exclusion of potential critics from instruction, promotion of potential supporters through giving privileged educational access, and the use of tuition for spreading supportive values — devices generally employed by every dominant group.

In England at the end of the eighteenth century, the security of Anglican domination was much more the product of lack of threat or opposition. The majority of facilities was owned by the church, but at elementary level it represented only a thin network of parish and charity schools.[6] Since Brougham's Royal Commission of 1820 branded England as the worst educated country in Europe, the Anglican monopoly was clearly not extensive.[7] It depended on the absence of organized opposition: a competing network of Dissenting establishments had yet to be consolidated, while the individual dame-schools plugged the gaps without constituting any concerted threat.

Anglican control of secondary and higher education was more firmly based. Not only were many of the endowed schools religious foundations, but also the clergy enjoyed a complete monopoly of educational personnel. It supplied the vast majority of staff and controlled the profession as a whole, since an ecclesiastical licence was needed to become a teacher. The classical curricula of public and endowed schools, reflecting the state of knowledge at their foundation, were definitions of instruction upheld by the church because of their relevance to ordination. The same was true of the universities where an entirely Anglican teaching and student body meant that higher education was permeated with religious orthodoxy[8] and largely geared to reproducing the Anglican oligarchy over time — between 1800 and 1850 nearly half of those matriculating at Oxford were subsequently ordained.[9] The governing elite provided supportive legal constraints, the most important being the Test Acts, limiting university graduation to Anglicans alone, and the judicial upholding of the statutes pertaining to endowed foundations which served to protect the Church's definition of instruction. In England a defensive ideology was not properly elaborated until Anglican domination came under attack.[10]

(a) The effects of domination on other parts of the social structure

The nature of the dominant group's definition of instruction gave rise to specific kinds of educational outputs which could be either a help or a hindrance to contemporaneous operations taking place in other parts of society. It is to these that we must now turn in order to investigate what supportive pressures the dominant group's activities in the educational field generated from other sectors of society, and where they met with the greatest opposition. Although this only represents a preliminary and conditional structuring of parties whose interests lay in the maintenance of domination and those whose interests lay in its overthrow, it bears an important though imperfect relationship to subsequent patterns of educational interaction. This, we will seek to demonstrate, is not simply a matter of correlation but a structural influence on group interaction, which in turn is modified or reinforced by other influences. If this is the case, then **the fact that the distribution of adventitious benefits and obstructions was very different in the countries concerned is of corresponding importance for understanding the educational conflict which took place.**

Because of their supreme control over education, the dominant groups in both England and France were able to design the form of learning which best served their purposes, with almost complete disregard for the requirements of others. It is not surprising, then, that in each case the narrowness of instruction and the homogeneity of its outputs [11] obstructed more activities than those which it accidentally aided. (A broader, more differentiated education would have produced more adventitious beneficiaries, each of whom would have gained something from different parts of instruction.) However, it is not the number of parties who were obstructed or aided which is crucial, but rather qualitative characteristics of groups of people in these categories — who they were, what resources they had at their disposal and how willing they were to engage in support of, or opposition to, the dominant group.

In France, Catholic domination sponsored a tradition of scholastic classicism which served its own purposes but increasingly meant that 'a gap widened between it and society'. To Diderot it was only useful to the most useless of occupations — the priesthood and the professoriat. [12] Similarly, in the mid eighteenth century, Rolland stressed its incompatibility with public administration and went on to underline its disservice to military and commercial activities, 'are public schools destined only to produce clergymen, judges, physicians and men of letters? Are soldiers, sailors, tradesmen and artists unworthy?' [13]

Even the *ancien régime* monarchy was not a clear-cut beneficiary. Certainly the Catholic definition of instruction which hindered social mobility, confirmed social privilege and stressed duties associated with station in life, served to reinforce the stratificational system upon which absolutism rested. But, on the other hand, Jesuit ultramontanism was antithetic to the monarchy's Gallican policy in religious matters, and its scholasticism was decreasingly useful to government service. It was only with the expulsion of the Jesuits and their replacement by the more modernistic Oratorians as the leading teaching Order, that the monarchy eventually became an unambiguous adventitious beneficiary, and the sole one at that.

In England, the developing capitalist economy was seriously impeded by the Anglican definition of instruction and the values it embodied. This taught deference to squire and clergy but not to entrepreneur and merchant, it defended hereditary privilege but not newly acquired property, it preached catechism and constitution but not industrial skills and the spirit of capitalism, it taught classics and pure mathematics but not accountancy and applied science.[14] Equally, it penalized other religious organizations since the constraints which prevented Dissenters from attending many endowed schools, from university graduation, and from entering the teaching profession, hindered a range of denominational operations.

On the other hand, the Anglican dominant group had a clear adventitious beneficiary in the political elite. Increasing working-class unrest in the early nineteenth century made the contribution of religious instruction to social quietism proportionately valuable. Equally complementary with the goals of both political parties was the social exclusivity of Anglican secondary and higher education — for the status characteristics which were confirmed through education were the same as those employed by the governing elite when making ascriptive political appointments. The production of churchmen was in no way incompatible with the production of statesmen.

(b) Support for the dominant group

Adventitious beneficiaries do not convert directly into supportive groups. Indeed, they may not move in this direction at all since other factors can neutralize or counteract the structural predisposition towards their becoming loci of support. To recap, those receiving rewards must be aware of it, and must not have social ties, values, or any other source of allegiance which militates against solidarity with and defence of the dominant group. In neither England nor France did such factors nullify the influence of educational relations on the formation of alliances for the maintenance of domination.

On the contrary, in France, conditional influences originating from *other* social relationships reinforced the educational predisposition for an alliance between clergy and nobility. As enlightened thought simultaneously became more secular and more radical, the nobility was not slow to recognize the rewards it received from clerical instruction. Furthermore, the clergy and the nobility constituted the two privileged Estates — they were united by social ties and similar vested social interests in the retention of privilege — a link which went far beyond their educational relations.[15] Once the Jesuits had been expelled in 1762 and the Oratorian Order, with its Gallican outlook and more modern curriculum, had stepped into the gap, then social, religious, political and educational factors encouraged the nobility to act in a supportive capacity.

In England, too, the education alliance between Anglican Church and political elite was cemented by other factors, although complicated by party politics. By the early nineteenth century, tories and whigs alike acknowledged the services of the church to social control and to legitimating elitist government: both supported the National Society for Promoting the Education of the Poor in the Principles of the Established Church. Social ties of family and class linked Anglican leaders to members of both political parties. Nevertheless, the traditional 'Church and King'[16] outlook was more prominent among tories than in the Whig Party, which increasingly received the Dissenting vote after 1832. Thus, while whigs remained consistent in their support of *religious* instruction, it was the tories who finally emerged as strong allies of *Anglican* education.

Assertion

Educational conflict need not prove damaging to the dominant group or lead to any change in its definition of instruction if the constraints and ideological pressures it develops succeed in containing or eliminating opposition. Furthermore, the support that dominant groups receive from other parts of the social structure may be sufficient to protect their control. Having discussed the preconditions for the endurance of domination and analyzed the specific types of support accorded to it in both countries, a parallel specification is now required of the conditions under which an assertive group *can* seriously challenge domination.

Only the necessary conditions for successful assertion are outlined, and these consist of the factors required to overcome domination — to evade its constraints, to reject its ideology, and to damage its monopoly. Without them there will not be far-reaching changes, but conflict may be resolved in favour of existing domination, for this depends on the outcome of inter-action itself. What is being specified, then, are only those factors without which latent opposition cannot be transformed into assertion and an assertive group cannot overcome the dominant group.

First, opposition must acquire bargaining power, i.e., sufficient numerical support and organizational strength to challenge domination. Both involve a desire for concerted action to transform educational control which over-rides social ties with the dominant group and any conviction that its legitimatory ideology may have carried. In other words, diffuse discontent must be consolidated into organized assertion if con-straints are to be subverted. To this end, a counter ideology is required, partly to inform the movement of its goals, to recruit participants from the obstructed institution(s) as well as sup-port from a wider audience, and ultimately to justify using the bargaining power at its disposal. But, above all, the ideology of the dominant group has to be challenged and negated by a separate philosophy which legitimates the goals and activities of the assertive group and specifies its new definition of instruc-tion. Finally, the assertive group must successfully engage in activities which are instrumental in devaluing the dominant group's monopoly.

Instrumental activities can take two different forms — substitution or restriction. (These, incidentally, correspond to two of the ways Blau outlines through which power can be undermined.)[17] *Substitution* consists in replacing the supply of educational facilities, which the dominant group had monopolized, by new ones. In practice, this means devaluing its monopoly by building and maintaining new schools and recruiting, training and paying new teachers to staff them. Here domination is challenged by competition on the educational market — the aim of the assertive group being to price the domi-nant party out of it or to relegate it to a small corner of the market. In either case, a transfer of control takes place and macroscopic changes are introduced. *Restriction*, on the other hand, consists of removing some of the facilities owned by the dominant group, or preventing it from supplying these resources to the educational sphere. Thus, the monopoly is devalued coercively; buildings may be appropriated, educational funds confiscated, or personnel excluded from teaching and administration. Here domination is challenged, not by market competition but by coercive power — the aim being the forcible transfer of educational control.

The nature and timing of confrontation between domination and assertion depends upon the balance of factors present on the two sides. There are two limiting cases: unchallenged domination, when no group has acquired any of the factors necessary for assertion (which corresponds to institutional stability), and, on the other hand, a situation where the prerequisites of domination are matched by the preconditions of assertion (which corresponds to overt institutional conflict). The three components of assertion may be developed simultaneously or over a period of time, but for analytical purposes they will be examined sequentially for the two countries.

(a) The consolidation of bargaining power

Bargaining power is essentially a matter of numbers and organization; it can obviously vary in strength and plays an important part in determining the relative success of different assertive groups. Several elements jointly contribute to influencing the bargaining power acquired. These can be classified as factors which restrain the development of a large and committed assertive group versus those which further its actualization. When the obstructions stemming from the prevailing definition of instruction all focus upon the same social group, a higher proportion of its members are likely to be active in the pursuit of educational change. Equally, if frustrations are experienced by different social groups which are nevertheless closely linked by other kinds of social ties, their alliance increases overall bargaining power. Both of these represent a particular type of mobilization, where a single assertive group develops with a large number of potential activists. Here there will be a polarization of conflict between domination and assertion. On the other hand, if frustrations are diffused among a number of different social groups which are not linked to one another, pluralistic assertion is more likely and each group will have a more limited pool of potential participants. Because each will have greater difficulties in acquiring strong bargaining power, educational conflict will be complex and protracted.

Other factors can operate in a cross-cutting or reinforcing fashion as was discussed in Chapter 2. Strong links, on grounds other than educational, with the dominant group or its supporters, can reduce the number of those actively opposing it. Similarly, the existence of social antagonism between the assertive group and other sections of society reduces the probability of recruiting allies and thus fulfils a similar restraining function. Bargaining power will then be stronger the greater the independence of the obstructed group from the dominant group and the greater its links with other parts of society, especially if these in turn are ill-disposed towards the dominant group on other grounds.

France provides a striking example of a country where the polarization of educational conflict was not restrained by other social ties or allegiances and the consolidation of bargaining power by the assertive group was correspondingly easy. Most important here was the fact that obstructed operations gave rise to frustrations which were experienced cumulatively in one group — the bourgeoisie. Not only was Catholic education irrelevant to its activities in commerce and finance but school enrolment and graduation placed it in an anomic position when its members could not gain appointments commensurate with their qualifications. 'Each year instructed, ambitious and intelligent young men graduated . . . but their legitimate ambition came up against unscalable obstacles, money, titles . . . The Army, high positions in the Church, judicial offices were all the prerogatives of rich and noble families.'[18] These multiple grievances led to the recruitment of activists from all sections of the bourgeoisie committed to educational change.

On the other hand, there were few links between the bourgeoisie and the privileged Estates to restrain participation in assertive activities. On the contrary, social, economic and political factors conditioned opposition to privilege itself — that is, to the First and Second Estates, the dominant group and its noble supporters. Simultaneously, the bourgeoisie could recruit allies from among the people, given that the latter were subject to indoctrination by clergy, repression by nobility and financial exploitation by the state.

Thus, predispositions towards educational assertion were superimposed on further sources of social division and political opposition. [19] Far from participation in educational conflict being restrained by other social ties it was encouraged by them, and assertive bargaining power was augmented proportionately. Educational conflict thus harnessed itself to social conflict structured by legal privilege.

By contrast, the factors influencing the formation of educational opposition in England were complex and cross-cutting, eventually resulting in the emergence of two distinct assertive groups. Initially, it seemed that middle-class assertion would not experience great difficulties in generating bargaining power since two of the major operations impeded by Anglican instruction — the development of the capitalist economy and the progress of Dissenting denominations — affected many of the same people. The entrepreneurial and Dissenting groups were not perfectly superimposed, but there was a large overlapping sector where frustrations were doubled — where fathers were compelled to become self-taught industrialists and their children were debarred from a polite education by religious affiliation and trade connections. At the same time, educational activism was tempered by the significant percentage of the middle class which remained committed Anglicans and by the high proportion of factory owners afraid to lose child labour. [20]

Nevertheless, during the first decades of the nineteenth century it appeared that alliance with the working class would considerably augment bargaining power. Shared opposition to the church as the educationally dominant group, and to its supporter, the political elite as the ruling class, promoted joint action. However, the non-enfranchisement of the working class in 1832 accentuated the divergent political interests of industrial workers and entrepreneurs. In turn, this signalled the emergence of independent educational assertion on the part of labour. Consequently, the consolidation of bargaining power became more difficult for both forms of assertion since they had to recruit participants to oppose the dominant group *and* the other assertive party. Unlike France, political alignments in England fragmented educational alliances rather than cementing them, and this partly accounts for educational conflict being much more protracted in England.

(b) The elaboration of ideology

The possession of an ideology performs three vital functions for an assertive group. **Ideology is a central factor in challenging domination, since the legitimation of educational control must be negated by unmasking the interests served, thus reducing support for the prevailing definition of instruction. Secondly, it is crucial in legitimating assertion itself and is thus related to the consolidation of bargaining power. Finally, it is vital for the specification of an alternative definition of instruction, the blueprint which will be implemented in schools if the assertive group is successful.** The elaboration of assertive ideologies can, as we have seen, be facilitated or hindered by cultural factors and the distribution of social values in a given country.

The analysis of educational ideologies is important for two reasons. On the one hand, ideological factors exert an independent influence upon educational interaction. As Weber argued, struggle in the realm of ideas parallels rather than reflects group conflict and, although related to the structured interests of participants, contributes something of its own to determining the outcome between them. Here we will see that educational ideologies played an important role in the recruitment of support and formation of assertive alliances — sometimes over-riding differences of interest, sometimes introducing cleavage within an interest group. On the other hand, educational ideologies are vital to the understanding of educational change. The precise definition of instruction advocated by a group cannot be derived directly from its interests. These interests do not dictate the content of the ideology adopted (for more than one educational philosophy may be compatible with them), nor within it the exact nature of the blueprint advance (for more than one specific curriculum, type of school, etc., may serve group interests and contribute to the attainment of group goals). Thus, to account for the aims pursued in assertion and the changes introduced if successful, the ideological source of the new definition of instruction must be examined.

In France, educational values encouraged polarization between domination and assertion and buttressed the alliance against the Catholic Church. Initially restricting themselves to anti-clericalism, rather than anti-Catholicism, the bourgeois assertive group appealed to French enlightened thought and especially to the educational philosophy of Diderot.[21] His stress upon utilitarianism, nationalism and meritocracy captured their aims perfectly, specifying precisely the type of education desired and negating the Catholic definition of instruction so successfully that even the monarchy supported the expulsion of the Jesuit Order. This particular strand of thought was, however, too explicitly elitist (though on meritocratic not traditional grounds) to recruit popular support, which the bourgeoisie needed in the educational struggle as in political conflict. To gain it involved papering over the divisions which threatened the unity of the Third Estate by legitimating educational assertion to the people as an inextricable part of their battle for political rights. The thought of Condorcet [22] and Sieyès [23] contributed much to legitimating assertion on a wide social basis, by relating the political attack on the nobility to the educational assault on the clergy, and blending the two into a single challenge to privilege itself — whose abolition could only be achieved by the united action of the Third Estate.

In England, on the other hand, cultural and ideological influences complicated alliances and prevented the clear-cut polarization of educational conflict. The existence of Dissent was initially helpful in crystallizing opposition to Anglicanism, for it represented pluralism in religious values. Almost immediately, however, strong denominational commitment reduced unity within the embryonic assertive group because it clashed with the secular utilitarian element. This strain was apparent during the early years of the British and Foreign School Society where schism developed between the secular and Quaker elements, which eventually left the society in Dissenting hands.

However, the victory of Dissent [24] (which became more pronounced when working-class unrest cast doubts on the restraining power of classical economics and secular ethics [25] and thus revalued religion for popular control), had a serious backlash. Effectively, it alienated the working-class leadership to whom secularism had strongly appealed, because it harmonized with the intellectual traditions most influential in popular educational thought — the secular rationalism of the French Revolution and early English anarchism. Ideologically, the working classes were as tenacious in their adhesion to secularism as was Dissent in its defence of denominationalism. It took other factors to precipitate the final break-away in the early 1830s — but secular socialist values then played a major role in the crystallization of an independent popular assertive group and in the corresponding reduction of middle-class bargaining power.[26]

(c) The development of instrumental activities
Use of either a restrictive or a substitutive strategy to devalue the monopoly of the dominant group is conditioned by the social distribution of resources. Thus, few assertive groups have free choice between the alternative kinds of instrumental activities.

For a group to begin assertion by means of a restrictive policy, it needs some degree of access to the national legislative machinery. The social distribution of political power, therefore, structures the availability of restrictive strategies to different assertive groups associated with various institutions. However, the fact that legislative influence is essential does not imply that any group initiating a restrictive strategy is synonymous with the political elite itself or possesses extensive political power, especially if the economic distribution is such that the adoption of a substitutive strategy is precluded. However, in such cases the use of restriction to damage the dominant group's monopoly is dependent on a concordance of goals between the assertive group and the political elite. This unanimity need not be present at the start but may be generated in the course of assertion. The support of governing elites can be won by convincing them that existing educational control is politically undesirable and by specifying an alternative definition of instruction which is more conducive to their aims. However, unless the political elite can be recruited as a strenuous ally, then only a substantial shift in the societal distribution of power to the advantage of the assertive group gives it any chance of executing a restrictive strategy.

It is because such political changes can occur in the course of interaction that the initial degree of access to governmental machinery does not determine the success or failure of assertive groups. However, ultimately, it is only when the assertive group is very closely allied to, or in fact co-terminous with, the political elite that restrictive strategies can be successful and engender macroscopic educational change.

For a group to begin its assertive activities by employing a strategy of substitution it needs access to some degree of economic surplus which can be directed to devaluing the existing monopoly of educational facilities. Although the economic distribution conditions the differential availability of this strategy to various assertive groups, once again it does not determine the outcome of assertion. First, the crucial factor in developing this kind of instrumental activity is not the absolute amount of wealth at a group's disposal, but the proportion of it which can be mobilized for educational purposes (thus relative bargaining power is significant here). Secondly, if the assertive ideology legitimates opposition among a wider audience of potential supporters, the resources made available to this end are increased. Thirdly, while the provision of alternative physical facilities in education is capital intensive, considerable progress can be made through concentrating on competition in the field of human resources (which is why so many assertive groups have made use of the Lancastrian method; [27] grossly deficient as a means of instruction, but strategically ideal in yielding maximum educational encroachment for minimum investment).

Thus, it can be seen that the economic distribution exerts an influence on the selection and development of substitutive strategies which exactly parallels that exerted by the power distribution on restrictive strategies. In both cases the initial adoption of a strategy is influenced by the original resource distribution, but the outcome cannot be predicted from it. However, in substitution, as in restriction, if the policy is to succeed, resources must be accumulated in the course of inter-action. This has the further implication that just as the political elite was considered to be the type of assertive group most likely to succeed in restriction, so the economic elite is best placed to carry through substitution. Indeed, the assertive groups which have the greatest probability of failing to develop either kind of instrumental activity are those which occupy the lowest position on both the wealth and power dimensions simultaneously. These in fact are usually the only groups which can be said to have a free choice between the two strategies — though progress with either is difficult, but not impossible.

In France we have seen that a variety of factors helped to structure a single assertive alliance and here the distribution of resources encouraged the pre-revolutionary bourgeoisie to follow a restrictive strategy. As a predominantly professional-commercial group rather than an industrial middle class, it was not poor but was far from being in an economic position to compete with the resources of the Catholic Church — and it is financial relativities which are crucial in substitution. Furthermore, the assertive alliance with the popular section of the Third Estate was not one which substantially added to the financial resources of opposition. On the political dimension, however, the bourgeoisie had influence only in the provincial parliaments which were consultative rather than decision-making bodies. Nevertheless, these could be employed as platforms for the expression of bourgeois views and the success of certain presidents (especially Rolland and La Chalotais) in initiating the expulsion of the Jesuits, confirmed the adoption of a restrictive strategy against the church. It encouraged the search for allies and the attempt to unite the Third Estate in order to strengthen bargaining power and exert greater political pressure, for in France political power would have to be augmented during educational interaction if assertion was to succeed.

The English case presents a complete contrast, for the middle-class alliance of entrepreneurs and Dissenters represented a group whose respective economic and political positions clearly favoured the adoption of a substitutive strategy. In terms of financial surplus they were, as their economists never failed to underline, the group making the greatest contribution to national wealth. However, despite having largely taken over from the landed interest as the economic elite, their political participation was minimal before large-scale enfranchisement in 1832: after it, parliamentary representation and cabinet influence still remained small for several subsequent decades. It is not surprising, then, that in the first half of the nineteenth century this group concentrated on devaluing the Anglican monopoly by substituting new establishments at all levels, either on a proprietary basis or through voluntary subscription.

On the other hand, working-class assertion came from a group which had neither political influence nor economic surplus and thus lacked the factors predisposing towards selection of either strategy. Indeed, the tactical debate about whether to engage in educational substitution as a basis for subsequent political change or whether to seek franchise reform first as a means for obtaining educational change later on, was to divide the Chartist movement.[28] Nevertheless, it was the substitutive strategy which was adopted immediately after and largely because of political disappointment in 1832. The chance of being in a position to manipulate legislative machinery for educational reform then appeared remote; substitution could be immediate, and the argument of Lovett that an instructed class had better chance of enfranchisement was influential. Relative to working-class resources, the sums mobilized for substitution of elementary schools, halls of science, and mechanics' institutes were impressive — but more as an index of class commitment to educational change than as a serious threat to the dominant group or the growing network of institutions founded by the assertive section of the middle class.

Educational conflict

Organized conflict rather than unco-ordinated opposition occurs when the three prerequisites of domination are matched by those of assertion, as was the case in both countries examined. The nature, length and intensity of educational conflict is influenced by a variety of factors, many of them non-educational, and these have been incorporated into the discussion but obviously cannot themselves be explained within the present analysis. They are taken as given in our theoretical approach, which is more concerned with their consequences for educational interaction. Hence, the points at which they impinge upon educational groups have been indicated and it now remains to examine the combined impact of all the factors discussed on the course of educational conflict. It will be possible to do this only in the briefest terms: only the most salient features will be accentuated and most attention will be given to the final state of play between dominant and assertive groups at the point when macroscopic change begins to take place in education. Discussion of the changes themselves is reserved for the next chapter.

France is a clear-cut case where an assertive group succeeded in devaluing the monopoly of the dominant group and gained educational control on the basis of a restrictive strategy. As such, it illustrates the important fact that possession of political power alone does not confer the ability to define instruction, although control of the legislative machinery is a necessary condition for restricting others and preventing them from doing so. For on the basis of this kind of strategy there are two stages involved in attaining educational control — one negative, the other positive.

The first is *restriction* itself which is essentially a destructive phase comprising the closure of schools, proscription of teachers, and dismantling of the previous apparatus for educational administration. It is not synonymous with educational control (although it is a precondition of it), precisely because it is negative and may merely destroy the functioning of education altogether for a time. The second stage, where control is attained and a new definition of instruction is imposed, involves the *replacement* of new educational facilities. For this to occur not only requires access to legislative machinery but also the political capacity to mobilize sufficient resources.

In France the Revolution in itself only gave the Third Estate legislative control through which to devalue the dominant group's monopoly, but did not enable them to proceed with replacement. The bourgeoisie was now politically powerful but still dependent on the support of the people in education as in politics and this severely constrained replacement. Not only did it invoke the problem of defining a common denominator of reform, acceptable to all sections of the Third Estate, which none of the three revolutionary assemblies succeeded in producing;[29] the more serious constraint consisted in the fact that popular support was incompatible with the high levels of taxation which successful replacement implied. A revolution which had been waged against the tax burden could not risk imposing new levies as one of the earliest actions of government.

The shift from assembly to consular and finally to imperial government meant that military coercion replaced popular support as the basis of political stability. With the return to strong government came educational *étatisme*: the immediate resurgence of the bourgeois ideology of the parliamentarians with its nationalism, vocationalism and Gallicanism as the definition of instruction endorsed by the imperial political elite. On a coercive basis, progress could finally be made towards replacement — of a kind which embodied these values.

The case of England is very different, for pluralistic assertive groups working on a substitutive basis led to the development of separate and alternative educational networks, outside the control of the dominant group. Middle-class substitution had begun early in the nineteenth century. Its immediate effect was to stimulate Anglican efforts to retain control and the National

Society was the organization designed for this defence. The assertive group counter-attacked with the foundation of a parallel organization, the British and Foreign School Society, geared to undenominational instruction. A combination of factors reinforced this partitioning of the elementary field among the competing parties. Distrust of state intervention on the part of Anglicans and Dissenters alike, coupled with tory unwillingness to employ it and whig commitment to educational expansion, represented a parallelogram of forces whose outcome was the voluntary system — where schools were financed through the two rival societies. In effect, control of the elementary level was left (and this was itself a product of substitutive conflict) to be determined by competition on the educational market. The factors which had produced the voluntary system (and the religious difficulty was only partly responsible), ultimately had the effect of entrenching it. The wealth of the middle class allowed it to make considerable progress in founding schools and recruiting teachers, though greater damage would have been inflicted on the Anglicans had the iron-masters been less concerned to retain profits from child labour and had the working class not been deflected to found its own network. Simultaneously, Anglican appeals enabled the church to increase its educational resources. Thus, strong, differentiated and autonomous networks of elementary schools continued to develop in parallel. The same was true at secondary level and again in higher education where the foundation of University College, as a product of middle-class assertion, was matched by the establishment of King's College and Durham University, as Anglican institutions.

Correspondingly, educational conflict did not result in a clearcut transfer of control to the assertive alliance as occurred in France. Instead, deadlock developed between the parties involved. The dominant group was threatened but not eliminated: the assertive alliance evaded constraints and entered the educational market but could not monopolize it. Competition was fierce but since neither party could fatally injure the other, their respective educational networks continued to develop in parallel.

Response to this deadlock was identical for the various parties concerned. The established church increasingly turned towards the state for political intervention in defence of Anglican control and to further its influence over the sectarian forces of dissent.[30] Partly because denominationalists feared the consequences of this, and partly due to their increased political influence, the middle-class alliance was also drawn into the political struggle in order to overcome market stalemate. Since working-class assertion with its limited resources had recognized the impossibility of educational reform without political change during the second stage of the Chartist movement, all the parties engaged in conflict now looked to political action for its resolution. The quest for politico-educational alliances which would exert pressure on political parties in Parliament developed in the 1860s. But it occurred when none of these groups had the exclusive prerogative of political influence and it took place in the context of two well developed networks of national education. What all parties sought from the state was defence and expansion of what they had already achieved, and the extent to which they got it depended upon a lengthy and complex process of political interaction. Resolution of the educational conflict therefore depended on resolution of the political conflict, and until the end of the century political deadlock was to parallel the earlier educational stalemate. Meanwhile, the separate educational networks retained their autonomy and continued to expand slowly.

4 STRUCTURAL ELABORATION: THE EMERGENCE OF STATE EDUCATIONAL SYSTEMS

This chapter is concerned with the final phase of the cycle, which is also, of course, the first phase of the next cycle. It deals with educational changes resulting from the social interaction just discussed, which will, in their turn, condition future interaction and further educational change. **The aim here is to link a specific mechanism of change (the interaction of educationally dominant and assertive groups) with its effects on the structure of education and the relations between education and society.**

These links can be summarized in two propositions, which are held to be universal for nations whose educational systems developed autonomously.

(i) Competitive conflict transforms the structural relations between education and society by inducing the emergence of state educational systems which are integrated with a plurality of other social institutions.

(ii) Simultaneously, this process of interaction introduces an internal restructuring of education itself, through the development of four new emergent properties: 'unification', 'systematization', 'differentiation' and 'specialization'.[1]

Universal characteristics of structural elaboration: multiple integration and state systems

This section concentrates on proposition (i) concerning the integration of education to the political centre and also to a plurality of social institutions as products of the interaction between dominant and assertive groups. In other words, the competitive conflict responsible for education losing its mono-integrated status also accounts for linking instruction to the central decision-making agency of a society and to other parts of the social structure.

Although both changes are the universal products of a competitive process of interaction, this does not mean that they follow from a uniform sequence of events. Instead, their development varies according to which of the strategies — restrictive or substitutive — was pursued to challenge the monopoly of the educational ownership group in any given country.

(a) From restrictive strategies

We have seen that successful restrictive strategies are two-stage affairs involving the destruction of private ownership and the subsequent reintegration of education with other parts of society. Failure to move from the destructive phase of restriction to the constructive stage of replacement simply annihilates existing educational provisions.

It is in this need to replace as well as to restrict, if a new group is to accede to educational control, that the mechanism is found which accounts for the emergence of state educational systems. The mechanism itself entails nothing superordinate to the actors involved, it is simply the result of an assertive group continuing to seek educational control and is contingent upon the consistent pursuit of this goal. Were an assertive group to falter in the face of difficulties with replacement, and to renounce its desire to define instruction, the predicted consequences would not follow. As in any sociological theory which focuses upon goal-orientated behaviour, it must be recognized that actors and groups of actors can change the goals they seek to attain, for to reject determinism is to admit that ultimately circumstances force no one to do anything. Nevertheless, for a theory of this kind to have explanatory power there must be good reasons why a particular goal is highly likely to be sustained by a group and thus lead to the predicted consequences.

Now here the assertive group initially sought educational control because the institutional operations with which it was associated were being seriously obstructed, and it thus wished to have the power to redefine educational services. Its activities continue to be impeded in the absence of educational provisions (for if its operations could dispense with such services, this group would originally have fallen in the neutral category) and may again be obstructed by the resurgence of the old dominant group if replacement does not occur. Thus, continuity in conditioning, represented by the endurance of obstructions, accounts for the assertive group's pertinacity in seeking educational control. It is the reason why groups which have accomplished the negative restrictive phase will struggle to achieve educational replacement.

To imply that replacement is a difficult task derives from the reasons which led an assertive group to employ a restrictive strategy in the first place, namely that it did not have financial resources commensurate with its political power. Thus, in France, economic wealth was concentrated outside the assertive group — in the hands of the landed aristocracy not the Third Estate, and the significance of this *negative* predisposition towards restriction does not stop there. Because of it, an assertive group which had waged a successful policy of restriction was then completely unable to replace educational facilities from its own resources.

However, when the assertive group and the political elite are co-terminous, the lack of resources does not preclude replacement. For the advantage such an assertive group possesses over any other is that it can use the central legal machinery to organize public educational financing rather than having to provide such facilities itself. To do this is not an easy or automatic procedure, if only because it is an innovatory one which involves withdrawing central resources from existing priorities and/or increasing the fiscal burden on the public. It is one, however, that presents the trebly irresistible attraction of allowing the assertive group to control educational output in conformity with its goals, to do so at national level and at public expense.

However, what takes place in this situation is not merely the integration of education to the polity, but the emergence of national state education. The assertive group does not simply replace the old dominant group, for it cannot subordinate education by making it dependent on resources it owns and supplies. These are public resources, and with their mobilization for purposes of instruction, educational ownership and educational control become separated for the first time. There was never any question of the assertive political elite being able to appropriate public funds and thus to constitute itself as an ownership group, for such wealth was not even centrally located. The amount which could be diverted from the national budget was totally inadequate to the task of replacement, whose completion involved supplementing central funding by the political mobilization of local resources.[2]

The budget of the Imperial University gives the clearest picture of the importance of central mobilization compared with direct central financing.[3] By 1811 the municipalities were charged with the upkeep of the *faculté*, *lycée* and *collège* buildings and the principal communes were compelled to create grants for secondary school pupils or pay a contribution into the treasury which was earmarked for this purpose. In sum, the elementary schools, *lycées* and some *facultés* were made self-supporting, and the university treasury had only to maintain in full the central educational administration.

Thus, the assertive group succeeds in bringing about replacement not through the supplies it provides itself but by use of its political authority to mobilize the necessary resources. It has gained educational control, not on the old basis of monopoly ownership of facilities but by virtue of its legislative power. Control ceases to be entrepreneurial and becomes managerial, for although education remains subordinate, it is dependent upon resources owned and supplied by the state, not by a dominant group. The capacity to define instruction becomes firmly linked to political position and, what is completely novel, can be lost with the declining political fortunes of a group. Thus, the emergence of national state education is the result of a group attempting to complete a restrictive strategy, but the control it gains over it is of a different and weaker kind than that previously enjoyed by dominant ownership groups.

So far it has been the development of the integration between education and the state which has been accentuated as the end result of the replacement phase. However, the same two factors — the assertive group's desire to gain educational control and its use of public resources to do so — also account for the simultaneous emergence of multiple integration. First, an assertive political elite faces considerable problems in arranging the public financing of education for the first time, especially when the emergence of a state system predates industrialization. The assertive group thus has to seek political support for large-scale public spending on education — support within the governing elite for giving it a high priority, and outside it for supplementing central educational expenditure. In turn, the latter groups make their support conditional upon their own educational demands being met by government.

The assertive group is now in a difficult position for it cannot gain control (by completing replacement) without support, yet support is conditional upon a diversification of educational outputs beyond the goals designated by the polity. This is one of the two sources of multiple integration and it is as important for authoritarian regimes as for those based on democracy. **It is, however, an unintended consequence, for the diversification of educational outputs in order to service a multiplicity of operations is the price the assertive group pays for the mobilization of resources. It is the cost of control without ownership.**

In addition, however, some of the new structural relations which develop between education and other social institutions are intended ones and stem from the assertive group itself, for by definition all political elites have a plurality of aims which impinge upon the operations of various institutional spheres. Specific changes in educational outputs will help in their attainment. Since no political elite is truly monolithic, sub-groups like the military may want educational outputs rather different from those sought, for example, by heads of civil administration — and demand them at the point when replacement becomes a practical reality. Problems of elite cohesion are solved by concessions which intensify multiple integration.

Ideally the assertive group would like to establish interdependence imperatively between education and those operations designated in its original blueprint; in practice this is modified because of the need for support from sectional interests within the elite and for public support outside it. Thus, the two sources of multiple integration, the intended and the unintended, intermingle and determine the exact nature of the structural relations which emerge.

The replacement phase in France (1805-33) gave steady priority to developing those forms of instruction from which political elites would gain most, while making shifting concessions to such sections of society whose support was needed. Given strong government but limited funds, initial replacement catered to the civil and military requirements of Napoleon's empire. For him — 'to instruct is secondary, the main thing is to train and to do so according to the pattern which suits the

State'.[4] Resources were concentrated at the top, founding a national network of *lycées* whose *baccalauréat* gave direct entry to state employment or to *grandes écoles*,[5] retailored to meet *etatist* requirements — St Cyr supplied army officers, *Polytechnique* furnished numerate civil servants and *Ecole Normale* stocked the highest reaches of the teaching profession.[6] Thus, ability was harnessed to state service and a diploma elite was created among the professional bourgeoisie, giving it vested interests in educational maintenance.

Although the individual had no right to instruction if the state had no need of it, the wish 'to use the masses for manual labour and above all . . . to obey and to die beneath the flag'[7] required a political socialization which would cost money. To provide this at state expense would have subtracted from secondary and higher provisions, but to concede to Catholic pressures for readmission to the educational field had the double advantage of securing church support for the new system while passing it the bill for elementary instruction. Thus, the forms of multiple integration developed under the empire linked post-elementary outputs as closely as possible to the military, bureaucratic and political operations of state, while the traditional interdependence between the church and elementary schooling remained basically undisturbed.

However, Catholic support proved nominal and despite stringent state controls[8] the church persistently exceeded its brief and pursued autonomous religious aims: 'the main goal of primary instruction was as before to instruct people in the Catholic religion.'[9] Given that the church increasingly used its position to contest rather than buttress the state system, the new bourgeois government of the July Monarchy replaced this support base by one which Napoleon had completely neglected — the economic elite. The establishment of vocational schools (*primaires supérieures*), in 1833, provided the skills now sought in commerce, industry and business administration, thus rupturing the previous integration between religion and elementary education and replacing it with a new structural relationship with the economy.[10] And this occurred without disturbing the connections previously established between higher levels of instruction and the state, which were simply too advantageous for subsequent political elites to dispense with — there Napoleon had rightly forecast that 'public education is the future and the duration of my work after me'.

(b) From substitutive strategies

Here the integration of education to the polity is an indirect and unintended consequence of interaction: those embarking on substitution aim to assume the position of the dominant group and to alter the part of society which education serves. Instead, the immediate effect of this type of assertion is to introduce a rudimentary form of multiple integration, while the ultimate result is the emergence of a state system — thus reversing the order in which these two features appear, compared with systems originating from restriction.

The immediate effect is produced because no assertive group enters market competition unless it seeks a very different kind of instruction from that provided by the dominant group. Consequently, the output from assertive schools is designed to serve institutional operations previously obstructed by the only form of education available. Furthermore, since there is no reason to suppose that the dominant definition of instruction will only prove a hindrance in one quarter, or that the leading assertive group can contain or accommodate all other educational grievances, there is nothing to prevent the mobilization of other assertive groups. If operational exigencies lead those from different social institutions to contemplate substitution on their own behalf, nothing but their own limited resources can stop them. But any new group engaging in market competition only does so because it is profoundly dissatisfied with the two definitions of instruction now in existence, and what it provides is something different again. Thus the mechanics' institutes and halls of science[11] of the English working class, developed a non-vocational definition of instruction, geared to popular enlightenment, and serving the political advancement of a group which both Anglican and entrepreneurial schooling repudiated or repressed.

This form of multiple integration is rudimentary because although 'education' as a whole now services a plurality of social institutions for the first time, the various independent networks of establishments are completely separate from one another. There is in fact no 'education as a whole' except in the sense of it being the sum of these various parts, owned by different groups, serving diverse institutional operations, and operating in isolation from one another. The networks are totally segregated in terms of roles, personnel, administration, financing, intake, examination and, above all, definition of instruction.

Moreover, all the networks tend to grow in strength, for the crucial thing about substitutive strategies is that they are incapable of forcing the old dominant group out of the educational market however successful and attractive the new provisions prove. Competition cannot ultimately exclude the dominant group for it cannot be deprived of the facilities it owns or the right to keep on supplying them. Here the factors originally predisposing towards adoption of a substitutive strategy have further implications. This course of action was followed by groups whose economic surplus outweighed their political influence and who generally lacked any access to the central legislative machinery (necessary for successful restriction). Such being the case, and no major redistribution of political power having occurred, the assertive group lacks the legal constraints to eliminate the dominant group entirely or to prevent others from entering the market and complicating competition.

However, the origins of multiple integration proper are found in these vigorous independent networks, each one embodying a different definition of instruction. Basically, this comes about through a process of incorporation as these segregated networks become connected together to form a system. This is not a simple additive process: the type of national education which emerges is not just the sum of these various sets of establishments. It is the product of negotiation, conciliation, concession and coercion, all of which result in modifying the original networks — accentuating some, altering others and partially suppressing certain institutions. Nevertheless, diversity in the emergent system stems from the incorporated networks retaining much of their early distinctiveness and continuing to supply many of the services for which they were originally established. Once again the mechanism which produces both universal changes is nothing other than the consistent pursuit of their educational goals by the conflicting parties. To trace the emergence of change from interaction is to focus on what competition does to the groups involved and to their prospects of attaining educational control.

The initial effect of competitive interaction is considerable educational expansion as the various groups seek to move forward against each other. The final result is that deadlock arises between them. The resources which can be mobilized by any group for educational purposes are not limitless and as conflict becomes protracted, each party is trying to run faster in order to stay put. No group makes headway against the others.

The situation in mid nineteenth-century England was typical — rivalry 'did not produce a surplus of schools and cheap education, as some educational "free-traders" expected, but tended to paralyse the activities of all parties, so that schools were built that could not be maintained and children were taught for such short periods that they could benefit very little from the instruction given'.[12] Increasingly, then, the independent networks were locked in conflict, and prospects of retaining or attaining educational control through further market efforts diminished accordingly.

From this situation of stalemate, pressures develop which culminate in the integration of education to the state. Each of the competitive parties seeks to break out of the deadlock and this can only be done in one of two ways — by obtaining considerable new resources or by acquiring legal constraints to use against competitors. It is obvious that the central government is the only source of the latter, but less self-evident perhaps that it is also the greatest untapped supply of wealth for educational purposes.

It matters little who makes the first move towards state intervention, although the competing group with the closest link to the political elite is usually the earliest to hope for legal protection (like the Anglican Church turning to its old adventitious beneficiary, the Tory Party and receiving backing, for the voluntary system undoubtedly worked in the Anglicans' favour). Education is irresistibly dragged into the political arena, for all competing groups are threatened if one alone makes headway with central government. Thus, profound educational conflict produces a strain towards state intervention as a means to advance or to protect the various networks. **The development of a state educational system does not originate from the goals of either dominant or assertive groups. It is the eventual and unintended product of all of them seeking state intervention for their own ends simultaneously.**

Because all competing groups do this simultaneously, the conflicting parties in education have to accommodate themselves to the structure of political conflict. Unless they can insert their aims prominently in the programme of an influential political grouping they have little chance of extracting governmental support and recognition. **Hence a period of alliance formation follows in which political opposition** (organized in parties in the case of England) meets educational competition (the independent ownership groups). Thus, the Educational League was formed after the liberal majority in 1868 to 'make the government go faster'[13] and dismantle the voluntary system, still favouring the Anglican Church.[14] It was an alliance of Nonconformists, radicals and entrepreneurs, together with the TUC in pursuit of national unsectarian education maintained from local rates. The counterpart of the league was the defensive National Educational Union through which the established church, sponsored by the Tory Party, sought to consolidate its position by 'judiciously supplementing the present denominational system of national instruction'.[15]

The alliances formed may vary in the strength of their political sponsorship, through the two-way accommodation involved. On the one hand, several educational groups might have to work through a single political party, one doing so through elective affinity, another perhaps through lack of alternative: the price of putting effective pressure on Parliament by working via the league, through the Liberal Party, was a dilution of goals for both the Nonconformists and the working class which had to abandon their denominational and socialist definitions of instruction respectively. On the other hand, the parties may differ in the strength of their solidarity with the educational pressure groups: the Anglican Union gained clear-cut support from the Tory Party, without substantial dilution of its educational goals, while the league was merely a pressure group within liberal politics whose effectiveness was muted by other party considerations.

These alliances transmit educational conflict from the market-place to the centre of the political arena. However, political struggles *over* education take place in the context of established market positions — of flourishing and functioning networks, for which their political allies seek central financial support and legal recognition.

Political conflict itself, then, has the effect of preserving the networks, sometimes through successive parties giving financial aid and legal backing when in government to different ownership groups (thus positively strengthening them), sometimes through opposition preventing government from undermining a network through financial or legal sanctions (thus defending them negatively), and ultimately through the compact they thrash out on the educational question.[16]

The settlement of 1870 reflected the balance of power between the two coalitions. It established the 'dual system': rate-aided school boards could be elected where the Education Department was satisfied that a shortage existed (a major advance for assertion); voluntary denominational schools were to continue receiving government grants but not to gain rate-aid (a continuing recognition of the Anglican Church which remained the largest proprietor). The liberal cabinet had steered a course between conciliating the forty MPs affiliated to the league and not alienating its Anglican members by depriving the church of the right to control what it owned. Non-decision-making was of paramount significance, for the party political defence of vested interests had militated against the introduction of a single national system of education. [17]

However, through this political process of concession, compromise and compact the independent networks do become increasingly public — they receive public funding and in return have to yield some autonomy to accountability — they gain legal recognition but have to cede some independence to incorporation. Central agencies are developed by government to control the public financing of instruction and to ensure adherence to the rules concerning legal recognition, with the national educational system emerging as the end-product.

How this works and who it benefits reflects the balance of power between the parties. The last third of the century was dominated by conservative rule. The 1870 liberal settlement proved a formula favouring the assertive alliance: after 1875 the Anglicans complained constantly of falling subscriptions, rising costs and competition from the school boards and succeeded in activating tory support for their cause. By a series of legal and administrative steps utilizing the new instruments of central control — auditing of school expenditure and intensified use of the code of instruction — the unseen grip of the Treasury tightened *differentially* on the networks. [18] Henceforth, conservative efforts were devoted to defending the established rights of the church at elementary level (still enrolling 64 per cent in the late 1880s), by pressing for rate-aid, and to protecting Anglican entrenchment at the secondary level, by seeking to dismantle the higher grade schools. [19]

Despite considerable opposition from the liberals, the labour movement and the Free Churches, these were the major components of the tory Act passed in 1902 which created a single central authority for English education and linked the networks together for the first time to form a national system. Thus, the types of interaction which link education to the polity are quite different from those which characterize systems with restrictive origins. There a political elite sought financial support to develop national education — here, educational entrepreneurs seek political support to consolidate their control. There educational systems developed centrifugally, by governmental initiative spreading outwards — here they emerge centripetally, from peripheric innovations which converge on government. In the former, **a powerful elite founds a national educational system in order to serve its various goals: in the latter, educational networks already serving different goals become incorporated to form a national educational system.** Systems with substitutive origins are then bred out of the private competitive networks by institutionalized political conflict; their final form being shaped by the interplay between government and opposition.

Since the two are rarely perfectly balanced, an interest group allied to a strong governing party will tend to see its network prominently placed in the educational system and will not have to make great concessions over its outputs and the parts of society these serve; one which has to work through a weaker form of opposition will tend to see its network relegated, subject to governmental modification, and loss of distinctiveness. Undoubtedly, the working-class definition of instruction lost out most, given minimal political sponsorship. It was virtually eliminated from national education since its main foothold had been in the higher grade schools which were now suppressed. In becoming part of a national system, elementary education had lost some of its earlier diversity although the various religious denominations succeeded in becoming incorporated without substantial loss of managerial autonomy.

Compared with the ferocity of elementary school politics, incorporation at higher levels was not overshadowed by a class threat and was settled by give and take among the party elites — feasible because the respective networks concentrated upon different types of tuition. Thus, the old Anglican strongholds retained their traditional definition of instruction in the public schools and ancient universities;[20] middle-class institutions were well accommodated, with technical education[21] coming under the aegis of the local authorities in 1902 and the university extension colleges[22] receiving grants and charters which upgraded them without entailing loss of autonomy or change in the services provided for business or commerce; denominational secondary schools[23] were inserted without diminution of their special kinds of outputs. Although the endowed grammar schools increasingly served the growing bureaucratic requirements of government, other parts of post-elementary education could preserve their distinctive definitions of instruction.

(c) Structural elaboration within educational systems

To turn now to the internal changes taking place in national education is partly to engage in an exercise of analytic convenience, in the sense that the transformations to be examined are not separate from those already discussed. Indeed, they result indirectly from the same processes of interaction and thus take place almost simultaneously. There appear to be four types of internal change which are universally related to the emergence of educational systems: unification, systematization, differentiation and specialization. The first pair are associated with the attachment of national education to the state and the second pair with its multiple integration to different social institutions.

Unification

The first universal characteristic of state systems refers to the scope and nature of educational administration. **Unification involves the incorporation or development of diverse establishments, activities and personnel under a central, national and specifically educational framework of administration.** In turn, this results in certain uniform controls emanating from the centre, and the standardization of certain educational inputs, processes and outputs on a nation-wide basis. Such unification may be partial, as some kinds of educational institutions, some forms of instruction and some types of teachers may remain outside the central administrative framework. However, as we shall see later, the degree of unification is not simply a function of the size of the free or private sector in education. Unification varies both in extensiveness and also in the intensity of administrative control.

Not every aspect of unification mentioned in the definition has its origins in the advent of state systems: both the French Catholics and English Anglicans could perhaps claim to have administered a national educational network, but their administrative agencies were neither linked to the political centre, nor were they specifically educational in character. Thus, the significance of state systems for this type of internal change is that only with them are all aspects of unification found in conjunction.

As the definition makes clear, unification is equally characteristic of systems with substitutive origins, which emerge through incorporation and of systems with restrictive roots, which develop through replacement. In the former, the development of a central authority for education is a slow and cumulative process which is not completed until incorporation has taken place. The administrative framework is gradually elaborated and dissociated from other bodies (Charity Commission, the church, Poor Law agencies, etc.) as a direct product of the networks seeking public finance and legal recognition. When systems have restrictive origins, unification is generally quicker and more dramatic. Once the restrictive phase has been accomplished, replacement immediately takes a unified form — it is centrally directed, national in scope and controlled and orchestrated by specialized administrative agencies, which are often (as in France) new organs designed for the purpose.

Unification is not synonymous with the centralization of education, although the former is clearly a precondition of the latter. The concept of centralization denotes specific relations between the unified parts. 'A centralized system is one in which one element or sub-system plays a major or dominant role in the operation of the system. We may call this the *leading-part*, or say that the system is *centred* around this part. A small change in the leading-part will then be reflected throughout the system, causing considerable change.'[24] A centralized system is thus a special type of unified system, but not all unified systems are centralized; to argue otherwise is to assume that in all forms of state education the largest educational changes follow from the smallest initiatives of the political elite. On this point one can fully concur with Cohen that it is simply not the case that state institutions always influence others more than the state is influenced by them.[25] The existence of a central administrative framework does not automatically make it the leading part. Centralization is thus regarded as a variable elaborative characteristic, whereas unification is a change which is universal upon the emergence of state systems.

Systematization

Accompanying unification, through which new educational boundaries are defined, are further internal changes which represent a transition from summativity to wholeness as the new systems become consolidated. Instead of national education being the sum of disparate and unrelated sets of establishments or independent networks, it now refers to a series of interconnected elements within the unified whole. **Systematization consists in the 'strengthening of pre-existing relations among the parts, the development of relations among parts previously unrelated, the gradual addition of parts and relations to a system, or some combination of these changes'.**[26] Two other aspects of systematization may be gradually refined in the decades following the emergence of the state system: first, a series of national examinations (or ones whose validity is nationwide), corresponding to the boundaries delineated by the administrative framework and graded in relation to the various levels; second, regular forms of teacher recruitment, training and certification, valid throughout the system and appropriate to the various levels. This progressive systematization is analytically distinct from unification, since the latter is equally compatible with summativity. Empirically, however, these two changes go hand in hand, for both appear to be universal upon the emergence of state systems.

One of the most important aspects of this change is the development of hierarchical organization, i.e. the gradual articulation of the different educational levels which may previously have been unrelated, controlled by different ownership groups, and completely unco-ordinated. Hierarchical organization develops because educational goals, even if focused intently on a given level of instruction, are hampered by a lack of complementarity with inputs, processes and outputs at other levels. The impetus towards this form of change is not provided by some abstract 'strain towards efficiency', but reflects the increased co-ordination required if a multiplicity of educational goals are to be attained and the pressure exerted by their advocates to see that they are met.

To avoid confusion, it should be stressed that the concept of hierarchical organization does not imply the existence of an educational ladder. While the former is a precondition of the latter, it does not constitute the sufficient conditions for its development. The co-ordination of inputs, processes and outputs at different levels of instruction does not necessarily imply that pupils can or do pass from the lowest to the highest level. Indeed, with reference to certain goals, it involves organizing processes at the lowest level in such a way that its pupils *cannot* enter the next level and do not have the qualifications to do so. Hierarchical organization can thus operate positively to encourage movement between levels, by dovetailing inputs, processes and outputs, or negatively to discourage them by placing barriers between the parts. Both the positive and negative aspects will be found in most systems, but the particular levels at which they operate depend on the goals pursued and the outcomes of political interaction.

Differentiation

In the antecedent period, one consequence of ownership was a relatively low degree of differentiation between education and the institution whose elite subordinated it — low in terms of the definition of instruction itself (usually confounded with the operations of the subordinator, education, for example, being considered as the formation of the Christian); in terms of the educational role structure (often completely overlapping that of its subordinator and illustrated most clearly by the religious teaching Orders); and finally, of course, in terms of its administrative framework. **Multiple integration, on the other hand, is associated with the development of a specialized educational collectivity, occupying a distinctively educational role structure, and transmitting definitions of instruction which are not co-terminous with the knowledge or beliefs of any single social institution.**

For the pursuit of diverse educational goals and the effective pressure of a plurality of groups, together prevent the new educational system from being organized at the same low level of differentiation. Quite simply, a form of education which remained confounded with, for example, religious practices and personnel, would hardly satisfy military or civil training requirements. If education is to service several operations simultaneously, it can only do so if it stands somewhat apart from all — for proximity to one will be prejudicial to the others.

Where restriction is concerned, the very plurality of political goals vis-à-vis education is itself a reason for educational differentiation, for these preclude the uniform and unifunctional type of education which is associated with a dominant ownership group. Certainly, there may be sections of the elite which preferred a low level of differentiation, with an intermingling of political and educational roles and activities, such that trained teachers represented loyal cadres and political ideology dictated the definition of instruction. However, the multiplicity of services sought from education by the various sections of society meant that the pressures they exerted did engender and sustain a higher overall degree of differentiation than was the case in the antecedent period.

The same factors are responsible in systems with substitutive origins, although they operate in a very different way. The political negotiations surrounding the incorporation of the independent networks fundamentally preclude a low differentiation of education. Since each assertive group works through its political alliance to defend the distinctiveness of its network while gaining state support, their interaction necessarily has the effect of opposing a tight relationship between education and one institution alone. Indeed, incorporation could not be negotiated were this the case, for all networks but one would have everything to lose and nothing to gain. Instead, the terms negotiated are essentially ones which deny any assertive group exclusive powers to define instruction, supply its personnel or control administration.[27] Thereafter, the conjunction of these different interests means that each acts as a waGchdog to prevent the re-establishment of exclusive links between education and another party.

Specialization
So far we have seen how a change towards hierarchical organization helps to avoid the various educational goals from being mutually exclusive. However, the co-ordination of parts and levels only helps in the negative sense of removing obstacles to multiple goal attainment. In itself it does nothing to ensure that education *does* serve a variety of demands and service a plurality of institutional operations. Indeed, logically, a

hierarchically organized system could be a unifunctional one; it could mean co-ordination of parts and levels for a single purpose.

The concept of specialization refers to a range of internal changes rather to any single one. To serve a particular demand may involve the development of new types of establishments or the pursuit of new activities in existing ones; the delineation of new roles, forms of recruitment and training; the increased complexity of intake policies and the development of branching paths of pupil allocation, within or between levels and types of establishment; additional variety in curricula, examinations and qualifications throughout the educational system; the development of special facilities, teaching materials and equipment. These are further effects of multiple integration where specialization in intake, processes and outputs develop to meet demands whose diversity is incompatible with unitary procedures.

In systems with restrictive origins we have already seen that some diversification of educational services is the price of elite cohesion and public support. Where substitution is concerned, specialization is transmitted to the new system through incorporation of the independent networks, and the more they were incorporated intact, the greater the initial specialization of the educational system. In both cases it is the possession of power that determines the demands which are given most specialized attention in the new system.

These four changes take place within the same system, they may occur simultaneously or sequentially, and are forms of growth which can go on indefinitely. Since each aspect of this internal elaboration derives from social interaction, the specific changes which result are not necessarily complementary. They are not synonymous with a better adaptation of the educational system to its environment or with an optimal arrangement of activities for giving maximum services to a variety of social groups. Therefore, no assumption can be made that they constitute a trend towards systemic integration — structural contradiction and social conflict do not necessarily diminish.

Structural elaboration: variable characteristics

If our theoretical approach can account not only for general types of elaboration, but also for *variations* in these changes, then it should be possible to advance further propositions. These would deal with the relationship between the four main internal changes in different systems and would give greater theoretical purchase on their specific problems of structural integration and further educational conflict.

It appears that variations in the elaborated characteristics are closely related to the way in which the educational systems developed — by incorporation or replacement. In particular these different social origins produce differences in the strength of the two pairs of characteristics (unification/systematization and differentiation/specialization) relative to one another. This in turn influences the relationships between these pairs and the problems of integration experienced within new educational systems.

(a) From restrictive origins

Unification and systematization are the pair of characteristics to emerge first and are inextricably bound together, for there is no intervening period in which a gradual transition is made from summativity to wholeness. Once restriction is completed and replacement begins the political elite seeks to institutionalize a new definition of instruction which is highly compatible with its requirements. Yet, if it is to ensure that the new establishments and personnel provide the services needed, then it must control them closely. Hence, one of the first innovations made during the replacement phase is the development of an administrative structure tailored to this task. This must simultaneously guarantee the responsiveness of educational institutions to the directions of the political elite and seek to eliminate countervailing or disruptive tendencies.

In founding the Imperial University (the name given to the new system as a whole), Napoleon could not have been more explicit that he was creating an instrument of government: 'schools should be state establishments and not establishments in the state. They depend on the state and have no resort but it; they exist by it and for it. They hold their right to exist and their very substance from it; they ought to receive from it their task and their rule.'[28] **In other words, if the aims of the political elite are to be satisfied, unification must be intense and extensive.** What is significant about such systems is that this group is in a position to design the unified administrative framework in accordance with its goals.

The central administrative agencies formed have a stong, hierarchical distribution of authority in which each lower administrative level is subject to a higher one and ultimate control is exercised at the apex by a political officer. In turn, this means a very low degree of autonomy of decision-making in the various regions or in individual schools. It is not uncommon for every decision concerning expenditure, appointments, examination, curriculum and recruitment to be referred to a higher authority. Similarly, the autonomy of educational personnel is not great and it is common in such systems to find that teachers are civil servants and thus subject to more limiting legal statutes than other professions.

This intensive unification is exemplified in the decree of 1808 creating the framework of the Imperial University. To ensure central control, a perfect administrative pyramid was erected which subordinated regional *académies* to the authority of a *grand-maître* who in turn was directly responsible to the head of state, the Emperor himself. This legislation proclaimed uniformity in instruction throughout the country and the government's right to enforce it.[29] In consequence, all schools at the same level were to impart identical instruction, to each corresponded a single form of organization and every qualification (*baccalauréat, license, doctorat*) became a national one. This is the origin, more than half a century later, of the remark made by the legendary minister of the Second Empire that 'à cette heure, dans telle classe, tous les élèves de l'empire explique telle page de Virgile'.[30] Central controls also reached out to enmesh the teaching profession as civil servants and to ally them to the state by more than statutory bonds. To Napoleon, 'il n'y aura pas d'état politique fixe, s'il n'y a pas un corps enseignant avec des principes fixe . . . Mon but principal dans l'établissement d'un corps enseignant est d'avoir un moyen de diriger les opinions politiques et morales'.[31] The loyalty of the teaching profession, modelled jointly on the Jesuit corporation and the military hierarchy, was to be ensured by a judicious mixture of training, incentives and surveillance.

Equally important is the fact that unification is very extensive. Thus, the decree creating the Imperial University also attempted to give the state educational system an absolute monopoly over all instruction. State controls over private education were elaborated and reinforced in 1811, thus greatly increasing the extensiveness of unification. The most important restrictions, which virtually made these establishments part of the public system, included governmental authorization before any school could be opened, subordination to *université* regulations and inability to confer their own diplomas. In addition, to prevent competition with public education, private schools were weakened financially by a per capita contribution to the *université* paid on each pupil, and academically by a requirement that all private pupils entering for the *baccalauréat* had to present a *certificat d'études* attesting that their last two years of study had been in a public *lycée* or *collège*. Fearing above all resurgence of the Catholic Church, their schools were limited to one per *département* and prohibited altogether in towns where *lycées* existed. Initially, at elementary level, the religious orders were allowed to continue teaching but as part of a dual policy to control the church in the state and the people in society.

However, the boundaries of the state system did not, in fact, become co-terminous with those of national education. Private confessional schools lost only about half their pupils after the stringent legislation of 1811 which sought to establish a state monopoly.[32] Indeed, the old dominant group continued to demand freedom of instruction and independent status for its own establishments. Nevertheless, even if these demands met with some success — as, for example, in France after the loi Falloux in the 1850s — the private sector does not achieve much independence as it cannot escape from the controls and common practices imposed by the unified framework. What to the state had been a partial failure in its policy for monopolizing public instruction, was a continuous and crushing blow to the autonomy of private education.

For instance, the existence of a single series of state-organized examinations limits the definitions of instruction which can be pursued within the private sector. Because of these factors unification is more marked in systems with restrictive origins, and the private sector is less able to create exigencies for the public sector because it is more closely controlled. Quite simply it is less problematic because it is less different. At the same time, however, the fact that the private sector is unified also prevents it from functioning as a shock absorber for the state system by serving unsatisfied demands and thus channelling a potential source of conflict away from public instruction.

From the start, systematization is equally pronounced for it develops in tandem with strong unification. Because restrictive strategies, unlike substitutive ones, present the opportunity for beginning largely from scratch, any successful political elite will avoid internal bottle-necks, contradictions and inconsistencies by dovetailing inputs, processes and outputs in its own interests. At first, such systematization will involve only those parts and levels to which the political elite has given priority in its replacement policy, although others are added later. Nevertheless, the principles guiding co-ordination are the operational requirements of the political elite.

Pressures towards further specialization and differentiation arise as has been seen from multiple integration, which is an unavoidable consequence of the quest for resources and support during the replacement phase. Ideally, the political elite would like to construct a tightly controlled educational system with just that degree and kind of specialization needed to meet the various *étatist* goals. Instead, realistically it seeks the maximum contribution and support from other parts of society in return for conceding the minimum amount of diversification.

In France, this aim was achieved by confining to the primary level those forms of specialization which were of little interest to the state. (An instance where systematization followed the negative principle of hierarchical organization — the educational ladder was quite deliberately lacking.) Thus, because demands for increased diversity were minimized and modified by the political elite, the concessions made to them did not reduce the high level of systematization or detract from the streamlined structure of the resulting system. Because they were introduced by government, the new specialized institutions did not escape central administrative control and thus lower the high degree of unification. In other words, systematization and unification remained the predominant pair of characteristics as specialization and differentiation were accommodated to them.

Such systems may properly be termed centralized — they have a distinct leading part in their respective administrative frameworks and small changes initiated through them have ramifications for all the other component parts of education. Since changes in the various elements are carefully monitored by the centre, their reciprocal influence is not of equivalent strength.

(b) From substitutive origins

The crucial point about substitutive systems is that **unification and systematization are superimposed on the networks which are already specialized and differentiated.** What this means in practical terms, is that the degree of unification brought about over the whole range of educational establishments is relatively low. In the same way, systematization is imperfect and various discontinuities in inputs, processes and outputs between different parts and levels witness to its incompleteness. The weakness of these two characteristics is a direct product of the interaction which leads to incorporation. It arises from defence of the independent networks in which specialization and differentiation are already entrenched.

As far as unification is concerned, each assertive group has a vested interest in retaining managerial autonomy over its network, since this alone guarantees the continued flow of those services for which the network was founded in the first place. Ultimately, pressures stemming from the assertive groups combine to ensure that unification will not be intense or extensive. The conditions under which a high degree of central administrative control could be introduced, would involve the dispossession of the assertive groups and nationalization of the networks. The political balance of power prevents this as each party sponsor protects educational property rights, as first the voluntary system and then the 1870 settlement in England illustrate. The role of the state was still principally that of central paymaster and the next quarter of a century did not fundamentally strengthen unification.[33]

By the mid 1890s a complex administrative picture had developed from the conflict between the political sponsors. Some reduction in autonomy had been the price of state aid and recognition, but not strong, rationalized administration. A patchwork of statutory instruments, financial regulations and a chaotic array of agencies made up the central machinery for educational control. The main authority for secondary education, in so far as one existed, remained the Charity Commission which had survived the Taunton attempt at organizational rationalization and represented an organ unresponsive

to government.[34] (As Forster later reported, 'I found no Ministerial power there . . . my vote went for no more than those
of anyone else'.)[35] Then the Science and Art Department,
originally merely intended to encourage study of subjects
neglected by traditional curricula, invaded both technical
schools and board schools in the course of awarding its grants,
an intrusion resented by both. Finally, the Education Department, supposedly concerned with the allocation of payments
to elementary schools, also overlapped with administration of
the higher grade level and the training colleges.

What is even more important as incorporation advances, is
that political action continues to repulse the emergence of a
strong central authority with extensive powers. This is largely
an effect of the politico-educational alliances themselves.
To a significant degree party hands are tied. However much a
strengthened form of central educational administration might
make political good sense, there is the support of the educational interest groups to consider. The latter, as highly
organized bodies for exerting party influence, constantly use
it to minimize such tendencies. The crucial point here is that
such pressures are being put on both or all parties simultaneously. In sum then, forceful political initiatives in favour
of a strongly unified system are lacking in such countries.

Thus, even the Bryce Commission (1895), which represented
a liberal attempt at administrative rationalization, underlined
that this was not synonymous with making 'secondary education purely a matter of state concern':[36] it accepted the
existence of a large private sector which would not be highly
controlled. It did not propose certification of teachers, only the
keeping of a central register; it did not advocate central examination, merely the regulation and co-ordination of those held
by the differing examining bodies already at work. Its careful
insistence on guidance, not control and on co-ordination rather
than nationalization indicates the low degree of unification the
liberals thought politically feasible. Yet it was to be an even
lower degree which was introduced by the tories in the next
seven years. This situation simply bears no comparison with
the total commitment of political elites to central unified control in systems with restrictive origins.

The 1899 Act, instituting the Board of Education,
represented the weakest form of unification, since it simply
brought together the Education Department, the Science and

Art Department and the Charity Commission, while guaranteeing that there would be a separate organizational method for dealing with secondary education. It was so weak that it was virtually unopposed: 'a phenomenon that might legitimately, if uncharitably, be ascribed to the fact that the Bill was agreeably innocuous. It afforded such benefits as might be derived from association with a Department of State, without their being obliged to surrender any fundamental liberties they enjoyed'.[37] It was unopposed precisely because it was, in the words of the chairman of the London School Board, nothing but 'a miserable little piece of Departmental machinery'.[38] Nevertheless, for the first time 'the existence of the central authority implied that the administration of all public instruction was essentially a unity'.[39] However, when compared with countries of restrictive origins, there is no denying that 'the rise of a central authority for English education had been a slow, tortuous, makeshift, muddled, unplanned, disjointed and ignoble process'.[40]

Furthermore, unification is not fully extensive, for important parts remain substantially outside the central administrative framework. Certain potential participants in state education simply withdraw, retaining their private status if it appears to them that their position in the unified system would be disadvantageous, and, if they have the resources to stay independent. This had been the strategy of the Headmasters' Conference from 1869 onwards: to ensure that the public schools 'should be free from any form of external guidance or control'.[41] The private sector in education develops from such cases (they are rather like companies whose directors find the terms of a proposed merger unacceptable). However, it is not the existence of a private sector per se which is the peculiar characteristic of systems with substitutive origins. It is the conjunction between incomplete and weak unification which is significant here. For it gives rise to a private sector which is the most independent in the world.

Turning to systematization, here again attempts to preserve the autonomy of the networks limited the extent to which it could develop, just as they had reduced the degree of unification which could take place. The two issues, of course, are closely related, for without strong unification it is unlikely that a high level of systematization can be maintained, and, in addition, the defence of specialist activities means repulsing intrusive central control. Again (in exact parallel to the argument about unification), if prominence of individual parts is the political concern of all, then a rational relationship between them is the political concern of none.

Directly reflecting this, the degree of systematization achieved by the English 1902 Act was the lowest possible, for it said nothing about the relations between secondary education and elementary schooling. In practice, the various institutions operating at these two levels showed the greatest discontinuities between one another: they were not dovetailed in terms of pupils' ages, their curricula or their examinations, but overlapped and contradicted each other at every point. This situation had arisen because the two major political sponsors had consistently pursued incompatible principles of hierarchical organization; the Tory Party advocating the negative principle and the Liberal Party the positive one. Neither of the political antagonists struggled for a rational relationship between *all* current types of institutions — their aim was to suppress, limit or transform their opponents' institutions and then to systematize relations between the remaining parts. It was precisely because neither party was fully successful in the preliminary ground-clearing operation that systematization could not be far-reaching. Thus, the Act of 1902 was not able to adjudicate between the two principles of systematization. Oppositional pressures had forced the inclusion of clauses making it obligatory for the LEA's to promote post-elementary education in relation to the needs of their areas. The Tory government had only managed to leave the relations between the two levels vague, not to impose its principle of complete separation. When the liberals finally returned to office in 1905, all they could accomplish was the introduction of 25 per cent of free places in secondary schools, so linking the two levels by competitive scholarships. Thus, all they could do was partially to impose their principle of hierarchical organization on their opponents' institutions.

At the secondary level itself, less was eliminated and (therefore) even less was co-ordinated. The middle-class technical schools and extension colleges survived, they remained linked together, but unco-ordinated with their opposite numbers, the public schools and older universities. Hence, the English system entered the twentieth century characterized by overall organizational discontinuity — with occasional links between pairs of institutions (witnessing to the partial success of their sponsors) but without any of the dovetailing devices such as a uniform teaching body or national curricula and examinations (testifying to the intransigence of their founders).

In other words, educational systems originating from substitution retain specialization and differentiation as their dominant pair of characteristics and these constantly create strains and problems which, as we shall see, are barely contained by simultaneous but weaker pressures towards unification and systematization. Such systems are frequently and properly referred to as decentralized — they indeed have no leading-part.

PART II
EDUCATIONAL
SYSTEMS IN ACTION

5 STRUCTURE: STATE SYSTEMS AND NEW PROCESSES OF CHANGE

The preceding chapters sought to explain the emergence of state education systems: we now turn to their consequences for subsequent interaction and further educational change.

Once private ownership had given way to state systems and mono-integration to multiple integration, educational interaction was immediately conditioned in a completely different manner. The context in which people now found themselves educationally, the problems they experienced, and what they could do about them altered radically. They reacted and interacted differently and this gave rise to educational change through processes other than the competitive conflict of earlier times. **Ultimately this means that once state systems have developed, the domination and assertion approach ceases to be appropriate for the analysis of educational change, since the structural relations which made it so have now disappeared.**

Interaction between dominant and assertive groups had been the historical 'guidance mechanism'[1] which repatterned the relationship between education and society, but concurrently it had transformed itself by destroying the conditions engendering this distinctive form of interaction. Henceforth, as education began to serve a plurality of social institutions, its control largely ceased to rest on the private ownership and provision of physical and human resources; most of them became publicly provided and thus their command was now the issue. Correspondingly, control over education became less direct: instead, struggles over it concerned indirect rights to deploy public finance for particular educational ends.

To understand the transformation of conditional influences which stem from the new systems is vital for the explanation of educational conflict and change in the modern period. However, two kinds of influences are involved: the general consequences of the emergent state systems, which will be examined first, and the variable effects of their different structures, which will be discussed afterwards. Because centralized and decentralized systems emerged respectively from restrictive or substitutive competition, their subsequent conditioning of educational interaction will not be identical. For different kinds of structural elaboration which developed in the past, in turn condition diverse forms of interaction in the present, and may then influence divergent patterns of change in the future.

(a) General effects on education

The first and most obvious consequence of the new linkages established between education and society is the loss of its previous mono-integrated status (associated with private ownership), many of whose educational implications also disappear. The fact that these systems are multiply integrated has the general effect of lifting education from its earlier position of total subordination. Now, four interrelated factors begin to inject a greater reciprocity into the relations between education and the institutions it serves. All of these stem from the fact that the resources used by education are no longer owned and monopolized by one party. Together they do not introduce balanced exchange, but although reciprocity remains imperfect, a significant amount of educational autonomy develops for the first time.

(i) To begin with, the fact that it is public resources rather than private means which now finance education does something to correct its supine dependency on a single supplier which can manipulate funding to call the tune and variations on it. The significance of this change is heightened because simultaneously education ceases to be a minority affair, for the competitive interaction giving rise to state systems also generated considerable expansion[2] — in both strategies this gradually meant that more and more children were being enrolled and an increasing proportion of people were practically involved, if only as parents.

From being completely without influence over formal education in the antecedent period, the position of the mass of the population has improved because of the pressures it can exert over public spending. Parental outcry and student protest are political prices which elite groups, directly concerned with transmitting public funds to education, must take into account. Consequently, educational spending increases, but at first this does not begin to approximate to 'fair exchange', for though monopoly has been lost, financial hegemony remains in the hands of a minority elite.

(ii) However, the very plurality of the institutional orders with which education is now integrated in itself fosters greater reciprocity. Their operations are distinct, and the groups associated with them will not seek identical outputs from education however strong the alliance between them or the mutual interdependence of their operations.

Reciprocity is encouraged through fear of the harm which would result for their own activities were educational services to be defined and commandeered exclusively by one party. Each group involved has a vested interest in preventing instruction from again becoming supremely dependent upon one among them. Thus, counter pressures operate against the re-emergence of the old mono-integrated and subordinate pattern. In the context of state systems, mutual policing seeks to prevent any one group from making the flow of public funds to education conditional on instruction meeting its requirements alone.[3] Since all integrated parties want different educational services and since all play the policing role towards each other, the overall effect is an increase in funds for education. This growth in reciprocity is the only possible compromise if no party is allowed to monopolize and all groups press simultaneously for their requirements to be met in full.

If the additional resources gained in this way result in any surplus over the costs involved in producing the agreed outputs, these may be devoted to the pursuit of internal goals. **Thus, this net consequence of multiple integration for education is a potential increase in autonomy, defined as the capacity for internal determination of its operations. This may not be extensive in certain cases, but its existence to some degree in every state system is in complete contrast with the total lack of autonomy which characterized education under private ownership.**

(iii) Obviously, this increased autonomy would be of little significance if educational personnel remained as tightly controlled and unable to articulate or implement their own demands as in the past. In fact, on the contrary, the changes just discussed go hand in hand with a third — the transformation of the teaching role itself — and their importance is due to this simultaneity.

As we have already seen, when education begins to serve a plurality of operations because of multiple integration, the definition of instruction becomes more complex. Specialization is the method by which a diversity of educational processes are accommodated with one another. It has profound occupational ramifications. First, educational personnel become clearly differentiated from the professional role structure of other social institutions — the mixed roles of priest-teacher or warrior-teacher disappear. **This has the important effect of creating professional educational interest groups for the first time — that is, people whose vested interests lie in the improvement of their educational positions because of their exclusive full-time employment in them.**

Secondly, the specialized activities in which teachers now engage gradually enable them to claim unrivalled expertise in educational matters. Even though the definition of instruction is still largely formulated elsewhere, there is no longer a body — such as theologians — which is more authoritative about the knowledge transmitted than the academics. This facilitates the transformation of a loose collection of teachers into a self-conscious profession, which seeks to acquire the same rights as other professional associations. Although this may take time, their increase in autonomy together with the greater flexibility of resources available can already be used to introduce some of the changes the professional interest groups want for themselves. **For the first time, educational operations are not determined exclusively by groups from other social institutions.**

(iv) However, professional organization has external as well as internal consequences. It is only after professionalization develops that direct transactions can be conducted between external interest groups and education itself. During the earlier period any such transaction was necessarily indirect: it was carried out perforce with the dominant group, by-passing education which did not enjoy the requisite autonomy for direct negotiation. Now professional interest groups may themselves initiate transactions with the exterior or be approached by outside parties.

Ideational influence comes into universal play, with external interest groups trying to convince the profession that certain courses of action are in both their interests — arguing, perhaps, that starting a new applied course would also generate extra teaching posts, protect against redundancy and improve facilities. Here the external agency is seeking to benefit by getting the profession to use its new freedom of initiative and surplus resources in ways which are advantageous to it. Alternatively, the profession tries to gain outside support for its own policies and with full professionalization, collective action gives more force to these views.

Secondly, there is a stronger form of direct negotiation which actually involves the exchange of resources for services. In certain systems the degree of autonomy acquired by the profession enables it to accept resources, in terms of research grants, buildings, equipment, etc., from outside parties, in return for increased intake, for laying on new courses or making special forms of training available and for undertaking applied research projects. Again, this type of transaction may be initiated by either party and again it will not be concluded unless it is felt to be mutually advantageous. The net result is therefore a novel and important process of change which not only enables the profession to accomplish more of its goals directly, but also does the same for certain groups in the wider society.

In sum, an extremely significant implication of the emergent state systems is that much more endogenous change must be anticipated now that education gains more autonomy through multiple integration. Since the teaching profession will collectively formulate its goals and plays a greater part in negotiating educational change, its activities cannot be ignored as in the antecedent period. In other words the explanation of change in state educational systems must alter now that their personnel have ceased to be passively controlled and have started to be professionally active. Explanation must now include reference to changes which are initiated autonomously within the educational system, whether this is due to the internal cumulation of resources or to transactions with external groups.

(b) Effects on other social institutions

The educational changes which have taken place universally affect other institutions, in terms of the services their members receive and in terms of the control that their members can exert.

Change in services is largely due to the development of multiple integration, change in control derives mainly from the linkage of national education to the political centre. The new relationship between education and society, consequent upon the emergence of state systems, is one in which both the capacity to control education and the receipt of educational services shift away from the (near) zero-sum situation which prevailed in the past.

In the antecedent period, if a group was the dominant group, then it enjoyed the most extensive powers over education, if it was not, then it was powerless to institute anything other than the most minor changes in instruction. As a basis of educational control, monopoly ownership was necessarily of that zero-sum type: the shift from private ownership to public funding annulled this formula. Educational control increasingly resided in the capacity to influence public spending, and its possession by one party no longer implied that others lacked it — if the military elite exerted a strong influence on educational spending this did not mean that the economic elite was correspondingly uninfluential. (This example also illustrates that the spreading of educational control does not necessarily entail a more democratic distribution of it.)

Multiple integration obviously has a very similar effect on the services received from instruction. Their distribution never approximated quite so closely to the zero-sum position as was the case for educational control, since although outputs were designed to serve the requirements of one group alone, certain other parts of society could sometimes make use of them. However, with the emergence of the state system, the fact that various institutional spheres are served by education now ceases to be a matter of adventitious benefit. Instead, the more specialized outputs are *intended* to service different operational requirements simultaneously.

The more widespread distribution of educational services has the immediate effect of abolishing the tripartite division between other social institutions into adventitious beneficiaries, neutral or obstructed institutions, according to the goodness of fit between their operational requirements and the education available. With multiple integration these stark contrasts fade. Sharp differences in kind are partly transmuted into differences of degree. The blurring of the tripartite division has the important consequence that it can no longer be used as a simple guide to identifying support for and opposition to the educational status quo. This becomes clear when we consider the new educational system in relation to our three previous categories.

(i) Compared with the old adventitious beneficiaries (which received something for nothing because of the harmony between their requirements and that dominant definition of instruction) **more parts of society now gain some of the services they seek upon the emergence of state educational systems.** Certainly, this is limited to those sectors which move into an integrative relationship with education during the interaction sequence generating the new system. Certainly, too, few of the new parties which do so, including the powerful political elites spearheading restrictive strategies, gain precisely what they want, and none gains what it does without concessions to other groups. But they do gain something and it comes with a bonus never enjoyed by adventitious beneficiaries — a measure of security. Because of this, they acquire a vested interest in the continuation of these services, even if they want to see their scale greatly extended or their relevance vastly increased. For the first time, a plurality of institutional spheres now have a lasting stake in the existing form of education.

(ii) The main change which takes place as far as the old category of neutral institutions is concerned is its drastic curtailment. **Compared with the antecedent period there are fewer and fewer parts of society whose operations are neither helped nor hindered by the prevailing definition of instruction.**

On the one hand, there is the push exerted by the expansion of instruction — inextricably related to the development of state systems — which now affects *all* social institutions. As school enrolment increased spectacularly, fewer parties could go their own way, inducting and initiating the next generation, independent of and indifferent to the prevailing type of instruction. For they were increasingly forced to recruit school-leavers and eventually could recruit nothing but them. In this situation, complete indifference to the skills and values they had acquired was impossible to sustain.

On the other hand, they were not simply pushed to seek interdependence because independence was no longer possible. There was also the pull exerted by the changed nature of their own operations. The salience of instruction grew with such broader social processes as bureaucratization, the application of science to production, the commercialization of agriculture, and the development of world markets. Few institutional spheres remained immune from all those influences. Obviously, formal instruction had no monopoly over the transmission of skills and many successful forms of in-service training developed. However, as the new systems were funded by these groups, like all others, it is unsurprising that the majority began to want value for money — a form of education better adapted to its operations, without paying twice over for it.

(iii) In the previous era, considerable significance was attached to the class of institutions whose respective operations were obstructed by the prevailing nature of education, and this still remains the case. However, two new propositions can be advanced about this experience of hindrance once the state system has emerged. Both concern the 'who' question and highlight important contrasts with that antecedent period.

The first is simply that since the new forms of national instruction are state educational systems, then it follows that the governing elite will never appear in the obstructed category. It will not gain precisely the services required because, *inter alia*, of inefficient planning, unintended consequences, a backwash from the private sector, and the interference of other objectives pursued in the system. But the fact that it is always imperfectly served does not mean that it is ever severely obstructed. Its legitimate control of resources is proof against this. Thus a fundamental contrast with the antecedent period is that nowhere will the state appear as an obstructed party in any serious sense of the term.

The second is that total obstruction will now be experienced principally by non-elite groups — it becomes concentrated among the people. This can be explicated by referring back to which parties successfully imposed (some of) their service requirements on the emergent educational systems. As far as systems with restrictive origins are concerned, what is obvious is that the more closely groups were clustered around the governing elite, the more say they had in defining instruction. With some over-simplification, the receipt of educational services can be pictured as a series of gradients: first, the governmental bureaucracy at the centre received most of its service requirements; secondly, sub-sections of the political elite were in receipt of many of the outputs needed for the institutional operations with which they were identified; thirdly, there was a partial satisfaction of educational demands among explicit supporters of government; and finally, a severe tailing-off of educational services to other uninfluential sections of the population.

Exactly the same occurred in systems with substitutive origins. Here the definition of instruction derived from the independent networks run by those who had been able to mobilize resources to found and operate them. During the consolidation of the system certain networks attained a prominent place, thus guaranteeing continuity of service to their sponsors while others were relegated, or even eliminated. Again, one can picture gradients in educational services received, with these tailing off for groups which had not been able to protect their definition of instruction from erosion during incorporation, and petering out altogether for parts of society which had never developed a competitive network. Thus, in these systems, too, the experience of total obstruction will be concentrated among non-elite groups, which lacked the resources to develop strong networks and the power to defend them.

Hence, in the new educational systems, maximal educational obstruction will, for the first time, show a strong tendency to be concentrated among the less privileged sections of the population. What has changed is that the experience of grave impediments is no longer shared with a number of important institutional elites, like the military, the economic or the political elite itself.

Thus, the inception of state systems alters the relationship between education and different parts of society. The loci of support for and opposition to the new definitions of instruction are still conditioned by benefits received from it and frustrations induced by it. However, the distribution of these rewarding and frustrating situations among different social institutions changes both quantitatively (in terms of the number of institutional spheres assured of services) and qualitatively (in terms of the degree of benefit or obstruction experienced and by whom). It remains to link these alterations in the social distribution of educational services and the parallel transformation of educational control to the question of interaction and change.

(c) Effects on the processes of educational change

Turning now to consider how change is brought about within the state educational system, this too is found to differ considerably from the earlier period. In the past, competition introduced sweeping educational changes whereas negotiation only produced minor modifications acceptable to the dominant ownership groups. The importance of competitive conflict then was due to the structural relations linking education and society — to the fact that only by displacing the dominant ownership group could macroscopic change take place. The transformation of these structural relations, with the advent of state systems, means that this is no longer the case. Instead, the conditions for successful competition became vastly more stringent at exactly the same time that the changes obtainable through negotiation increase enormously in scope. These two factors will be considered in turn to account for the fact that negotiation is now the most important process of educational change.

(i) Direct competition loses most of its viability in the new state system, for the chances that any dissatisfied group could gain educational control by either of the old competitive strategies are drastically reduced. On the one hand, the resources upon which educational control now rests are no longer concentrated in the pockets of a single group. This implies that strategies based on substitution are extremely unlikely to succeed because of the volume of public resources now absorbed by education, which rises as a corollary of multiple integration (more resources are needed if different kinds of services are to be provided simultaneously, more and more are forthcoming for this to be done because of the conjunction of pressures exerted by powerful interested parties). Thus, the chance of private suppliers being able to compete with public ones becomes increasingly inconceivable over time.

Equally, a restrictive strategy launched by a dissatisfied group would be most unlikely to succeed. To do so, it would have to overcome the governing elite (which obviously now thinks that state education is in its own best interests) as well as undermining the other parties whose activities are being adequately (if not ideally) served. As has been seen, one of the main results of multiple integration is the development of a plurality of groups with vested interests in the prevailing form of education. Thus, because it would have to contend with a defence of the educational status quo which is now centrally directed and socially extensive, restrictive competition ceases to be a realistic remedy for those finding education grossly inadequate for their purposes.

In effect, there is now only one way in which competitive conflict can still succeed and, although it will happen, the necessary conditions are severe enough to make it a very rare occurrence. Quite simply, unless social disintegration is extremely far-reaching, large-scale educational change will not be brought about by competition. It is only likely to occur as part of a general social transformation in which the state itself is overthrown and educational grievances can merge with other, more important causes of revolution.

(ii) However, transformation of the process responsible for macroscopic educational change is not due simply to the impossibility of the old methods, but is co-determined by the new possibilities which open up with the spread of control over education. What is crucial here is not merely that many parties get something out of education, for it could still be argued that they have more to gain from change than to lose from the status quo. It is also that their newly acquired influence over decision-making now provides an alternative means for modifying the definition of instruction. The possession of resources, which in the past could only produce change through competitive substitution, can now be employed to *transact* modifications. Similarly, political influence, which then could only serve to spearhead restriction, can now be used to *negotiate* changes in the state system, through pressurizing the central government to which it is attached.

Processes of negotiation were irrelevant to large-scale changes while educational control was vested in private ownership, because transactions remained limited to those found acceptable by the group subordinating education. However, in state systems the spread of educational control means that no single party can impose its limitations on what may be negotiated. Just as the definition of instruction is no longer designed to serve one party alone, so too no single group can veto the introduction of far-reaching changes if these are sought by others. The only limits to what is negotiable are those imposed via the interaction of the influential parties themselves — the way in which they block one another, the compromises they mutually enforce, and their concern that changes should be compatible with the present services which they require.

However, there are no grounds for expecting that less change will occur after the emergence of state systems than in earlier times: all that alters is the process predominantly responsible for bringing it about. On the one hand, radical change may be sought jointly by a group of parties which together are influential enough to transact it. General societal changes can alter the operational requirements of several sectors simultaneously (as in the aftermath of war) and lead their members to press for similar or compatible forms of educational change. On the other hand, smaller changes negotiated from month to month can accumulate until they represent a considerable departure from their starting point.

The checks, balances and compromises are no homeostatic mechanism guaranteeing the maintenance of the educational status quo. On the contrary, the pursuit of their own interests by all parties gives rise to transactions which alter the educational context: as each transaction is accomplished, groups realign according to how it has affected them, and further interaction produces new departures.

Thus, instead of negotiation being of limited importance, it becomes the process which accounts for most of the change most of the time in most countries. On the whole it is less dramatic: sweeping changes are introduced less precipitously, important modifications may be transacted without polemic, and innovations can be initiated unobtrusively. As a process it is also vastly more complex: with competitive conflict one set of relations was crucial for change (that between the dominant ownership group and others), whereas in negotiation several sets of relationships between education and society account for the changes taking place. Consequently, as the interaction leading to change becomes more complex, so, too, must the nature of the analysis which seeks to explain it.

(iii) The general process of negotiation can be broken down into three different kinds, all of which come into play with the development of state educational systems. As will be seen, the three kinds of negotiation are not equally accessible to all social groups, so that to examine them is to investigate three different sets of relations between education and society. The changes which are observed to take place will stem from the three in conjunction.

The first type of negotiation, *internal initiation*, has already been touched upon in the previous section. It was seen that their increased autonomy enables professional educators to play a part in determining the rate of exchange between resources received and services supplied. Surplus resources can then be devoted to accomplishing professional goals within the educational system. In other words, this source of change is the school, the college and the university. It can be brought about on a small scale by independent initiative in a particular establishment, and on a much larger scale by collective professional action. The relations which are significant here are those taking place between professional educators on the one hand and the suppliers of resources on the other.

The second form of negotiation, *external transaction*, involves relations between internal and external interest groups. It is usually instigated from outside educational boundaries by groups seeking new or additional services. As before, the profession is one of the groups involved in these negotiations, but the other party opts into the transaction of its own accord: it is this which distinguishes external transactions from internal initiation. Groups which, in the past, could only pursue change indirectly by dealing with the dominant group, can now negotiate directly with education itself. Given the increased autonomy of the new educational system, the outside world can now approach it. It is not suggested that these direct transactions will predominate over indirect ones (conducted via the political centre), indeed in some countries they will be of very limited scope. In others, however, they make an extremely important contribution to educational change.

Thus, certain parties which do not receive all the educational services they require will try to rectify this situation by entering into negotiations with the profession, offering more resources in exchange for better services. Basically, then, the external agency will try to buy the educational change it wants (although the currency need not necessarily be monetary). For example, a particular local firm may offer equipment and facilities for a college to lay on a specialized form of training, the armed services may provide scholarships in return for the enrolment of their cadets, the police, farmers and various professional groups may sponsor or support specialized establishments and industry may negotiate applied research in return for grants, professorships, laboratories, etc. This list is illustrative, but the fact that it is vastly more extensive in reality does not mean that any outside party can negotiate everything it wants provided it has the necessary resources. There are two major obstacles to unlimited transactions.

On the one hand, the profession itself has the power of veto.

Like other groups it is motivated by vested interests and will refuse transactions which compromise these. If the services sought by outside agencies are held to be professionally degrading (e.g., involving 'training' rather than 'teaching', the presentation of pseudo-knowledge or the dissemination of unacceptable values), the terms will be rejected. If they imply a less attractive work-situation, worse conditions, longer hours, more pupils, lower standards, they will probably suffer the same fate. Similarly, terms which are advantageous in their own right will not be accepted if they are likely to damage other desirable negotiations or to prove disruptive. For example, a university may turn down an attractive military research contract to avoid student outcry. Thus, in seeking to advance and project itself professionally, the educators also filter external demands and conclude transactions only where these are held to be reputable, profitable, and compatible.

On the other hand, as the major supplier of resources, the governing elite also enjoys the power of veto in certain circumstances. It will try to prevent transactions taking place which are contrary to its current policies, at least as far as public education is concerned. However, not all external transactions will meet with political censure and some indeed will be welcomed — if services are provided in exchange for private resources they take the strain off the system both financially and in the sense of removing pressure from government. Furthermore, the composition of governments varies and what might once have been vetoed, may become acceptable, pass into established practice and survive future political change. Finally, the private sector of education, in certain countries, can enable external transactions to take place even if they have been politically vetoed for public instruction. Changes introduced in this manner may well have important repercussions for the state system itself.

It is probably clear from the foregoing that external transaction is a form of negotiation which is open only to those groups which have substantial resources at their disposal. Thus, both processes of change discussed so far involve relations between education and rather restricted parts of the social structure. The same is not true of the third kind of negotiation, *political manipulation*. On the contrary, this is the principal resort of those who have no other means of gaining satisfaction for their educational demands — despite the fact that they may also be the least successful at manipulating the political machine. This form of negotiation arises because education now receives most of its funds from public sources. In turn, a whole series of groups (depending on the nature of the regime) acquires formal influence over the shaping of public educational policy. It is this, of course, which encourages popular groups of various kinds to use the political channel in the absence of alternatives. In the endless quest for support and party votes, it is this, too, which focuses much of the public dialogue about instruction on popular or democratic themes, though it does not imply a commensurate degree of political action on these lines.

However, this does highlight some important breaks with the past which accompany the development of state systems. First, educational influence is not tightly restricted to those parties which are already closely integrated with it: instead all groups can attempt to work through the polity, wielding whatever political influence they possess, to modify national educational policy in their favour. Secondly, while the distribution of educational control remained relatively static as long as the monopoly of vital resources was maintained by the dominant group, now that ownership and control have largely been dissociated, educational influence becomes much less stable over time since it varies with the balance of political power. Thus, the question of which groups receive educational services, and to what degree these coincide with operational requirements, may receive different answers as time passes and the composition of the governing elite alters. Thirdly, then, to understand educational changes stemming from governmental directives we need to analyze the political interaction through which various groups negotiated their introduction. Obviously, the groups which enjoy the greatest continuity of political power will receive a complementary and uninterrupted flow of educational services, and vice versa. Nevertheless, since this is not a zero-sum situation there will be a whole series of political pressures, alliances and concessions whose result is the continuous modification of the definition of instruction. The final contrast with the earlier period is that because the state everywhere plays a major role in the regulation of resources flowing to public education, it will always be a party to the process of structural elaboration in education, although political manipulation will not be the only process involved.

In sum, the three new forms of negotiation add up to a much more complicated process of change than the old style of competition. To analyze it involves examining group interaction at the levels of the school, the community, and the nation, and the inter-relations between them. For these different types of negotiation do not take place in isolation from one another. Political manipulation influences negotiations between government and the profession, thus affecting the amount and type of internal initiation which can occur. It also helps to determine the nature of external transactions, partly because of the power of veto and partly, too, because it helps define which groups engage in such negotiations, i.e., those whose demands are not well served by public policy. In turn, external transactions, conducted with the profession, increase the surplus resources of the latter and thus influence the scope and sometimes the character of changes brought about by internal initiation. Together, the changes introduced in these two ways modify the definition of instruction independently of the political centre. This alters the services available in ways which will be favourable to some groups and detrimental to others, thus affecting their policy orientations and the goals they subsequently pursue through political manipulation.

Thus, each form of negotiation and the changes to which it gives rise has repercussions on the others. This then is the complex network of interaction and change which must be unravelled in order to explain the transformation of educational systems. If our explanations are to do justice to this complexity, then the relative simplicity of the domination and assertion approach must be left behind, where it belongs, with the period antecedent to the emergence of educational systems.

(d) Structural relations
conditioning educational interaction

Structural factors only influence interaction because they shape the action contexts in which people find themselves: what affects them is their own educational system and their place in it. Yet, as was seen in Chapter 4, there are differences in the structure of the new educational systems which co-exist with the universal changes in structural relations. In particular, restrictive competition shaped a centralized system, whereas substitution fostered a decentralized one. Thus, the actual situations to which people react, and which predispose them to act in particular ways, are moulded by their national system: this system will reflect universal changes but it will present them to people as part and parcel of its own particular structure. Thus, to explain interaction we must leave the general discussion of universal changes behind and get down to the question of how these are mediated and modified by differences in the structure of particular educational systems.

In considering structural influences on interaction, the same two factors — the distribution of educational services and control — need examining in greater detail. The former course helps to determine which groups will be pursuing change actively while the latter helps to account for the ways in which they go about it. Here it will be shown that the emergent centralized and decentralized systems exert dissimilar influences upon interaction because of differences in their distributions of services and control.

In decentralized educational systems

Earlier it was seen that systems originating from substitution are much more loosely structured. Because specialization and differentiation were entrenched in the independent networks before the development of state education, they remained the predominant characteristics. The interaction surrounding incorporation defended much of the autonomy and integrity of the networks and thus limited the degree of unification and systematization taking place. Hence, such systems are decentralized, they have no leading part, and are raggedly integrated.

The predominance of differentiation and specialization leads to a distinctive set of strains which persists because unification and systematization remain too weak to provide the coordination which would prevent it. On the one hand, the system is sluggish and unresponsive to administrative control, its parts going their own way, often contradicting and obstructing central policy through their activities (as is most evident in the case of the strong private sector with its elitist practices). On the other hand, this same autonomy threatens the internal integration of the system leading to bottle-necks and barriers,[4] which persist because each element defends its own specialized practices and none is strong enough to make order among them.

These strains represented by unresponsiveness to central control and internal disjuncture, are experienced by various groups as deficiencies in educational services. To some groups this means that they will have access to certain levels of instruction but are debarred from entering higher establishments or elite enclaves; to others, frustration may consist in certain studies not continuing beyond a given level (it may be impossible to gain a degree in technical or applied disciplines). Each of these will be experienced as personal frustrations by pupils (and their families), and as recruitment problems (in a broader sense than the occupational) by those concerned with other institutional operations. In addition, the latter often find that the types of specialization carried over from the competitive stage of educational conflict, run counter to those they now require.

These exigencies in turn condition pressures for change from the various groups involved. However, they do not experience the same problems as one another (those debarred from prestige institutions are not the same people, by and large, as those whose recruits lack the training required). Also, the exigencies differ in that some could be overcome without substantial change in the system (by modifying course composition or admissions quotas). In conjunction, these two points indicate that the distribution of services and dis-services in decentralized systems discourages the emergence of a single solidary oppositional group committed to far-reaching educational change.

This fissiparousness is encouraged by the variety of things the discontented can do about their grievances, for the spread of control in the decentralized system means that change can be initiated in a number of ways. What is of supreme importance here is the rough parity between the three forms of negotiation as sources of educational change. Not all of these are open to every discontented group: its position in the social structure largely determines which ones it can use successfully. But the fact that different groups can pursue change in different ways is a further reason for not expecting the development of a united oppositional movement. Instead, it is anticipated that fragmentary interest groups will initiate change through different forms of negotiation in the decentralized system.

(i) First, *internal initiation* is an extremely important process of change here. In decentralized systems the profession rapidly becomes an active participant in the formation of educational policy. Because of its greater initial autonomy and its access to independent resources in terms of endowments, bequests, subscriptions, fees and earnings, the process of professionalization occurs early. It is not so subject to legal control nor so financially dependent on the polity as to preclude the formation of professional associations. These emerge first from the richer networks, whose very resources give them special interests to protect (like the Headmasters' Conference in late nineteenth-century England). It may take longer for them to develop in other parts of the system, but in none is control or dependency strong enough to prevent it.

Their consolidation means that the profession can begin to negotiate with the polity on an organized basis, and to affect policy formation in a variety of ways — gaining representation on advisory committees to government; independently initiating changes which are then used as 'evidence' or 'precedent' in subsequent political bargaining; refusing to implement central policies or subjecting them to considerable modification at the local level; as well as negotiating continuously for better pay and conditions. The relationship thus becomes a two-way one with education no longer passively receiving directives but with teachers collectively helping to frame legislation and mould practice.

Its independence enables the profession to make substantial internal innovations on the basis of its own experience, the teaching situation it faces, and the collective goals formulated by its associations. In decentralized systems the range of changes which can be introduced in this way is broad and often includes the capacity to alter curricula, texts, examinations, teaching methods and disciplinary processes, to accept or reject *in situ* the demands voiced by pupils and students, as well as to improve the professional work situation. In this type of system, internal initiation serves professional interests but also benefits other parts of society by rectifying locally perceived deficiencies. The increased resources earned in the process in turn reinforce autonomy and extend the future scope of internal initiation.

(ii) Secondly, *external transactions* represent a process whereby certain groups negotiate substantial changes in decentralized systems. Those parties which dispose of considerable resources and have aims acceptable to the teachers can often gain satisfaction from the public sector. Transactions are more numerous with the more independent parts of the state system. In England, accordingly, it has been the technical schools, colleges and universities which have been involved in the majority of external transactions — their own evolution being shaped by this process.

When wealthy groups fail to obtain the changes they seek from public education because their demands are unacceptable to the profession, are too specialized or focus on levels which are virtually closed to external transactions, another possibility exists in the decentralized system. There, strong private sectors of education flourish with relatively little interference from the administrative framework and such groups can gain satisfaction by buying what they seek from existing institutions or by founding new ones. These transactions account for the development of pre-school education, of preparatory establishments, of experimental or specialized secondary schools devoted to music, the arts, sectarianism or minority cultures, and commercial and industrial training; of technical, theological and trade colleges; of business schools and even of an independent university. The variety is as great as the list of buyers, for there are few barriers to entering the private market in education, especially where the older age groups of pupils are concerned. Obviously, this openness means that a number of disreputable institutions (like the self-styled colleges selling degrees) will be found among them, but what is significant about the private sector in a decentralized system is that its parts are not condemned to be second-rate.

Because they are not compelled to enter pupils for state examinations or to follow standard curricula, they are not forced to ape the public sector and thus to dilute their own activities. Instead, they can develop clear and distinctive courses which establish their own prestige and/or award qualifications which are recognized for their relevance in appropriate areas. Success is not guaranteed but it can be attained equally by a short trade course, a secretarial college, an elite business school or a trade-union college. Hence, various groups can introduce the educational changes sought, without standards comparing unfavourably with those in the public sector. This form of external transaction is, however, restricted to groups with surplus resources at their disposal. In the decentralized system it is not difficult to buy educational change but neither is it cheap.

(iii) While government has certain powers of control over educational institutions, their greater autonomy prevents *political manipulation* from being the distinctive form of change in decentralized systems. Thus, the third form of negotiation tends to be most important (a), where external transactions are least possible, and (b), for those who are least able to engage in them. On the one hand (a), although unification is weak when national education has substitutive origins, certain parts and levels emerge with less autonomy from the political centre than others. Because interest groups cannot transact services directly, they have to work indirectly to influence governmental policy and to counteract the political pressures of other parties in order to shape these particular public institutions in conformity with their needs. Thus, political manipulation will be most intense, and most important in accounting for change, when alternative courses of action are most limited.

It will also be used most intensively, (b), by those whose demands have little chance of satisfaction through other methods and, in general, the majority of the population is not in a position to use the first two forms of negotiation. The lower classes, immigrant groups and ethnic minorities cannot engage in external transactions on a significant scale because they lack the resources. Generally, too, the nature of their sub-cultures does not harmonize spontaneously with prevailing academic values and they do not gain much advantage from internal initiation. Partly this discourages them from trying to influence the profession but also many of their practical demands (like opening playgrounds early, running holiday activities, incorporating foreign cultures or integrating handicapped children in the local school) would not improve the teachers' work situation or enhance professional status.

Thus, it is via political manipulation that non-elite groups seek to gain any kind of educational change. (It is significant that even the powerful trades union movement makes most use of this form of negotiation and only dabbles in external transactions to meet its own bureaucratic needs.) By continuously dragging class, ethnic and minority claims to the centre of the political arena, other groups are irresistibly drawn to debate in these terms when defending their own interests. For this reason, most of the central legislation passed will be found to concentrate on such issues. However, the public prominence accorded to the educational problems of the underprivileged should not mislead us about the character of educational change in general: in the decentralized system other kinds of changes can be introduced unobtrusively through different forms of negotiation, without visible political struggle or social polarization.

Hence, it follows that the most outstanding feature of interaction in these systems with substitutive origins is its complexity. If change is to be explained satisfactorily, then all three kinds of interaction must be examined, together with the interrelations between them. Analysis will have to concentrate on the distribution of educational deficiencies, on the differential availability of the three sources of changes according to the position of the groups affected, and on the different forms of negotiation themselves.

In centralized educational systems

In the last chapter it was seen that systems with restrictive origins have a tightly integrated internal structure. Because their emergence was orchestrated by the political elite, the various parts were co-ordinated from the start to protect its own educational requirements from interference by other services which had to be provided simultaneously. Because such elites sought a system which would be uniquely responsive to their changing needs, the administrative frameworks were expressly designed as the leading part of each such system. Through them educational change could be filtered and monitored so that it never escaped the control of the governing elite.

In turn, the problems of integration found here are of a very different type from those common to systems with substitutive origins. Instead of the strains which develop representing a constant threat to the internal co-ordination of the system and a danger to governmental control, here the exigencies generated by a tightly articulated and centralized system create problems for groups in other institutions. **Thus, in the centralized system tensions will manifest themselves between the system as a whole and other parts of society, because the dominant pair of characteristics limit the degree to which education can become diverse enough to meet its demands.** Parents and pupils confront a system which provides them with relatively little choice. Other groups will find themselves compelled to develop various forms of in-service training in the broadest sense of the term; they will experience recruitment problems because of the prestige attaching to mainstream education and its outlets into state service; they will suffer from the implicit or explicit denigration of their activities and values by the official definition of instruction.

These deficiencies which condition pressures for change clearly structure educational opposition very differently in the centralized system. To begin with, the uniformity of public education means that there are more groups which gain very little in terms of services from it. In turn, this means that there is less chance that each deficiency will be experienced discretely by isolated groups. Added to this, the severity of educational grievances provides more opportunity for various groups to discover common ground. Taken in conjunction, these factors imply that the development of a united opposition group or groups is less unlikely in systems with restrictive rather than substitutive origins. The final contrast with the decentralized system is that tighter central control makes it difficult to remove the pool of grievances gradually, by a series of direct transactions — different in kind and spread over time and space.

(i) First, *internal initiation* will be less significant in centralized systems, both in terms of who can use it and what can be accomplished through it. The most outstanding difference is that, by and large, it is not a channel through which external or consumer demands can be filtered and satisfied. Instead, this process tends to be the exclusive prerogative of the profession itself, although the scope of changes which can be introduced internally is also more limited due to the lower degree of professional autonomy. Compared with its counterparts in decentralized systems, the professional body receives more directives from the centre and is able to initiate fewer in return.

Professionalization takes place with greater difficulty and over a longer period in the centralized system. The teaching body starts off with relatively little autonomy from the administrative framework which defines its training programme, supervisers certification and organizes placements. Usually, to ensure continued control, teachers are made civil servants and are subject to the same restrictive statutes which withhold the right to combine or engage in political action. Teachers' associations thus emerge late, after a hard battle for recognition of professional expertise and the eventual lifting of the most repressive statutes. What results is not a uni-directional relationship, but one in which the profession is very far from being an equal party in negotiations with government.

Their relative lack of autonomy also means that teachers and academics cannot negotiate directly with external agencies or earn extra resources from them. They themselves are too closely controlled to be able to offer the kinds of modifications sought by various groups in the community. They cannot alter courses, curricula, assessment, examination or selection procedures, for these are established centrally and are not susceptible to local variation. Thus, the most important issues are removed from the negotiating table. Local groups cannot hope to influence the profession to make good the deficiencies that the former experience in educational services. They are well aware that the teachers' hands are tied and that their own efforts are better directed elsewhere. Thus, formal contact between the profession and external interest groups will not be great at local level. What is missing here is the hard, practical and productive deal-ing between them, characteristic of decentralized systems.

The internal changes which the profession can introduce (by using any surplus resources extracted from government) are usually limited to those which are acceptable to the political elite and compatible with the existing organization of the system. On the whole, these are modifications which are of con-cern to professional advancement but matters of indifference to government — intensification of intellectual specialization, accentuation of the pure over the applied and extension of research activities. Hence, the changes it can and does initiate internally are those which benefit itself alone: in the cen-tralized systems the profession can only function as a vested-interest group.

(ii) *External transactions* are also of limited importance as a process by which major changes are negotiated in the central-ized system. No part of the public sector is independent enough to introduce new services in exchange for resources. Because it cannot earn, its autonomy remains low and state education stays closed to transactions, however great the resources offered by the external groups and however acceptable their proposals might be to the teaching profession. It may seem to follow that negotiations with the private sector will therefore be a more important source of change in the centralized system, precisely because of the closed nature of public education. The opposite is in fact the case.

Certainly, groups with adequate resources can found new establishments or negotiate changes with existing private institutions; however, the services acquired in this way are rarely adequate to meet their demands because the private sector is subject to heavy state interference and finds it difficult to offer a proper alternative to public instruction. First, the effect of strong unification is that private establishments are more closely controlled in terms of their inputs, processes and outputs. They are subject to state inspection, certification and often examination, and because of this such establishments are irresistibly drawn to imitate public education. For instance, if their pupils or students are to sit for national examinations, then they must follow public curricula, use the set texts and appoint teachers adept in the appropriate methods, otherwise their failure rate will exceed that of the public sector. Thus, schools set up for confessional purposes constantly find that religious instruction, far from dominating the timetable, is being squeezed out by examinable subjects. Here, the problem for these institutions is that their external sponsors and parental fee-payers are not going to invest in something which they can get free of charge anyway.

Alternatively, if the private sector attempted to award its own qualifications, these would have little chance of establishing their value on the educational market since this is far from a free one. Only state qualifications are recognized for a whole range of purposes which are of vital concern to those taking private diplomas — university entry, deferred military service, public appointments or possession of a degree. Private institutions are in a cleft stick, for they go it alone in the knowledge that what they have to offer cannot compete with the advantages and prestige attaching to public certificates. By following this alternative, they by and large condemn themselves to being second-rate and to giving a corresponding lack of satisfaction to those they serve: in the centralized system the private sector is not the elitist one.

Yet external interest groups seek neither the second-rate nor a carbon-copy of public instruction, they want a different kind of service from private education, but this difference is precisely what the remorseless pressure towards standardization, which emanates from the state, also militates against. The private sector thus remains weak, for too many groups seeking substantial educational change know that they can only get a modicum of satisfaction from it. Among them may be the rich elites which could buy the services they require in a different kind of system. Here, since their demands are scarcely met by external transactions, they are forced to (re)present them through the last form of negotiation.

(iii) Thus *political manipulation* is by far the most important form of negotiation in centralized systems. Because education as a whole has so little autonomy from the government and because groups seeking change have few alternative means of obtaining it, most pressures converge on the political centre. The provisions which do exist for serving other parts of society are those which the political elite had to concede historically because of its need for support and resources. This remains the case for future changes in the definition of instruction — these stem predominantly from processes of political interaction. In other words, the parties seeking new services must accumulate their demands, form alliances and organize themselves to work through the political machinery.

This is the case for most groups, including the teachers and academics, for when their demands exceed the bounds of professional self-advancement and involve broader educational issues they cannot introduce these directly. Instead, they must go outside the system in order to influence it, by joining a national political organization or external pressure group. The same applies to the majority of affluent groups which cannot transact changes directly; it, too, must seek to transform public policy through political manipulation. **This represents a major contrast with the decentralized system, for instead of political interaction being the resort of the underprivileged, it is the main channel through which all social groups work to bring about educational change. Consequently, a more restricted area of social conflict needs to be examined to account for a change in the centralized system, compared with the decentralized system. Analysis will have to concentrate on the distribution of educational deficiencies, the differential ability of groups to exert political influence, and the nature of political interaction itself.**

(e) Determinants of educational interaction

As in the preceding period, due allowance has to be made for the influence of other structural and cultural factors, which are non-educational in origin, upon the processes of interaction and the resulting patterns of change. The transition from the first to the second cycle is a historical process of quite lengthy duration and thus considerable social change will have been unfolding concurrently. In starting to discuss the second cycle we must now insert those alterations in the social context of educational interaction which distinguish it from the social environment of domination and assertion in the past.

The growing complexity of social structures, which develops as societies move towards full industrial status, involves the mobilization of broader sections of society, the differentiation of a larger number of corporate interests, and the interpenetration of diverse collectivities. The social environment of education enlarges correspondingly (practically no one remains disinterested in the definition of instruction), and becomes more complicated as the nature of educational demands undergoes a parallel diversification (matching the greater social differentiation of interests). In all new systems, this spells greater educational activity as do the concomitant cultural changes which have taken place. The increasingly international nature of value systems, consequent upon mass communication, mass literacy and mass mobility means that limited access to alternative legitimatory values no longer operates as a barrier to the organization of opposition, except perhaps in countries with very efficient forms of censorship. On the contrary, there is a growing fund of inter-continental ideologies, of schools of thought propagated by educationalists, ensuring that no ignorance of alternatives holds back the potential forces for change. However, this new environmental context has different consequences for the two types of systems.

The nature of the decentralized system is such that the greater social differentiation of interests and values, structured elsewhere in society, can find educational expression without difficulty. Given three different outlets for change, there is high probability that different interests and pluralistic values will be pursued through them. In other words, there is no longer the need to accumulate, articulate and then dilute demands, as in the old alliances of the past. Instead, particular social interests can and will attempt to negotiate their requirements in all their detailed specificity. Of course, this is not to deny that the more influential parties remain linked by kinship, class or overlapping membership (e.g., businessmen in Parliament, politicians as churchgoers and shareholders, teachers as members of political parties), the more they will defend common interests at all three strategic points — the school, the community and the central political arena.

On the other hand, in the centralized system, the supreme importance of political manipulation still places a considerable premium on the ability of both government and opposition respectively, to hold together if they are to be successful in the maintenance of the status quo or the transaction of change. Thus, if the spread of control has increased the social and cultural diversity of the controllers, mutual accommodation is still needed for them to arrive at a common programme.

Equally significant, given the attachment of every new system to the political centre, are the differences in the national structuring of political power. Thus, the relative closure or accessibility of state power will have far-reaching consequences for educational interaction in every system. This is absolutely crucial in the centralized system, since political manipulation is the main process for negotiating change. It is still very important in the decentralized system, although the effects of political closure can be offset, to some extent, by the intensive use of the other two processes. Thus, in contrast to the antecedent period, there is now an interface between education and the polity in all countries where educational systems have emerged.

(f) Patterns of educational interaction

Taking the whole of the foregoing discussion together, the different patterns of interaction which are conditioned by the two different kinds of educational system can be summarized in the following basic diagrams. These stand in the same relation to the second cycle as did Figure 3 (Chapter 2) to the first cycle, when educational change was heavily conditioned by ownership, mono-integration and subordination. The fact that there are now two diagrams for the second cycle reflects the importance attached to the centralization and decentralization as conditional influences on subsequent interaction. Both diagrams have been deliberately simplified at this stage in order to accentuate the different patterns of educational interaction to which the two systems give rise.

FIGURE 4
The structural conditioning of educational
interaction in the centralized system

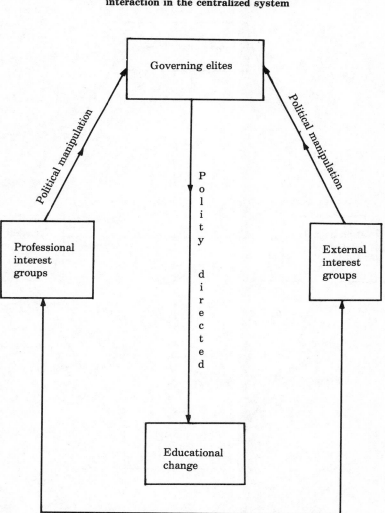

Aggregation of demands

FIGURE 5
The structural conditioning of educational
interaction in the decentralized system

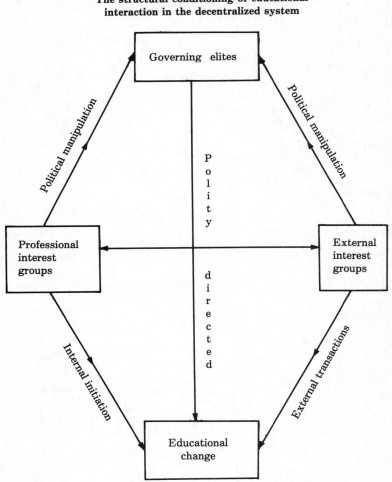

Figure 4 shows the typical convection currents of action conditioned by the centralized system, where demands originating in the school or community have to be aggregated, passed upwards to the central decision-making arena and negotiated there before being transmitted down to education in the form of polity-directed changes. In contrast, Figure 5 presents the more complex cross-currents of interaction conditioned by the decentralized system. Due to the fact that there are three different outlets for the negotiation of change, there is no necessity for demands to be cumulated or passed upwards, since changes can be introduced locally or internally. Hence the greater complexity of the typical action pattern.

These two basic diagrams involve considerable oversimplification.[5] The gross interaction patterns for both kinds of system are like road maps which show nothing but the motorways: complex transactions between sub-groups, parties and organizations, have been eliminated to allow the figure to stand out from the ground (see Appendix 1 for expanded diagrams relating to the two kinds of systems). However, in the following two chapters, dealing with interaction in the new educational systems, it is necessary to go beyond these simplified pictures and to magnify the two basic diagrams until they bear a closer resemblance to models of empirical reality, rather than schematic representations of dominant traits.

6 INTERACTION: EDUCATIONAL NEGOTIATIONS

Three processes of transacting educational change

Three processes of educational negotiation have now been distinguished: political manipulation, internal initiation and external transactions. Each of these involves the exchange of resources or services (wealth, power or expertise) against one another by the interest groups involved. Educational change is the product of such transactions and its nature is therefore determined by which group succeeds in accomplishing which form of negotiation in the course of interaction. Success depends upon the negotiating strength of one party relative to the other in any transaction. For this concept is a bilateral or relational term, it is not a generalized capacity possessed by some groups but not by others, but pertains to interaction itself.

Since each of the three processes of negotiation involves the exchange of resources, an unslavish use of Exchange Theory [1] helps to conceptualize what gives one group greater negotiating strength in relation to another. Furthermore, since power and control are derived as the emergent consequences of exchange, then the outcome of negotiations accounts for the development of either dependence, reciprocity or domination of one group in relation to another and to education.

Let us begin this discussion of relative negotiating strengths by isolating three crucial elements of any given piece of educational interaction, viz: (a) the participants, (at least) two educational interest groups, X and Y; (b) the resources they respectively command, X^{r1} and Y^{r2}, which constitute their bargaining positions; (c) the exchange (or non-exchange) of r1 and r2, which expresses the relative negotiating strengths of X and Y. These elements determine the degree of change, if any, occurring in this particular case. They also decide who exercises educational control in this situation; it can be X, if Y finds r1 irresistible, or Y if X cannot do without r2, but control is not necessarily a zero-sum matter, for a reciprocal exchange of r1 and r2 gives X and Y shared control and joint responsibility for the changes introduced.

We can now begin to consider the nature of the relationship between these two groups and what will give one high negotiating strength vis-à-vis the other. It has been argued that an interest group has the best chance of concluding an educational transaction in its favour the more irresistible are the resources it supplies to the other party involved. In his discussion of exchange and power in social life, Blau has provided a useful classification of the situations in which such irresistibility arises.[2] X will have the highest degree of negotiating strength when it supplies resources to Y under four conditions: (a) when Y cannot reciprocate; (b) Y cannot get the needed resources from elsewhere; (c) Y cannot coerce X to supply them; and (d) Y cannot resign itself to doing without them.

From these can be derived the strategies required to attain or sustain educational control on the part of X in relation to Y. X must try to establish rates of exchanges which are highly favourable to itself; bar Y's access to alternative sources of supply through monopolizing the resource or legally controlling the processes of exchange; discourage any attempt at coercion on Y's part; and prevent Y from being indifferent to the benefits it offers. Equally, Y's defensive strategies, aimed at keeping up its own negotiating strength, can be deduced by corollary. It must do everything it can to avoid being reduced to complete dependence on X. This involves a constant effort to prevent the exchange rate from becoming too unfavourable, by increasing the desirability and exclusivity of its own resources or services to X. It must work at keeping alternative supply lines open and accumulating supplies, thus increasing independence from X; developing strong organizations to compel X to behave differently; and propagating counter-ideologies which undermine X's right to use resources in the way it does.

(a) Interest groups, exchange and the three processes of educational negotiation

So far, the exchanges which are the backbone of educational negotiations have been treated in abstract and skeletal form. They begin to be fleshed out when we relate them to the three processes responsible for introducing change into education.

Internal initiation

The principal resource commanded by the education profession is its expertise (i.e., the specialist knowledge possessed by teachers, their capacity to impart skills and to inculcate values). Basically, internal initiation involves the profession exchanging the expert services it can offer for other kinds of resources which it needs, namely the financial means and legal rights required to translate its own goals into reality. To do this it depends on getting a good rate of exchange for educational services against the financial resources supplied, in return, by external interest groups. But these transactions themselves may be subject to political veto so the profession also has to increase the value of its expertise to the political authorities in order to prevent their imposing such embargoes. The latter is merely one aspect of a broader negotiation with the polity in which expert services are exchanged against increments in autonomy (the legal rights to do x, y and z). Only if the profession succeeds in improving its wealth and autonomy in these ways will it be able to increase the amount of educational change produced by internal initiation and ensure that its direction coincides with professional interests. **Thus the main task, on whose accomplishment internal initiation depends, is the exchange of expertise for financial resources and legal rights on favourable terms.**

External transaction

The principal resource commanded by external interest groups is their wealth, or more strictly their liquid assets, which can be devoted to the quest for educational services of various kinds. External transactions fundamentally consist of the exchange of financial resources for educational expertise, e.g., a professional undertaking to receive certain pupils, provide a particular form of instruction or produce a specific kind of output in terms of the knowledge, skills or values of those completing the course of study. The financial resources offered against expert services have to be sufficiently attractive to the profession to overcome their inertia (unwillingness to add new teaching burdens, devise new curricula or invent novel methods of assessment), and any repugnance or reluctance felt towards performing and providing the services required (if, for example, they involve longer teaching hours, collaboration with non-professionals, lower entry standards, or constraints on the knowledge transmitted). Simultaneously, the external interest group must be able to evade or overcome any political resistance to these transactions taking place; for only if it does both will it be able to instigate those educational changes needed to service its particular institutional operations. **Thus, the main task, on whose completion external transactions rely, is the successful exchange of financial resources for expert services.**

Political manipulation

The principal resource commanded by political authorities (both central and local) is their legal authority and capacity to impose negative sanctions. This includes their ability to pass laws and impose regulations, to withhold benefits and recognition, as well as to penalize irregular practices and offending parties. Political manipulation, therefore, consists of those groups which dominate the central or local decision-making arenas using their official powers to extract the educational services desired and to preclude undesirable outputs. At either level, it involves the exchange of politico-educational privileges (ranging from salary increases for teachers, through the institutionalization of professional advice, to the recognition and regularization of internal initiatives) in return for increased educo-political services. Alternatively, it can involve the application of political sanctions, in other words the withholding of certain rights or requirements in order to overcome professional resistance or to veto unwanted transactions. The services extracted or suppressed in this way are used to keep educational activities in line with political requirements. **Thus, the main task, on whose execution political manipulation rests, is the exchange of power resources for expert services.**

Obviously, the designation of these 'main tasks' involves considerable over-simplification. First, each of the groups concerned (be it professional, institutional or political) possesses more than one type of resource which comes into play in processes of negotiation — the financial powers of government are simply a clear example of this more general point. Secondly, it is indeed many of the same people who engage in the three kinds of transactions: some members of the population may only participate at the lowest level in one of them (e.g., by voting), a much smaller proportion will participate in all three (e.g., by being an active member of a political party, a parent-teacher association and a chamber of commerce), while between these extremes there are varying degrees of educational activity and of overlap between participants. The existence of overlap means that actors themselves come to know that what happens via one process of negotiation then has an influence upon others, and that there is more than one way of getting what they want. Thirdly, the actual processes of negotiation have been entirely left aside by concentrating on the objectives of the 'main tasks' rather than the strategic action through which they may or may not be accomplished.

(b) Negotiating strategies

Each of the three processes of negotiation operates rather differently in the centralized and the decentralized system because of initial and enduring differences in the bargaining positions of the three main parties involved — the governing elite, professional educators and external interest groups. Nevertheless, the negotiating strategies are identical. Hence, formally, we are concerned with the same strategic interplay between the three main parties, with how each played the hands that the resource distribution dealt them, although the cards were stacked differently in the two kinds of system. For it is these negotiating strategies which in combination ultimately shaped educational change.

Political manipulation

Over time, the central authority seeks to maintain or strengthen its educational control in order to be able to attain its own goals and does so in the four following ways, all of which are hedged by the initial and subsequent distribution of resources among the three main parties to negotiation.

(i) The first strategy is to try to reduce the capacity of education to reciprocate for the resources supplied to it by the state. The aim here is to attain the educational equivalent of the state's position in a command economy, where it controls the rate of exchange, prices, production and distribution. Here the polity's leverage consists in its ability to confer benefits and this accounts for so many governments continuing to increase their investment in education, even when they have become the majority suppliers. As a strategy, however, this can prove double-edged, for to invest generously may be to allow the internal accumulation of surpluses with which the profession can pad itself against political prods whose thrust derives from withholding resources. However, if strategy (ii) is successful, then dependence on the state can be coupled with a low rate of exchange.

(ii) The effectiveness of the first strategy is thus related to the second — barring access to *alternative suppliers* by imposing legal limitations on exchange processes. Here the polity will refuse legal recognition to certain diplomas, establishments, personnel or courses, thus reducing the attractiveness of the services that the profession could offer to external groups. This discourages external transactions by damaging the professional bargaining position, but it is only one branch of a two-pronged attack. The other involves the imposition of legal vetoes and the refusal to authorize certain negotiations at all. The crucial element in this connection is the degree to which the external interest group is itself politically influential (and can deflect projected embargoes) or is capable of marshalling legal defence (to repulse or lift such vetoes). Ironically, this means that the polity's strategy will be most effective against the weaker suppliers, which have least to offer the profession but which also present least threat to the educational ambitions of governing elites.

(iii) Since the main problem for the governing elite is resistance to its policies, the third strategy is to undermine the autonomy which makes this possible. Thus, legislation can reduce local and institutional autonomy, making the system more responsive to central directives, if the governing elite is strong enough to deploy the whole battery of central sanctions to this end. But two things may stand in its way: the political influence and positions already acquired by educational interests, and the hostility of opposition parties (which may indeed accept state intervention in principle, but fear the consequences of placing this instrument in the hands of its opponents).

(iv) Consequently, most political elites will strategically promote ideologies favouring political intervention, often justified on totally different grounds but sharing the self-righteous assumption that it would be justly used in their hands alone. The left usually seeks to identify state intervention with eliminating social discrimination; the right generally associates it with guaranteeing value for taxpayers' money. Both strands can be met by ideological opposition from among their own supporters (interest groups defending educational autonomy because it advances their aims) and this itself may constitute a powerful normative contribution to the maintenance of the status quo.

However, the initial distribution of resources placed the governing elite in a very different strategic position upon the emergence of the decentralized and the centralized systems. The original distribution of resources was much less favourable to the political centre in decentralized systems and made its 'main task' of exchanging power resources for educational services considerably more complicated than where centralization prevailed. Other groups were also in strong bargaining positions and education was not exclusively dependent on the resources supplied (or withheld) by the central political elite. For example, the profession retained property and sectional autonomy, defended during incorporation; it maintained alternative suppliers and the relationship between internal and external interest groups was mutually supportive, protecting the 'free market in education'; organizations had formed to resist central encroachment on professional autonomy or the acquired rights of external interest groups and these continued to insert themselves at all levels of decision making so as to cushion the impact of political directives on education as well as generalizing values which mobilized opposition to political veto on educational matters. **Consequently, any change in the decentralized system involves a broader set of transactions. Every legal change introduced from the centre entails negotiation with professional interest groups to ensure its implementation, and with external interest groups to prevent its vitiation or evasion.**

Thus, in the decentralized system political manipulation involves a struggle, not only on the part of those wanting to influence governmental policy, but also in order to translate official policy into educational practice. Because of the initial distribution of resources, the polity is not in an unassailable bargaining position and, since the enduring aim of interested parties is to defend if not to improve their own positions of influence, this tends to keep it that way. In this context, parts of the system continually escape political control and introduce changes independently, thus creating new problems for government: while with equal pertinacity the polity struggles to contain such developments and keep education in line with governmental policy.

On the contrary, in centralized systems, the governing elite has been from the start in a vastly stronger strategic position. In terms of our earlier notation, the polity X supplied resources to education under the four conditions which made the professional groups Y^1 completely dependent upon it, and unable to increase their autonomy through dealings with other interest groups Y^2. The rates of exchange between X and Y^1 consistently favoured the former, the profession having neither the finance nor the freedom to alter its services and thus manipulate a more reciprocal rate; X's political veto on direct transactions between Y^1 and Y^2 prevented resources from being acquired elsewhere; while neither Y^1 nor Y^2 could resign themselves to the situation. The profession, both as a body morally committed to providing educational services for the community and as individuals with vested interests in job security, could not dispense with centrally provided resources. Moreover, in the modern period, we have already seen that few external interest groups can remain indifferent to the receipt of educational services. The only weak point in the polity's control was its capacity to contain counter-coercion on the part of Y^1 and Y^2, precisely because the negotiating strength of X itself generated so much discontent and opposition. Hence, of course, the pattern of intermittent explosions directed against X, which represent a major source of change in the centralized system.

Consequently, in centralized systems it is possible to concentrate almost exclusively on interaction which culminated in the passing of legislation, decrees or regulations because both internal and external interest groups had little alternative but to accept these measures since the polity was continuously in an unassailable position. In contrast, because of the weaker strategic position of the political elite in decentralized systems, the following forms of negotiation will be of greater significance there.

External transactions
The 'main task' of translating financial resources into the expert services required involves direct negotiation with professional groups. The political aspects of such transactions have already been discussed, so here we will concentrate on the factors

determining the relative negotiating strengths of external and internal groups when they (can) face one another in interaction. Although wealth of resources is usually translated into a high level of negotiating strength, it will be rather rare for any external interest group to reduce education, or a particular part of it, to a position of total dependence. Instead, when transactions occur they are more likely to be of a reciprocal nature for several reasons.

The fact that a professional group has been approached for services means that it has something of value to offer and this it can play upon in negotiations. Also, if it is propositioned by several external groups simultaneously, then the teaching body can pick and choose, bidding up the rate among the alternative suppliers of resources and only settling on advantageous terms. Finally, and most important, no external interest group can force the profession to supply services it does not want to provide (on normative grounds) or does not think are worth providing (at the price offered). On the contrary, the onus is upon the external group to make its terms as attractive as possible to the educational institutions involved. Given this defensive position on the part of the profession, what the external interest group must try to do is to ensure that a transaction takes place at a price which is reasonable to it.

They will be most likely to succeed when four conditions hold, and these constitute their negotiating strategies:

(i) When the external interest group proposes a generous exchange rate (leaving the profession a surplus over the actual cost of providing the services required), which implies that it has considerable resources at its disposal and/or devotes a high proportion of them to educational ends.

(ii) When the offer it proposes compares favourably with those made by other interest groups. However, such deals are not concluded exclusively on financial grounds — if the profession promotes its own goals through transacting with a particular group, the cash element will play a smaller part: if it feels it is degrading itself or endangering state aid through inviting political veto, then the financial inducement will have to be much greater. Nevertheless, the two above conditions hold good because wealth always enables an interest group to transact with the private sector, even if it makes no headway with public education.

(iii) When a group can 'square' a deal in advance with the polity, through the governmental influence or favour it enjoys, the educators are more likely to get down to the negotiating table for fear of future political reprisals.

(iv) When a group is convinced ideologically that it cannot dispense with educational services, the more likely it is to obtain them — partly because it will devote a greater proportion of its available resources to getting them, and partly because it will strive to meet the above conditions if it did not do so in the first place.

If the final condition holds, yet the group in question fails to bring about a direct transaction, it can still pursue its educational goals through political manipulation: indeed, many groups will be engaging in both forms of negotiation simultaneously. However, it is important to note that repeated repulsion by the profession can lead some groups to resign themselves to doing without educational services altogether. These will be the poorer groups whose lack of resources had given them weak bargaining positions with the profession, and especially those whose political influence was equally low. For minority groups, in particular, their failure in one kind of negotiation may produce general discouragement and mean that the profession has played a part in organizing certain issues and problems out of educational politics. This is true of both kinds of system, but will be more pronounced in centralized ones because external transactions themselves are fewer and less far-reaching.

Internal initiation

Here, where the main task is the translation of educational expertise into other kinds of resources (which increase autonomy and internal self-determination), different sections of the profession find themselves in different bargaining positions. The initial distribution of resources, vertically among the various educational levels and horizontally among different kinds of institutions, gave certain groups of teachers and academics better starting points than others. This should be borne in mind when recalling the points made about professional negotiating strength in the discussion of the other two processes. Rather than repeating these, we can extract from the earlier analysis those conditions under which the educators are most likely to succeed in transactions, and express them in such a way that they can refer to the profession as a whole or to particular parts of it.

Theodore Lownik Library
Illinois Benedictine College
Lisle, Illinois 60532

From the foregoing discussion it appears that professional groups will do best in negotiation, and in turn be able to introduce more of the internal innovations they desire, when they employ the following strategies:

(i) Offer services which are attractive in terms of their inputs, processes and outputs. One of the most important aspects of this is professional upgrading through which a higher quality of service is made available. By raising expertise itself, a higher exchange rate can be asked, thus increasing the market value of professional skills.

(ii) Control the certification of expertise, both in terms of the quantity and quality of those admitted to the profession, so as to create a *de facto* if not a *de jure* closed shop which bars alternative supplies of 'teachers' or 'lecturers', or so raises the prestige of the certificated professional that the latter are at best 'instructors' or 'trainers' and at worst 'crammers' or 'unqualified'.

(iii) Participate in official processes of educational control and administration in order that they themselves play a part in moulding official policy rather than being reduced to modifying, resisting or sabotaging it at the stage of implementation.

(iv) Reinforce and legitimate the above activities, as well as encouraging the need for expert services, through disseminating appropriate educational values. In this the profession alone can make direct use of the learning situation to spread its values, and also by its very nature it can make good use of public media.

(c) The bargaining positions of educational interest groups

So far we have analyzed negotiating strategies without reference to the vital question of who can use them. This is the point at which the distribution of resources in society connects up with the structural influences upon interaction exerted by different types of educational system. For the former defines the bargaining positions of the various social groups in relation to educational negotiations. Bluntly, the social structure determines *who* has the three kinds of assets, while the educational system is decisive for *what* they can do with them. Resource distributions obviously change largely in response to non-educational factors: they are thus inserted into the present analysis but cannot be explained by it.

In advancing a series of propositions about educational interaction, the intention is to remain neutral towards the general sociological debate between those who emphasize a uni-dimensional social structure (with a superimposition of the class, status and power dimensions) versus those stressing divergence and multidimensionality.[3] The relative merits of these views (for any given period) are left to manifest themselves through the analytical framework used here. For example, if class analysis alone is adequate to account for educational interaction, this will become apparent since the line-up for each process of negotiation would reflect little other than class divisions.

This deliberate neutrality (and the correspondingly guarded vocabulary of elites, groups and parties) is also prompted by the specificity of our problem which is to theorize about the intricacies of who really exercises and contests control, with what degree of success and under which conditions. Without this specification, class or any other concept of structured inter-action remains at too high a level of generality to give purchase on the course of institutional stability or change. In other words, theories claiming greater universality themselves need to specify the precise interactional mechanisms through which their 'key group' penetrates the educational field. It is exactly this question of how the social structure and educational system interpenetrate that is the concern of the present theory.

In particular, it is maintained that since political manipula-tion is the most important process through which change is introduced in the centralized system, then it is the social distribution of power which is of prime concern in explaining the course of educational politics. Conversely, since the three processes of negotiation enjoy a rough parity of importance in the decentralized system, then it is the distribution of all three resources — wealth, power and expertise — which shapes the contours of educational politics there.

Thus, the social distribution of power[4] in the centralized system and of power, wealth and expertise in the decentral-ized system constrain: the nature and number of people admitted to educational transactions; their initial bargaining positions and changes in them; and the volume and kinds of demands which can be negotiated at any time.

The concentration of power in relation
to the decentralized system
Thus, in the centralized system one variable exerts a crucial

influence on the course of educational politics, namely the structure of political decision-making.[5] Here the vital aspect of different political regimes is how broad or narrow, open or closed, accessible or inaccessible they are in structure. For this directly affects political manipulation since it helps to determine what kinds of changes are negotiable and who can engage in negotiations.

A simple formal classification in terms of degrees of governmental closure seems adequate here for differentiating between different political structures at different times. Closure is defined and identified by the accessibility of the main organs of government. Such organs are considered inaccessible if socially significant parties can make no use of them and are systematically turned down by them, if such organs give no hearing to issues held important by these groups, or if such organs operate coercively or manipulatively to exclude these parties, their issues or their interests. The main organs of national government are thus taken to delineate the central political arena and its degree of closure is the main structural characteristic to be accentuated: because our interest is centred on the manipulation of the former it is their manipulability which is stressed.

Consequently, a simple form of classification which is comparative, minimalistic, problem-oriented (and susceptible of later refinement), distinguishes three broad types of state frameworks:

A. The impenetrable political centre;
B. The semi-permeable political centre;
C. The accessible political centre.

Obviously, the simple typology used here is a static device and any country is likely to change category with regard to closure over time. Reasons for these political transformations lie outside the scope of this study, which merely takes account of them by using the classificatory scheme as a template which is moved longitudinally through history. This enables a nation's past to be divided into periods when its political centre was of the A, B or C variety and then allows the comparison of patterns of educational interaction and change when different countries displayed similar degrees of closure at different times. It is anticipated that the greater the penetrability of the political structure, the larger the number of parties able to gain redress for their educational grievances and the broader the range of changes introduced in centralized systems.[6]

From this we can advance three basic hypotheses:

Proposition 1: With an impenetrable political centre, only sub-sections of the governing elite will be able to negotiate educational demands by political manipulation.

Proposition 2: With a semi-permeable political centre, sub-sections of the governing elite, together with government supporters, will be able to negotiate educational demands by political manipulation.

Proposition 3: With an accessible political centre, governmental opponents, too, will be able to negotiate educational demands by political manipulation.

However, the effects of each type of political structure are themselves affected by the nature of elite relations within them, and the latter are logically and empirically distinct from the former.[7]

Relations among such elites are variable: at one extreme they may display unity, homogeneity and superimposition (sharing the same background, similar or compatible interests and consciousness of belonging and working together), at the other extreme they can be heterogeneous in origin, have cross-cutting affiliations and pursue disparate goals. Potentially, both kinds of elites can be found in conjunction with each type of political centre outlined above, which is precisely why the two should not be conflated.

Attention is given to governing elites for the simple reason that they always have the capacity to command political attention (they merely differ in the extent to which this is exclusive to them alone). Because of this, elite relations everywhere exert an influence on the kinds of educational changes which are introduced or blocked. Obviously, this influence is most crucial where the political centre is impenetrable, because then the governing elite alone constitutes the restricted circle of those with direct access to decision-making organs. Under these circumstances, the type and diversity of educational change sought (or the extent to which existing educational practice is defended) will be highly dependent on the relations between sub-elites, their relative independence from one another, and the extent of their unanimity about educational goals. It seems likely that the greater the homogeneity of the governing elite, the more standardized and undifferentiated will be any educational reforms introduced. Lack of unity, homogeneity and super-imposition between sub-elites, on the other hand, encourages a more diversified educational policy. However, it also seems to be the case that the effect of their divergent educational interests can often block change, especially where the different sections are evenly balanced. Finally, it must not be forgotten that governing elites which are divided on decision-making may be united on non-decision making. For example, military and civil service heads can seek very dissimilar types of curricula without any disagreement about which class of people should receive either kind of instruction. Empirically, one of the greatest problems of analyzing elite relations is thus to tease out and stress the quiet areas of educational accord as well as accentuating the blatant conflicts over policy.

The concentration of power, wealth and expertise in relation to the decentralized system

Whereas in the centralized system the bargaining positions of educational interest groups are determined by the relative concentration of political power, in the decentralized system it is the relative concentration of all three resource distributions which plays the corresponding role. The availability of all resources is conceptualized in a similar manner. Thus, wealth and expertise are also considered inaccessible in so far as significant social groups do not possess them, cannot make use of them, or to the degree that other groups can employ them to exclude further parties and their interests from either external transactions or internal initiation.

At all times, every educational interest group will have a place on the hierarchical distribution of each of the three resources considered. The general position of a group is made up of its placings on the hierarchies of wealth, power and expertise. However, it is methodologically impossible to express this overall position mathematically, because of the incommensurability between the three hierarchies, and the absence of a common denominator to which they could be reduced. In view of this, we are forced to work in rather gross terms, merely designating groups as having high or low access to each resource.

However, within these limitations, it is possible to advance three propositions which link groups and resources to educational interaction. (These represent the broad equivalents of propositions 1, 2 and 3 about who can negotiate change, given different concentrations of political power, in the centralized system.)

Proposition 4: Groups with low access to all resources will be in the weakest bargaining position (Position 1)

Proposition 5: Groups with differential access to the various resources will be in a stronger bargaining position (Position 2)

Proposition 6: Groups with high access to all resources will be in the best bargaining position (Position 3)

By corollary, groups are likely to receive educational services in reverse order. Therefore, it is groups in the latter position which will tend to be responsible for the majority of changes, whereas those in the first position will probably not be able to introduce significant educational modifications. However, it must be recalled that it is the degree of concentration which is crucial, for the less concentrated the distribution of resources, the fewer the number of parties which will find themselves in position (1) above, and the greater the proportion of groups which will be capable of benefiting from educational transactions. The opposite is equally true, a very high concentration of resources places a very restricted section of society in position (3) above. Along the same lines, a differential concentration of the three resources maximizes the number of interest groups finding themselves in position (2) above.

However, in contrast with the centralized system there is a much lower premium on 'good relations' among the resource holders: for, in the decentralized system, where the three processes of negotiation operate simultaneously, superimposition and organization are not necessary for effective transactions and may even prove counter-productive. For example, local firms working quietly through external transactions may gain the exact services they seek from colleges in their vicinity much more readily than if an industrial confederation sought the transformation of further education en bloc. Indeed, united inaction (in repulsing the educational ambitions of the resourceless masses) is probably the most important form of concerted action, for where positive changes are sought, the sub-elites will tend to pursue their specific institutional requirements independently. Finally, this does indeed imply that the less the unity among resource-holders, the greater the diversity of educational changes introduced. Unlike the centralized system where all protagonists cluster in and about the political arena, often blocking one another and producing overall immobility, the existence of three processes for negotiating changes reduces the extent to which groups cancel one another out and contribute to stasis.

These considerations lead to an important conclusion:

Proposition 7: The superimposition and organization of interest groups are only advantageous in decentralized systems to the extent that they increase collective resources.

The increase can be purely quantitative (e.g., wealthy groups getting together to found high quality private establishments) or may improve the variety of resources available to a collectivity (e.g., when a powerful group and a rich one collaborate). But unless this condition holds, collective action carries no automatic bonus for the negotiation of change.

However, where political manipulation is concerned, this condition nearly always does hold. The greater the intensity of organized pressure, whether at the level of voting in elections, shaping party policy or influencing decision-making, the stronger the impact — because numbers, commitment and organization are the stuff from which power is made. And this, of course, is why superimposition and organization were always advantageous to interest groups in centralized systems, for to them political manipulation was the only process of negotiation available. Another way of looking at this is that the centralized system is a special case where collective action always increases resources. However, it is only a particular case of a more general rule, whose full workings are displayed only in the decentralized system, with its three processes of negotiation, namely that combination promotes effective transactions only when it enhances the bargaining position of educational interest groups.

Interaction in the decentralized system[8]

Although we are dealing with the same generic process of negotiation when examining interaction in the two kinds of system; although this is conditioned by the same fundamental relationship between the distribution of resources in society and the structure of educational interest groups; and although the same basic strategies are responsible for generating educational change — the decentralized and the centralized systems differ in the *complexity* of the interaction patterns they engender. In other words, although the same theoretical framework will be employed for both systems, the patternings of interaction which it has to encompass are extremely different. Once again, substantive variation provides a challenge to theoretical unification.

Because of the supreme importance of political manipulation in the centralized system, the majority of interaction is narrowly clustered at the interface between education and central government. In turn, this serves to simplify the task of both description and explanation. There it is possible to describe educational interaction as a continuous political story, with characters, plot and outcome; and to explain educational interaction in terms of its relationship with the political structure.

Both description and explanation differ considerably when dealing with the decentralized system. On the one hand, interaction cannot be described as a story, because three different kinds of negotiation proceed simultaneously and at three distinct levels (the school, community and nation) instead of being restricted to the last of these. Thus, there is no single historical epic but only a vast collection of short stories (like 'going comprehensive'), often varying in scope, sometimes involving different personae, but whose outcomes are frequently intertwined (for the consequences of each transaction introduce shifts in educational control and the definition of instruction which alter the context in which subsequent negotiations occur). Explanation, on the other hand, involves making sense of these myriad episodes by relating them to a set of more general relationships which account for their patterning.

We will begin with the more complicated case of the decentralized system where, because the three forms of negotiation are of roughly equal importance, an account of educational interaction must be broad enough to embrace those transactions conducted autonomously by the profession and those introduced directly by external interest groups, as well as those taking place in the political decision-making arena. The centralized system then emerges as a special case (in the theoretical not the empirical sense) whose particular structure limits interaction to one part of a much wider range of negotiation, which is only displayed where decentralization prevails.

Since bargaining positions are intimately connected with the shifting distribution of resources in society, data on the latter are fed into the following discussion of England in the twentieth century. Four periods capture *major* shifts in the societal distributions of resources and corresponding alterations in the bargaining positions of different groups in society. Although alternative periodizations might be preferable for a more detailed analytical exercise, here they suffice for the disengagement of basic propositions concerning relations between resource distribution, negotiating strength and change in the decentralized system.

1902-18

In Table 1 it is clear that high degrees of concentration and superimposition are the outstanding characteristics of the

TABLE 1
Summary of the social distribution of resources: 1902-18[9]

Power
Highly concentrated: absence of universal suffrage; lack of an effective united party representing the masses until the end of the war; weak trade unionism enfeebled by legislative and judiciary constraints. Parliament dominated by the (mutually antagonistic) Liberal and Tory Parties of privilege: the nascent Labour Party forced to work as a liberal pressure group. A period of prelude to full parliamentary democracy.[10]

Wealth
Highly concentrated: capital holding restricted to the top few percentiles; large inter-class income differentials (mean deviations for male employment categories 67 percent, 1913-14), no serious improvement in real wages throughout the period; liberal reformism (pensions, National Insurance, super-tax, etc.) of little redistributive significance. Shrinking intra-class differentials did substitute a working class for the plural 'labouring' classes of the nineteenth century.[11]

Expertise
Highly concentrated: among the small group of 2,000 graduate academics in universities. Expertise of elementary teachers very low, certificated teachers being immersed by uncertificated personnel. The NUT worked to weed out the untrained, promote registration, improve low pay, status, autonomy and influence and to weld the intensely sectional groupings of teachers into a single profession.[12]

distribution of resources in society. Thus, before the end of the First World War, the vast majority of the population were in the weakest possible bargaining position, none but a tiny band of academics had differential access to resources, and only the socio-economic elites were strongly positioned (see propositions 4 to 6) — a privilege they would never again enjoy in this completely unrivalled form.

External transactions

The 1902 settlement recognized a number of groups as suppliers of educational resources: the religious denominations at all levels, the entrepreneurs in technical instruction and the upper middle class in prestige private schooling. However, the fate of the three main attempts to extend external transactions clearly demonstrated the indispensability of wealth if new demands were to be accommodated through this process.

The simplest case was the rise of the 'New Education Movement'. The 'progressives' were a loose association of prominent and usually wealthy individuals whose methods accentuated 'freedom' and 'individualism' on broad Montessori lines, becoming a more organized interest group after the 1915 Conference on New Ideals in Education.[13] Since they were prepared to maintain and staff experimental schools, the launching of the progressive movement required nothing from either polity or profession. It constituted no threat, it made no demands, and above all it confined itself to the private sector throughout its genesis — where external transactions are usually possible if funding is forthcoming.

The other pair of cases is instructive because two groups, one the most affluent, the other the least wealthy, both tried to negotiate directly with the same institutions — the universities. The success of industrialists and the failure of organized labour directly mirrored their respective negotiating strengths.

That of industry was exceedingly strong.[14] It could pay lavishly by university standards (strategy i) and make offers which no other social groups could better (strategy ii). It had 'squared' the polity (strategy iii), for the foundation of the Department of Scientific and Industrial Research (DSIR, 1916) to act as a broker between manufacturers with problems and universities with expertise, indicated all-party support for such transactions. Finally, the growth of the large firm convinced industrialists that the servicing of research and development requirements was imperative. In comparison, the negotiating strength of the academics was distinctly weaker, for in the absence of other bidders (state grants did not begin to cover overheads), they were in no position to pick and choose: even Cambridge was undergoing financial hardship and universities without the backing of big business were almost going under. Acquisition of new laboratories or libraries offset repugnance towards investigating the bio-chemistry of cheese-ripening, the composition of German detergents, etc., but implied that much teaching and research were determined outside the universities.

In sharp contrast the adult education movement, spearheaded by labour and TUC representatives (with the aim of improving their own leadership), proffered the begging-bowl not the wallet. Its negotiating strength was near zero and the significance of this profound imbalance became clear when developments in adult education affronted the dons and threatened to confront the government.[15] The Oxford colleges patronized 'impartial' WEA classes but would not tolerate the independent socialist Ruskin College founded by American philanthropy. The famous Ruskin strike only demonstrated that an external interest group cannot coerce the profession. On the contrary, imbalanced exchange means the weaker party must submit if transactions are to continue at all: submission took place, Ruskin's socialist principal was removed. The genuine labour colleges which the 'Plebs League' founded in response met with equal resistance from the polity, since this partisan instruction was officially blamed (1917) for unrest in the Welsh minefields. Henceforth, polity and profession hustled adult education along 'harmless' WEA lines, giving legal recognition and financial support provided its classes worked under academic surveillance and without institutional autonomy. Thus, the weak negotiating strength of the working class meant that it had not been able to introduce a socialist definition of instruction through external transactions.

Internal initiation

The general effect of the resource distribution was to place the profession as a whole in such a weak bargaining position that internal initiation made little contribution to educational change at this time. Instead, the majority of the teaching body was preoccupied with attaining the negotiating strength to participate later on — the conditions of which had figured in the NUT charter since 1870, but which only the academics achieved by 1918.

School-teachers made minimal headway on any of the four strategic fronts. Their upgrading was prevented while the Board of Education and the impoverished religious denominations shepherded an 'army of unqualified practitioners' into the classroom: [16] none of the NUT's exertions could weed them out since the board refused to terminate its Acting Teachers' Examination. Self-regulation, pursued through the establishment of a Teachers' Registration Council (1912), had derisory effects, since it had no sanctions to compel registration or to penalize those unsuitable for it. Little progress was made with insertion, while sectional divisions (voluntary vs. council teachers; graduates vs. non-graduates; trained vs. untrained; men vs. women; heads vs. class teachers; the certificated vs. the non-certificated), precluded consensual professional values and meant that the polity could capitalize on disunity to enfeeble strategic action on the first three fronts.

In contrast, the academics already enjoyed high expertise: their problem was how to turn it into a convertible currency. This was attempted by offering more attractive services (strategy i). Not only did academics respond to business demands (examined under external transactions) but many reached out to create new industrial demand for different services (especially in economics and commerce) — though initially without great success. The breakthrough was the war itself, [17] for the successful co-operation of scientists, firms and officials subsequently allowed academics to approach both of the richest institutions in society to offer what they would for what they could get.

By obtaining *two* wealthy suppliers the academics had achieved a prime condition for increasing the market value of professional skills. Successful *insertion* through the consolidation of the University Grants Committee (UGC) as an academic body, was important in protecting against central encroachment and providing a buffer against industrial intervention. [18] It was also an official sign that *self-regulation* was formally recognized. This combination of high expertise, increased earnings and enhanced autonomy introduced a positive feedback loop which fostered substantial internal initiation in the next period, while the school-teachers remained trapped much longer in their original bargaining position.

Political manipulation

The enduring concentration of political power meant that the rise of the Labour movement only succeeded in placing educational democratization on the parliamentary agenda. It could influence the topics of debate but not their outcome; for in the liberals' last great piece of educational legislation, the 1918 Act, the governing elites continued to perpetuate inegalitarianism in education.[19]

Prior to the war, political interaction demonstrated the yawning divide between labour's view of secondary education as a right and the liberal conception of it 'as an exceptional privilege to be strained through a sieve, and reserved, as far as the mass of people were concerned, for children of exceptional capacity'.[20] Essentially, the liberals were willing to abolish the half-time system by raising the school-leaving age but saw the subsequent instruction of the majority as taking place in part-time continuation classes, quite separate from the secondary schools for the selected few.

Nevertheless, by the end of the war the polity was geared for some reform to appease public and professional demand. Parties and pressure groups lined up now legislative change was in view, but since the Labour Party remained in the weakest parliamentary position, its chances of challenging liberal policy were small indeed. The new bill, drafted in 1917, showed the power elites closing ranks: its minor concessions to the left were coldly received because of the massive act of non-decision-making they concealed, namely the determination not to alter the basic structure of the educational system. Small as it was, the concession incited intense hostility from industrialists, especially the northern manufacturers, represented by the Federation of British Industry (FBI), who saw the end of the half-time system producing major industrial dislocation.

To get the bill through and propitiate industrial opposition, the introduction of continuation schools was postponed for seven years, though the subsequent economic depression prevented them from ever being realized. In reality, then, the Act had done nothing more than abolish the half-time system: it represented the effect of collective inaction on the part of the socio-economic elites vis-à-vis structural change and the incapacity of labour representatives to make any impact through political manipulation, given the distribution of power in society.

Conclusions

The greater the concentration of resources in society, the fewer the social groups which can utilize any of the three processes through which educational change is negotiated in the decentralized system. The majority of the population is prohibited from participating by its weak bargaining position: instead, it concentrates on acquiring the strategic prerequisites for subsequent participation. Furthermore, the greater the superimposition among resource-holders, the more all three processes of negotiation benefit them alone and the more non-decision-making is to their advantage. Finally, the conjunction of an extremely high concentration of resources and superimposition among resource-holders means that initial bargaining positions largely determine negotiating strength. Strategic interaction has little free-play to affect the outcome of changes transacted in education.

The inter-war years

The changes in the social distributions of the main resources were of a divergent nature in this period, as summarized in Table 2. Power underwent redistribution, wealth showed an intensified concentration, while expertise displayed a growth which spelt increased diffusion. The main consequence of this for the three processes of negotiating educational change was that it placed a variety of important social groups in a differential bargaining position for the first time.

External transactions

Wealth alone contracted and intensified in concentration during this period: its consequences were to reduce the social groups participating in external transactions, to prohibit new interest groups from starting direct negotiations, and to worsen the bargaining position of those who were weakly placed before the war. The latter is particularly clear where denominational, progressive and adult education were concerned, but their very different relationships with polity and profession mediated the impact of austerity upon them.

TABLE 2
Summary of the social distribution of resources
in the inter-war years [21]

Power
Reduced concentration: Union support and liberal demise meant labour became the chief opposition party, assuming office in the 1920s, thus realigning politics on a class basis. Effects of redistribution were neutralized by: the General Strike, enfeebling the Unions (membership only recovered its 1918 density by 1944); the parliamentary weakening of labour after MacDonald's failure to push the party into a national government and the repudiation of his leadership; the resultant conservative landslide in the 1930s. [22]

Wealth
Intensified concentration: economic crisis and depression increased financial disparities; unemployment disproportionate among manual workers and in double figures throughout period; widening income differentials (mean deviations for male employment categories rose from 67 percent 1913-14, to 75 percent 1922-24, and stood at 70 percent by 1935-36); manual earnings then registered an absolute, not a relative increase; collective assets of working-class organizations declined correspondingly in contrast to the growing resources of the FBI. [23]

Expertise
Deconcentration and growth: by the 1930s graduates increased among elementary personnel and trained teachers among secondary staff: by 1944 the term 'elementary' teacher had disappeared. In between, the board terminated its Acting Teachers' Examination and relinquished responsibility for certification to a national committee with NUT representation; groups of training colleges were formed round the universities, thus academics (who had doubled numerically) acquired greater cultural hegemony over the entire profession. [24]

The voluntary religious schools, facing straightened circumstances [25] as subscriptions fell away and church affiliation declined, were rescued by the fact that none of the three political parties was strong enough to alienate old supporters. As the liberals were traditionally committed to the free churches, the conservatives to protecting Anglicanism, while labour was under serious Catholic pressure, the National Government introduced a compromise measure whereby the LEAs made generous grants towards building voluntary schools to meet Hadow reorganization. For strategy (i), the non-punitive pouring-in of funds, was the only one all parties could countenance. Denominational education was saved thanks to the differential bargaining position of the churches, whose political influence was disproportionate to their resources.

The salvation of the progressive movement came from the profession not the polity. The post-war spate of experimental establishments (including Summerhill, the Malting House School and Beacon Hill) was pared to the bone by the downturn of the economy. Only a few would have remained as isolated showpieces but for the fact that child-centred education was taken into protective custody by the teachers. [26] Professional values had been seeded with progressive ideas and their victory was subsequently accomplished through internal initiation.

By contrast, adult education went to the wall — its deteriorating financial position coinciding with the internal acrimony which weakened the Labour movement. Following this severe check, the Labour Party made no future attempt to introduce socialist instruction through external transactions. [27]

Hence, the industrial elite proved the only group capable of extending direct negotiations, given its relative wealth plus strong official support for transactions which could help surmount the economic crisis. However, changes in the negotiating strength of the profession released the universities from supine dependence in their exchanges with industry. First, the wartime revaluation of their expertise allowed them to bid-up the exchange-rate and devote the surplus to their own ends (e.g., Manchester serviced numerous companies and simultaneously developed pure science under Rutherford, Bragg and Bohr). [28] Secondly, the existence of an alternative supplier in the state (providing one-third of university income by 1930) allowed academics to be more selective about their clients, as did the bipartite University Grants Committee which provided a buffer against crude business demands. Finally, a small but eminent group (Flexner, Laski, Bernal, Huxley) was becoming critical of offering anything, provided the price was right. Hence external transactions with industry proliferated steadily if much more selectively. They ensured continuing growth, despite economic depression but its direction was still markedly influenced from outside. [29]

Internal initiation

The inter-war years witnessed a reduced gulf between the bargaining positions of school-teachers and academics, thus leaving both poised for really substantial internal initiation once an economic upturn allowed the transaction of surplus resources. The four strategies of the school-teachers proved mutually reinforcing. Qualifications rose and advances were made in self-regulation as the LEAs involved the NUT in school reorganization and elementary teachers entered the inspectorate (freeing them from classroom censure by those unfamiliar with their problems and antipathetic to their values). Insertion took a step forward since the attention attracted by the seven reports (including the Hadow ones) of the Consultative Committee culminated in the creation of the Central Advisory Council for England (1944), with the new right to investigate topics of its choice.[30]

Underpinning all this was the development of a new set of educational values which had been hammered out in the private experimental schools. By the mid-1930s 'most of those who wrote books on education, spoke at conferences, produced official reports or sat on important committees, trained teachers, or contributed to the educational journals came to accept progressive views as a basis of their own thinking'.[31]

Together, these four improvements in negotiating strength allowed a quiet classroom revolution for freer child-centred methods to begin: it was held back by financial limitations on equipment and architectural adaptation, but the first serious piece of internal initiation by school-teachers was off the ground.

In the universities, continuing transactions with industry were offset by government spending cuts, thus precluding the egalitarian developments that the Association of University Teachers was advocating by 1942 — the creation of extra-mural departments and people's colleges. Professional values now exceeded the pursuit of vested interests — the pay scales had fallen from the AUT's eyes — but new innovations had to await more abundant resources. Generally in this period, internal initiation was limited, but not eliminated, by the overall shortage of funds.

Political manipulation

While the economic situation made the majority of the population exclusively dependent on political manipulation for expressing its educational demands, internal strife meant that the Labour Party could never satisfy them by introducing 'Secondary Education for All'.[32] What the working class received was largely on conservative terms. As the first decade of class politics, the 1920s set the scene with the tories driving brutal economy measures through the political breach, stopping Hadow reorganization in mid-stream and thus retreating from reformism to blunt retrenchment.

With the beginning of economic recovery in the late 1930s the Consultative Committee published the Spens Report, which played-up agreement between right and left on the need for differentiation (by proposing grammar, technical and modern schools) and played down their division over the principle of hierarchical organization (by giving the three schools parity of status). Given their political strength, the conservatives simply shelved Spens and substituted the Norwood Report (elicited from the more traditionalistic Secondary Schools Examination Council). This neatly inverted the Spens notion of parity between secondary schools by ranking them vertically and became the basis of the tripartite policy.[33] This was endorsed by R. A. Butler when he circulated 'Education After the War' (1941) in the run-up to a major piece of legislation. But with labour ministers now in the National Government, the Labour Party endorsing multilateral schooling[34] and the TUC, NUT and WEA banded together in Campaign for Educational Advance, there was substantial pressure for an Act providing equality of opportunity.

As drafted and passed the bill was a masterly piece of political manipulation, recognizing the significant difference between what the Campaign for Educational Advance desperately sought (raising the school-leaving age, gratuity, uniform amenities and universal secondary education) and commitment to a particular form of organization — the multilateral school. Accordingly, the 1944 Act gave secondary education to all: it made no mention of types of secondary school beyond stressing variety.[35] Since the bill had not prescribed tripartite reorganization nor legally proscribed the multilateral school, there was no formal barrier against supporting it. What it did do, however, was to create the necessary conditions for imposing tripartism or any other kind of organizational uniformity by creating a minister to 'control and direct' a 'national policy'.[36]

TABLE 3
Summary of the social distribution of resources,
1945-64[37]

Power
Substantial deconcentration: Although the conservatives had more time in office, they could not ignore the opposition as the parties were never more than a few percent apart in the five elections after 1945. Balance spelt further deconcentration, as both parties bid for the support of interest groups, and prompted consensus politics — 'Butskellism' with its bipartite endorsement of the managed economy, Welfare State and political corporatism.[38]

Wealth
Substantial deconcentration: Initiated by the first majority Labour government (1945) and its redistributive measures (National Insurance, rent control, progressive taxation, etc.), but mainly due to the expansionist economy of the 1950s resulting in: low levels of unemployment, steady rises in real income, substantial increases in disposable income, shrinking income differentials (mean deviations for male employment categories dropped from 70 percent in 1935-36 to 48 percent in 1955-56). Although capital only spread-out within the top 20 percentiles, poverty was no longer co-terminous with class.[39]

Expertise
Moderate deconcentration: Upgrading of school-teachers proceeded slowly — two-fifths of graduate teachers now worked outside the grammar schools, but the demographic 'bulge' brought in 35,000 staff under an emergency training scheme — regressive in relation to the ideal of a graduate profession but progressive in completely eliminating the unqualified. Academics emerged from the war with a greatly enhanced reputation and able to promote considerable university expansion and further intellectual specialization.[40]

Conclusions

The broadening of any resource distribution increases the range of social groups which can participate in educational negotiations (as illustrated by both power and expertise): but participation itself does not guarantee a successful outcome (as reference to the power dimension demonstrates), for this depends on negotiating strength. Furthermore, when the three resource distributions are no longer isomorphic or superimposed (i.e., many groups are in a differential position), then initial bargaining positions no longer nakedly determine the outcome of transactions, for negotiating strategies become more influential in shaping educational change.

1945-64

In our terms, the dawn of the 'affluent society' represented a growing availability of all three resources to larger sections of the population than ever before. It remains to be seen whether this generalized improvement in bargaining positions enabled new groups to participate successfully in educational negotiations for new purposes.

External transactions

The post-war period of economic recovery was particularly rich in external transactions, for greater affluence brought them within the reach of an unprecedented portion of society. Their proliferation was due partly to private affluence, for personal investment in private schooling reached record levels in the 1950s,[41] generating growth in public schools, a marked resurgence of experimental progressive schools, the proliferation of 'crammers' to ensure grammar school entry (thus institutionalizing the diffuse transactions developed by the lower middle class as their disposable income had allowed — the elocution teacher, maths coach and 'front-room' tutor), and the burgeoning of nursery schools as women workers filled a lacuna in public provisions.

Equally, corporate growth fostered the dramatic expansion of collective transactions.[42] Industry and commerce entered into novel exchanges with further education and the partnership between the state and industry (the educational face of corporatism) legitimated this by giving employers strong representation on the governing bodies of the new advanced colleges of technology, founded after the Percy Report of 1945. Henceforth, employers became the effective mentors on further education and could negotiate a host of diverse training requirements and then monitor and modify them.[43]

Where the universities were concerned, the bargaining position of the economic elites was better than ever before, but negotiating strength is a relational matter and it was precisely the relationship between buyer and seller that had changed. Industrialists were convinced of their need for research and manpower services (they were now the largest employer of graduates),[44] business was booming and could offer terms with

which none but the state could compete — and the latter itself
endorsed expansion (conferring five new university charters) on
the assumption that this would automatically strengthen the
economy. But, for the first time, academics could now outmatch
them: exceptionally, the exchange rate was to their advantage.

Academic expertise had never been more sought after and
private finance flowing to the universities reached new peaks
in the 1950s. The greedy absorption of all graduates[45] and the
proliferation of research sponsors increased academic independence — this being unintentionally reinforced by increased state
funding meant to enable the universities to respond more fully
not more selectively. Though transacting more intensively than
ever, the academics could finally afford the luxury of a cons-
cience — foregoing particular transactions without threatening
their own survival and giving priority to intellectual considerations in development decisions.

Internal initiation

School-teachers won sufficient autonomy for them to have virtual freedom to define instruction in any establishment up to
the grammar school.[46] Given the balanced nature of party
politics, attempts were made to woo the teachers, largely by
conceding increments in self-government. Consequently, as the
'statutory limitations on what can be done in a school are very
few indeed'[47] the contents and methods of instruction became
the prerogatives of teachers. These then reflected their progressive values, which had swept through the primary level,
now percolated up through the secondary moderns, and were
only held back by the examination barrier from inundating
higher levels.

For the first time, teachers too became able to participate
in audacious structural reform, thanks to their insertion at local
level. For the partnership which emerged between the profession and the local authorities was tantamount to an alliance
against the centre. (Frequently the LEAs aligned with the NUT
not the DES[48] and in turn the NUT opposed any administrative
erosion of local government powers.) This alliance was vital,
since the LEAs made all the running in structural innovation
at this time, pioneering comprehensive reorganization in opposition to central policy, which would have been impossible without
strong professional support.

By contrast, the increased impact of the academics was due to their strength in market terms. An unprecedented amount of state aid was now forthcoming, industrial benefactions doubled in the period 1952-63, and external funding of research represented the largest increase in any source of university income.[49] Yet the AUT calculated that, in 1957, less than half of the latter was actually devoted to industrial research — the majority of these earnings was therefore capital accumulated by the academic community and devoted to their own ends. Revelling in their new-found wealth, they developed the 'pure' rather than the 'applied', the social not the natural sciences, 'professional' not 'executive' training, and the PhD rather than the MSc. The financial scope for internal initiation had never been greater, but danger signs were present (the UGC was more intrusive, especially in steering research through ear-marked grants, and the government had quietly become the major supplier — it provided one-third of university income in 1938-39 but it furnished two-thirds by 1951-52).[50] Although this threat to autonomy did not materialize while the economic boom continued, the profession was becoming strategically vulnerable, for any collapse of industrial support (i.e., the natural equivalent of strategy (ii), the barring of alternative suppliers) would open the door to the central forces ready to undermine university autonomy (via strategy (iii)).

Political manipulation
The question of how to organize secondary education dominated political manipulation in the three decades following the 1944 Act, given that the lower classes could command continuous political attention while other social groups turned to make use of external transactions and internal initiation, since both had widened in terms of who could use them.

The interaction surrounding political manipulation fell into two phases. The first mirrored the political consensus of the period and witnessed Labour and Conservative governments successively employing their new central powers to introduce a higher degree of uniformity than ever before in English education — the tripartite system.[51] Labour would only sanction limited innovations (when it quit office in 1951, only twelve comprehensive schools existed): the conservatives only countenanced 'judicious experiments' (like London and Coventry) or made allowance for 'sparsely populated areas'. Yet from the mid-1950s onwards, conflict intensified 'between local authorities wishing to establish comprehensive schools, and the Ministry, wishing to prevent this development, except on its own terms'.[52]

While the conservative response was to shore up tripartism, protecting the grammar schools by allowing advanced courses in the secondary moderns, the reaction of many areas was to dispose of it completely. Although plans for comprehensive reorganization continued to be rejected, the local authorities took over the running from government and ministry in a manner inconceivable in the centralized system. The Leicestershire experiment crept in under the official net by using nothing but existing buildings: fifty comprehensive schools were now functioning, attracting considerable attention from other LEAs, and making their own pragmatic contribution by concrete example; finally, the Crowther Report (1959), underlining the need for a more flexible structure of secondary schooling, encouraged the snowballing of anti-tripartism among the local authorities. Even Edward Boyle bowed to Bradford's abolition of the 11 plus, a sign that 'in the early 1960s there was apparent the beginnings of a movement to do away with the selective system at the secondary stage, one which represented a reversal of the position established in the late 1940s when the central authority lead firmly contained development on these lines. Now it was the central authority which retreated before local authorities, though still uttering some final vetos as it went'.[53]

Conclusions

The greater the growth of all three resources and the deconcentration of their distributions, the more intensively are all three processes for negotiating educational change used, and the higher is the volume-cum-diversity of changes introduced. However, as the range of social groups which can participate in educational change expands, each group makes most use of that process in relation to which it has the best bargaining position. A major implication is that the lower classes turn to intensive political manipulation, the two alternative channels for introducing change being dominated by other social groups. Finally, the more intensive the employment of all three processes of negotiation, the more important is the interplay between them and their outcomes. [54]

TABLE 4
Summary of the social distribution of resources 1964-75 [55]

Power

Relocation and reconcentration: Under labour, the alliance between the state and the unions snapped with the proposed Industrial Relations Bill, removing the linchpin of consensual social democracy and the reason for conservative restraint. This rupture displaced power away from Westminster and towards the organized Leviathans, spelling an overall decline in effective representation for the majority, given simultaneous disorientation of the parties — without coherent philosophies, attracting support by sectional accretion, facing substantial electoral volatility and challenges to the two-party system itself. [56]

Wealth

Relocation, reconcentration and recession: Growth of multinational companies and institutional investment led to a parallel concentration of capital resources away from the state, rendering them less amenable to government control. Correspondingly, as Britain's economic position deteriorated in the 1960s, successive governments tried to balance the books by altering the labour side of the equation through wage freezes and incomes policies, thus widening pay differentials. Simultaneously, intensification of recession and inflation also reduced the disposable income of the middle classes. [57]

Expertise

Growth and deconcentration: Slow upgrading continued for school-teachers. The Robbins Report placed their training in the orbit of higher education and initiated the BEd. This did not create the all-graduate profession (only 10 percent stayed on for the degree in the 1960s) but meant that certification was no longer an end-stop, condemning teachers to semi-professionalism. For academics, Robbins brought huge expansion (the new universities, upgraded CATs, the CNAA) but also represented the climacteric of their growth, influence and valuation. [58]

1964-75

The years of unremitting growth of the main resources (and their rather more limited redistribution) were ending. Replacing them was another phase during which changes in the resource distributions were unsymmetrical, again producing various groups with differential bargaining capacities. However, current negotiations, even in straightened circumstances, took place in the context of past gains and this prevented recession and retrenchment from reducing the negotiating strength of any group to zero or from rendering any process of transaction nugatory.

External transactions
The start of this period was a prolongation of the last — there were continuities in the patterns of both personal and collective investment — but its finish saw a severe cut-back in external transactions, mirroring the deepening economic recession. Personal transactions with the private sector remained the preserve of middle-class groups (as they drifted further beyond the financial reach of working-class parents) but significant numbers made use of the 'voluntary aided' and especially the Catholic schools, regardless of religious affiliation, believing that these preserved standards and provided a protected environment. Given all-party agreement that church schools should not suffer from comprehensive reorganization (80 percent building and maintenance grants were made available to them),[59] the existence of this ready clientèle preserved the remains of the dual system.

The new post-Robbins universities represented a massive expansion which itself changed the market even before the economic downturn reduced the number of buyers, for it could no longer be assumed that the occupational structure would automatically absorb their products. Certainly some of the new universities (Essex, Lancaster and Warwick) rapidly entered intensive transactions with industry, but others remained completely disengaged, turning their autonomy more to their own account than to that of the national economy. Not only did this incur political opprobrium (an embargo on further universities) but industrial reactions revealed an ambivalence unknown in the antecedent period. Undoubtedly, some of the new developments in management sciences, industrial relations, business administration, data processing, etc., were distinctly advantageous to industry, commerce and bureaucracy,[60] but the foundation of an independent university was an indicator of growing dissatisfaction with the values communicated, if not with the training available in higher education.

If a feeling was spreading among their suppliers that the negotiating strength of the universities was excessive and leading to excess, then rectification was accomplished by recession which cut industrial transactions back hard.

Internal initiation

If the previous period was the high-water mark of academic influence, the present one was the best yet for the school-teachers since the scope of internal initiation widened enormously. The abandonment of the 11 plus relocated selective functions within the school, making teachers' assessments paramount for pupils' destinies, the Plowden Report (1965) witnessed the universalization of progressive pedagogy, all of this being crowned by the teachers winning control over the new Schools' Council. This was a signal piece of insertion, accomplished by the professional unions supported by local authority associations for, when first mooted (1964) the council was to be a 'commando-like unit', assisting the Secretary of State on matters of curriculum and examinations. When it emerged as an autonomous body, outside the department, it meant that the chief agency concerned with the definition of instruction was now commanded by teachers, thus officially reversing the respective roles of profession and polity as inherited from the nineteenth century.[61]

In contrast, after 1966 when the Robbins proposals took on flesh, the last vestiges of consensus politics dispersed, and the economic downturn established itself as here to stay, the academics had won everything they were going to achieve for a long time. Henceforth, they were engaged in a fort-holding operation which basically resulted from the universities' financial dependence on government. World recession and English inflation meant that alternative suppliers began to dry-up from the late 1960s onwards. For the first time academics were left alone with the state as the sole agency on which they depended for funding. Both parties had employed strategy (i), pouring in funds until all the universities had to offer was reliant on government resources. This now paid off and in turn allowed strategy (ii) to be activated — the strenuous use of political veto (always most effective in the absence of alternative suppliers). This was illustrated by the refusal to implement Robbins fully and by the imposition of the binary policy. Hence, once financial dependency was established, the exchange rate could be lowered, thus reducing surpluses available for internal initiation. The way was also open for the reduction of institutional autonomy (strategy iii), through the growing dirigisme of the UGC — which became more an agent of state than a neutral mediator between government and university.[62]

Political manipulation

The end of the social democratic consensus issued in a more hostile period of party politics — fully reflected in educational policy and only modified by LEA resistance to any government in office. In a period when power was increasingly displaced on to the most strongly organized collectivities, it is not surprising that the local authorities benefited — they were always there to press their case(s), whichever party was in power, and were obvious candidates for the tactic adopted by both parties of appeasing sectional interests.

Hence, when labour returned to power in 1964 it effectively sponsored the more 'progressive' authorities. When Circular 10/65 *requested* all LEAs to submit proposals for comprehensive reorganization, not only did this eschew legislative coercion of the local authorities but also the 'central guidance' it claimed to give 'amounted to passing round to all authorities what the DES had found in its suggestion box in 1965'[63] i.e., the six main models already operating at local level. Comprehensivization remained essentially local in character under the next Conservative government (1970-74), which stood to gain educationally from the intransigent authorities and politically from defending local rights. Their replacement circular of 10/70 condemned monolithic reform and committed itself to the defence of 'good schools' in the plural. Thus the conservatives decelerated and diluted comprehensive reorganization rather than stopping it, as many comprehensive plans were passed providing they left the grammar school intact. When labour resumed office in 1974, determined that reform should not be stranded 'halfway there', it still reined-in short of strong compulsion or standardization.

Why, then, did successive governments baulk at the legal imposition of a coherent policy from the centre? Largely because the sequence of interaction, encouraged by both parties, giving local initiative its head or intransigence its way, had gradually structured vested interests in local definitions of the comprehensive school (middle school, upper school, sixth form college, etc.) and these then conditioned resistance to the legislation of 'the' uniform comprehensive school. Thus, thirty years after the 1944 Act, positions had again been reversed with the authorities becoming more influential than the ministry as the result of the interaction surrounding political manipulation over the three decades.

Conclusions

Reconcentration, recontraction or relocation of each resource does damage or affect the respective process of negotiation. However, this is a more attenuated influence than in the past. Present negotiating strength is no longer quite so sensitive to the contemporary fluctuation of resources. For once the main educational interest groups have acquired significant negotiating strength, they tend to retain many of their past gains and to remain active parties in the negotiation of educational change. Thus, over time negotiating strength slowly and partially distances itself from temporary variations in bargaining positions. Nevertheless, a major effect of reconcentration and recontraction is to prevent any new social groups from participating in educational transactions for the first time.

Interaction in the centralized system [64]

The following discussion explores the nature of political manipulation, given that this is the most important process through which change is introduced in the centralized system. It remains so there because governing elites continuously wield the four strategies which ensure continual educational dependence on the state. The aim is now to move on to an analysis of its contours, course and consequences within such systems, for without this it is impossible to explain comparative and historical variations in political manipulation.

Particular patterns of interaction and different outcomes of political manipulation are held to derive from two factors: (i) the penetrability of the political centre and elite relations inside it; (ii) the superimposition and organization of supportive and oppositional interest groups in education. Obviously the formulation and testing of hypotheses about such combinations require an array of cases, covering all permutations of the key variables. As a single case study, France at least has the advantage of furnishing unequivocal illustrations of the three types of political centre with their different degrees of closure or accessibility:

A. The impenetrable polity — the Second Empire (1852-69)
B. The accessible polity — the Third and Fourth Republics (1875-1958)
C. The semi-penetrable polity — the Fifth Republic (1958 to date)

TABLE 5
Interaction in the impenetrable polity[65]

Framework of the state
Impenetrable political centre: Strong presidential government concentrating executive powers on Louis-Napoléon and away from the elected assembly which had no right to initiate legislation. An amalgam of plebiscitary and autocratic practices where presidential powers derived directly from the electorate without organized parliamentary bodies of right or left effectively respresenting public demands. Closure was so great that government and democracy were 'two separate poles, too far apart for the vital spark of democratic government to flash between them'.[66]

Elite relations
Elite disunity: Deep cross-cutting fissures fragmented the assembly, weakening its tenuous constitutional grasp on policy-formation. At one extreme were ultra-conservative monarchists, divided into Bourbons or Orléanists, but united in Catholic orthodoxy; in the middle were counter-revolutionary liberals, Bonapartists and liberal Catholics, capable of alliance but divided upon the role of state in society and of church in state; at the other extreme were minority republicans, repudiating clericalism and strong government. Even the broad class interests common to deputies (as bourgeois professionals, bankers or landed gentry) were split by the rural-urban divide.

Structure of educational interest groups
Fragmentary interest groups: Social divisions produced a variety of sub-cultures with divergent educational interests, while political repression (limiting freedom of the press and of association) deterred interest-group formation. Together they meant that educational pressure groups emerged tardily and separately, were weak in numbers and organization and without impact on the general population. Typically they were loose gatherings associated with specialist journals — like *L'Univers* (orthodox Catholic), *L'Opinion Nationale* (anti-clerical), *Journal des Economistes* (progressive industrialists), and *L'Atelier/Bibliothèque Utile* (republican working class), none of which was superimposed or even allied with any other.

This allows for a fairly rigorous assessment of propositions about the influence of political structure upon educational interaction and change. Unfortunately, an equivalent range of variation in elite relations is not provided in French history, as high elite disunity prevailed until the last period. Thus, it will be necessary to supplement the theoretical discussion with side references to other countries. Much the same is true of the organization of educational interest groups, since fragmentation remained their dominant characteristic throughout in France. (See Appendix 2 for a summary diagram of the complete permutations of relationships and their effects on the negotiation of change in education.)

The Second Empire, 1852-69

At the political centre
The nature of educational politics provides clear substantiation for Proposition 1, since they were dominated by the elites belonging to the charmed circle of the closed polity and directed by the changing balance of power between them. Hence, educational policy in the 1850s was shaped by the alliance between imperial government and the Catholic Church. Louis-Napoléon saw Catholicism in instruction as a counterweight to republican forces in society:[67] the church in turn made the seemingly innocent notion of 'liberty of instruction' a condition of their support for the president. But once this had been achieved (by the loi Falloux),[68] the liberal drapery clothing the freedom of instruction was stripped away to reveal the church revindicating educational control of the *université*, founding a competing network of confessional schools, and contesting control of the entire system. This, plus the Italian war of liberation in which Napoléon III received Papal denunciation as a traitor, finally ruptured the church-state alliance at the end of the 1850s.[69]

Having repudiated its supporters on the right, the government sought to build them up on the left, but paid the price for the alienation of the latter in the previous decade. Teachers had become unco-operative under their double surveillance by church and state, the Saint-Simonian bankers and industrialists disgruntled at the failure to harness education to economic development, and the republicans disillusioned by the repudiation of universal primary instruction. Yet these discontented groups could neither ally in a common cause nor could a common denominator be found among their grievances. The *universitaires* clung to their academic traditionalism, their sole claim to social status, to be protected against spiritual or temporal despoilation: but this tenacious classicism was irrelevant to the industrial elite, which sought scientific instruction, and its associated elitism was unacceptable to republican leaders who wanted universal schooling. Given the dead weight of the conservative majority in Parliament, this was a formula for inaction.

Consequently, various attempts at liberalization and modern-ization lacked the political strength necessary for execution, and it was the lowest common denominator of entrenched political, social and educational interests which passed into legislation. The attempt to universalize elementary schooling ended in a modest bill (1867) giving municipal councils the discretion to abolish fees; mainstream secondary education bowed to aca-demic conservatism and traditional classicism was left intact in the *lycées*; the demands of the new middle class for practical professional training were propitiated by the introduction of 'special education' inside existing *lycées* — deficient because of its expensiveness, lack of specialization and its social discrimination.

Thus, elite disunity had precluded the pursuit of a positive and coherent educational policy. It resulted either in sectional legislation favouring a particular elite alliance (as in the 1850s), but dissatisfying other elite groups which received too few of the educational services they required, or to collective inaction, because of mutual blocking (as in the 1860s). Under these cir-cumstances, non-decision-making was the most significant product of political closure. In particular, popular interests were organized out of the central arena for policy formation — since the only dimension of political unity was the negative bourgeois consensus. Here a comparison with the USSR is instructive as it presented a similar degree of political impenetrability but accompanied by more united elite relations in the post-revolutionary period.[70] This combination, on the contrary, facilitated the smooth downward flow of polity-directed changes which represented packages serving the common interests of the governing elites.

Professional interest groups

Teachers and academics are generally closely controlled under the impenetrable polity, which prevents effective co-ordinated action and the development of any of the four strategies for professional advancement. While the church-state alliance lasted,[71] this conjunction of authoritarian powers meant that centralized control grew at the expense of academic influence — detailed directives stemmed directly from the minister's Rue de Grenelle offices, via the inspectorate and prefecture to each classroom. Teachers had, for example, to keep notebooks on topics taught and exercises given so that the authorities could verify that the new restricted programmes had been observed. The stringency of surveillance was indicated by the dismissal of over 800 *instituteurs* for their suspected socialist opinions. Upon the break with the church and the withdrawal of the reserve inspectorate of parish priests, attempts were made to replace coercion by compliance, to woo back the profession by a limited amount of consultation, which did not warrant the name of insertion, but involved the signal concession of recognizing professional expertise.

Yet, even minor concessions, meant to increase teacher co-operation, tended to be counter-productive. The small increment in autonomy was used to intensify obstructiveness in defence of academic traditionalism. As a marginal social group, promoted from the people but not yet assimilated into the bourgeoisie, they clung tenaciously to the *culture générale*, which marked them off from the masses and forced Minister Duruy to retreat from his policy of modernization. Even his attempt to minimize Greek merely prompted the formation (1867) of the Association for the Encouragement of Greek Studies, the first essay in corporate action on the part of the profession. That it was harnessed to academic traditionalism here was circumstantial: it indicates that in a centralized educational system with an impenetrable polity, in so far as the profession is not simply obstructive it is driven to act as a vested-interest group. Under stringent control it cannot respond to the demands of other social groups, so any small increment in freedom of action will be used for the advancement of its own interests.

External interest groups

Obviously, tight central control over public instruction repulsed external transactions: there was no question of squaring a deal with a polity which did not consider that state education was open to negotiation. Less obviously it deterred negotiations with the private sector for the 'liberty of instruction', won by the church and available to others,[72] was not synonymous with the freedom to diversify education (because of the standardizing influence of state examinations).[73] Alternative suppliers could not extract alternative supplies which met the specialized requirements of external interest groups because of the low

TABLE 6
Interaction in the accessible polity[74]

Framework of the state

Accessible political centre: The political centre of gravity moved downwards as power shifted away from president and senate to be vested in government by assembly. The Chamber of Deputies, elected on direct male suffrage, exercised detailed control over public policy. Constitutionally, every group had access to the decision-making arena: in practice each nuance of public opinion could gain parliamentary expression and, in the absence of strong party organization, all could work through the shifting coalitions to press their demands. Punctuated by the Vichy and Provisional governments, the Fourth Republic was effectively a continuation of its predecessor — a prime index of lasting openness being that 30 percent of legislation was sponsored by the opposition. However, the fact that Parliaments had more control than governments contributed to political instability — eighty ministries collapsed under the Third and twenty-two under the Fourth Republic.

Elite relations

Elite disunity: This was mirrored in the fragmentation of political parties, due to cross-cutting social cleavages (clericalism, monarchism, class and militarism) which survived the introduction of mass suffrage. At the turn of the century, the extreme right was isolated through its legitimism and Catholicism, while moderate conservatives were united only in anti-clericalism and defence of business interests, the division of the bourgeoisie being completed by the Radical Party of the centre. Parallel divisions paralysed the twentieth-century left — permanently divided between Socialist and Communist parties, incapable of durable alliance. Party fragmentation spelt political 'centrism' as only combinations of the centre parties could form governments — the pendulum swung between the margins of centre-right and centre-left. In turn, political 'centrism' meant political 'immobilism' — legislation being restricted to the minimum programme which the governing coalition would endorse.

Structure of educational interest groups

Fragmentary interest groups: The weakness of political parties made them court every complementary interest. This encouraged the mobilization of many educational pressure groups: (i) *professional* associations: primary, secondary, technical — loosely united in the FEN by 1946; (ii) *sectional* groupings: Catholic organizations, industrial bodies, labour federations; (iii) *pressure* groups: of parents, students, reformers and educationalists. As their common target was national politics, they were all organized on a national basis since interest groups reflect the structure they seek to influence: local organizations are pointless if local negotiations are impossible. Interest groups proliferated but their aggregation was so difficult that they neutralized one another politically. Fragmentary political parties meant that the interest groups gave them guarded support for temporary pledges rather than a permanent unity of action developing for the political manipulation of educational change.

autonomy of private education. More importantly still, such groups lacked the organization necessary to engage in successful political manipulation and to introduce change through modifying public policy. This in turn highlights the fact that the impenetrable polity is never confronted by an organized and united source of opposition, regardless of whether it enjoys solidary elite relations or not. This absence could not be explained away by reference to class antagonism, since by the end of the Second Empire a common ideology of *laïcisme* was beginning to unite liberal industrialists and urban workers under the banner of secularism in education. Instead, the consolidation of opposition was deliberately prevented by limitations on the freedom of association — thus non-elite interests were organized out of the central decision-making arena imperatively.

The Third and Fourth Republics, 1875-1958

At the political centre
In the last two decades of the nineteenth century the intensity of *laïcisme* provided enough political cement for the Republican Union to steer through substantial legislation. The introduction of free, compulsory and secular instruction by Jules Ferry [75] in the 1880s involved the strengthening of all four strategies for increasing education's dependence on government. Underpinned by the ideology of *laïcité*, public educational funding increased; institutional autonomy diminished as primary schools were reduced to agencies of state and secular curricula were imposed throughout the system; alternative suppliers were banished when religious personnel were prohibited from teaching in the public sector — a policy which culminated in the full separation of church and state in 1905, given the intensity of clerical resistance to this secularization of the *université*.

Thereafter, bold legislation came to an abrupt end, although the parliamentary expression of demands remained unproblematic. The question of why such a highly accessible political centre did not produce a commensurate proportion of the educational changes pursued by different groups can only be explained by the basic lack of political cohesion between them which now became salient. In the past, clericalism had successfully driven a wedge into the conservative opposition, thus allowing

republican legislation to get through. It had also been vital
in postponing a split over educational modernization and
especially democratization between the centre and the left: the
only political combination capable of steering elements of these
on to the statute books. However, once *laïcisme* had triumphed,
it could no longer perform this role and the *école unique* issue
(the demand for a single, democratic middle school which
dominated educational politics thereafter) became the most long
drawn out example of political manipulation which failed
through lack of party unity.

The brief history of the Cartel des Gauches in the early 1920s
wrote the scenario for the rest of the Third and Fourth
Republics. In their electoral alliance the *école unique* had figured
prominently in the minimum programme which both radicals
and socialists could endorse. With support from the major
labour union (CGT) the Cartel won, but useful as educational
reform had been for covering party differences during elec-
tioneering, it became subordinate to destructive disputes over
economic policy when in office.[76] Perpetual division on the left
spelt a prolonged exercise in non-decision making: the battle
of the projects continued,[77] those of Zay (1937), Langevin-
Wallon (1947) and of Marie, Delbos, Depreux, Berthoin and
Billières (under the Fifth Republic) being killed in the cross-fire
over other issues or buried by the fall of ministries. Certainly,
the openness of the political centre could not be blamed; entirely
different effects will be found when accessibility, accompanied
by a stable party system, is examined in England. Immobilism
was the result of profound disunity among governing elites,
preventing the consolidation of stable units for political
manipulation (parties, alliances, coalitions) and generating the
crippling instability that dogged both Republics. This precluded
the steady downward flow of polity-directed changes. It was
unsatisfactory to both government and opposition, and merely
benefited conservative interests in society since protracted inaction was a welcome 'decision' to perpetuate educational
privilege.

Professional interest groups
Under the Third Republic, teachers remained constrained by
a battery of central regulations which prevented the *corps
enseignant* from engaging in internal initiation. As the

instituteurs were freed from the local tutelage of *curés* and *notables* to become civil servants, the state immediately enmeshed the primary school too in its familiar net of prescribed duties and proscribed activities. Since change of any magnitude at any level (in curricula, timetables, courses, examinations, pupil intake, etc.) required parliamentary or administrative sanction, the profession was driven towards political manipulation if it was to have any voice in policy formation.

To be effective through it, the profession had first to organize, but the path towards legitimate association was long and rough, paved with organizational repression and personal dismissals, until the Cartel des Gauches (dubbed the 'republic of professors') gave legal recognition to the *Syndicat National des Instituteurs* (SNI) and the association of secondary school teachers in 1924. Significantly, then, the first precondition of successful political manipulation, had itself depended on political change — on a brief shift of power to the left.

Henceforth, the centralized structure of education predisposed towards the formation of large national associations to exert parliamentary pressure.[78] If these were to succeed in the political negotiation of change they needed strong party sponsorship and concerted professional action. Given the social origins of the *corps enseignant*, their obvious allies were left of centre. However, the inability of the *Fédération Générale de l'Enseignement* (FGE), in the 1930s, and of the larger *Fédération de l'Education Nationale* (FEN), in the 1940s, to unite with any of the (warring) labour federations or (divided) parties of the left[79] precluded the exertion of strenuous and continuous political pressure. But internal disarray was as important as external failure to coalesce with others in vitiating effective political manipulation. The FGE could place its weight behind the *école unique* movement while projects remained safely on paper, but the FEN found no mantle of unity to cover the divergent interests of primary and secondary teachers after Jean Zay's clutch of experimental *classes nouvelles* had become a reality. In turn, this paralysed the FEN's potential for shaping public policy on educational democratization and it crippled the *école unique* movement itself.

Thus, within the accessible polity the contribution of the profession to educational change is not limited to negative obstructiveness. Teachers and academics can influence policy through extra-parliamentary association in conjunction with political sponsorship, but the condition for effective political manipulation is lasting unity of action between the three kinds of groups.

External interest groups

As before, stringent control of the *université* left the private sector as the only part of education open to external transactions, but the standardization of private schooling meant most interest groups abandoned negotiations with it and rapidly turned to political manipulation instead. The fact that secular private education steadily declined from the middle of the nineteenth century indicates that external interest groups could gain nothing from strategies (i) and (ii) (offering generous, competitive terms) and were driven to rely predominantly on the strategy (iii) — the attempt to 'square' a deal with the polity. Since the political structure of the two Republics encouraged interest group activity, squaring deals with a party sponsor was easy,[80] but the relative weakness of each party[81] made its delivery of the goods just about non-existent.

Equally deleterious for effective manipulative action were divisions among the interest groups themselves, since the accessible polity places a premium on their coalescence. Instead, clericalism and communism dissolved the unity of labour (dividing it into three groupings) and disaggregated consumer grievances (separating defenders of privilege, like the organization of lycéean parents from equally privileged protectors of Catholic rights: or alienating respectable radicalism, like the *Ligue de l'Enseignement, Compagnons de l'Université Nouvelle* or *Ligue des Droits de l'Homme* from disreputable forms of *gauchisme*).

The two factors interacted. Socio-ideological cleavages coupled with the constant availability of political sponsorship meant that in the course of political manipulation, any rebuff produced regrouping, any setback generated schism and any serious failure induced a complete falling apart. Thus the divisive relations characterizing the political elites were paralleled by those of the interest groups,[82] the two exacerbating one another and sacrificing the potential for negotiated change held out by the accessible polity — by reinforcing disaggregation of interests, organization and action.

TABLE 7
Interaction in the semi-penetrable polity [83]

Framework of the state

Semi-penetrable political centre: The antidote to past instability was to confer greater constitutional powers on president and government, to contain an unruly assembly. Presidential powers enabled certain issues to be resolved imperatively, over-riding the warring factions, but since the constitution vested most executive powers in the government, a strong president required a majority in the National Assembly — hence the development of a disciplined Gaullist Party. Government itself was strengthened in order to limit the ability of Parliament to overthrow or obstruct it: now legislation which was not officially sponsored sank to less than 10 percent of the whole. However, since Parliament was still the bedrock of power, a premium was placed on a strong opposition. Deficiencies in this respect on the left reduced democracy at the political centre beyond the constitutional diminution of openness.

Elite relations

Asymmetrical elite relations: The Gaullist Party (UNR then UDR) signalled growing unity on the right and gave the president an advantage unique in republican history — a decade with a working majority in the National Assembly. This increasingly streamlined party transformed the Fifth Republic into one of stable government and unstable oppositions, compared with the opposite under the Fourth Republic. The fragmented parties of the left and centre were the greatest force for Gaullist domination over public policy. Political arithmetic made their coalition imperative, but two factors inhibited it: hopes for a centre revival, excluding the communists, bifurcated the opposition and its potential for challenging the UDR; antagonism between the Socialist and Communist Parties prevented a genuine union of the left. This asymmetry, with unity on the right and disarray on the left did not change until the 1980s.

Structure of educational interest groups

Fragmentary interest groups: Factionalism and particularism weakened employers' federations, professional associations and workers' unions: *groupuscules* spawned on the right and the left. Both counteracted the consolidation of united national organizations, necessary for confronting the centralized state. Political manipulation was thus limited to lightning opportunistic alliances on specific issues. Since interest groups require party sponsorship, the absence of a united left in the face of a united right made disunity more of a penalty for some pressure groups than others. It spelt an asymmetry of influence where right-wing interest groups had the ear of government while their left wing counterparts scarcely had a hearing in the National Assembly.

The Fifth Republic, 1958 to date

At the political centre
The focal points of interaction represented a return to the earlier preoccupations with secularization, modernization and democratization. But in each area the changes introduced and the processes involved bore the marks of increased political closure and the asymmetrical access of different groups to decision-making. Each measure reflected the augmented powers of government, especially its devices for by-passing Parliament. [84] Each was passed in the face of substantial opposition from the left, the teaching profession and external interest groups, thus creating a growing reservoir of discontent. Finally, each selectively rewarded political supporters of government and penalized critics of the regime, while calculatively taking into account manifest and dangerous sources of discontent.

Yet even the loi Debré, a straightforward recompense for the Catholic vote [85] (passed as a motion of confidence), made strong contracts of association the condition of aid to Catholic schools. Effectively this was a central charter for standardization since it eliminated the last stronghold of diversity in French education — by intensifying strategy (iii), the undermining of institutional autonomy. A similar defence of *étatist* control accompanied those improvements in vocational training with which the Fouchet reforms rewarded the industrial backers of government (including the development of long and short technical courses at secondary level and the creation of university institutes of technology, as a 'short' alternative to the full degree). This was evidenced by the inclusion of education in the national plans, for these were bureaucratic not democratic exercises, involving the official interpretation of group interests rather than interest groups negotiating their specific demands. The Berthoin reform (1959), imposed by decree, was intended to defuse and diffuse the discontent which had built up following the repeated failure of the *école unique* movement. [86] It was a compromise measure which merely created a two-year observation cycle taking place in existing establishments — with all their self-fulfilling consequences. The intention was to give a little to those who had wanted substantial democratization, yet not to subtract much from those with vested interests in the educational status quo.

In sum, educational negotiations and the educationally

negotiable altered now that the four political strategies for inducing educational dependence on the state operated with a renewed vengeance. As the new style of government asserted itself in educational politics, discontent grew but the concessions made were too modest to contain seething hostility. Hence the outburst of the 1968 May events. Initiated by students, joined by an unprecedented total of 8 million strikers (including professional as well as industrial workers), and enjoying considerable popular support,[87] this extra-parliamentary movement owed nothing to party or union organization. It was a crisis not only for the government but for the official left, too, as direct action was a direct condemnation of the left-wing parties' failure to deliver the goods through political manipulation.

Consequently, all parties were predisposed towards panic legislation — hence the unanimity with which the *Loi d'Orientation de l'Enseignement Supérieur* came into being by November. This set a new pattern for the remaining Gaullist and the Giscardian periods: generous reformism in initial legislation was followed by administrative reneging on the more radical clauses. Alienation and opposition henceforth characterized relations between government and the profession. Although the solidarity of May was not recaptured, de Gaulle, Pompidou and Giscard d'Estaing had earned themselves an intransigent if disunited opponent whose intermittent outbursts vitiated every central move for educational rationalization or modernization, and which was later to present the Socialist government (1981) with half a century's frustrated aspirations for secularism, democracy and, above all, autonomy in education.

Professional interest groups

From the start, relations with the Gaullist government were ones of frigid mistrust as many teachers had refused to support de Gaulle in the 1958 referendum, on good republican grounds of commitment to open government, distrust of right-wing militarism and total repugnance for Catholic conservatism. In reprisal the *université* was made to writhe under the intrusive control of Minister Fouchet, active in the Algerian campaign and bringing military discipline to the educational system.

The new ministerial style of direct control in instruction by very detailed decrees meant that the profession was subject to a great many policy directives which it had neither helped to shape and which it was powerless to modify. Correspondingly, the profession's direct links with the central decision-making arena were reduced (appropriate commissions were often not even consulted) and its local and classroom activities became more circumscribed. Teachers and academics had little freedom to respond positively to external community demands or especially the internal demands of pupils (disoriented, for example, by the semi-annual changes in the *baccalauréat*) or students (bewildered by the changing course requirements attending the ministerial programme of modernization). Whatever their sympathies, they could not make a direct response through internal initiation nor could they play an indirect role by piloting change on to the statute books through political manipulation. The profession is in an intermediary position here in relation to the other two kinds of polities. Its corporate and consultative role is smaller than in the open polity, while its organization is greater than in the closed polity. It shares with the former the ability to form alliances with parties and interest groups outside the educational field but it shares with the latter the inability to play any other peaceful role than that of negative obstructiveness. These two aspects are intertwined in encouraging direct action when the negotiation of change fails. [88]

External interest groups
Lack of diversity in instruction invited all discontented groups to address themselves to the source of their frustrations, the state educational system itself: when coupled with the internal inflexibility of the centralized system, it constrained them to do so in a particular way, through the process of political manipulation. However, two factors made external interest groups less than successful in using the latter to negotiate change.

On the one hand, the French social structure still favoured fission rather than fusion. Even the main industrial organization, the *Conseil National du Patronat Français* failed to represent the small firms and shopkeepers: in parallel, trade unions did not organize more than a quarter of the active population and traditional ideological cleavages precluded rapprochement between the four main unions, cancelling out the advantages of their national structure and preventing a link-up with teachers' associations which still dared not put all their eggs in one basket. Instead, there was a plethora of pressure groups of all kinds, on the right as on the left (Meynaud lists over 300), [89] which reinforced particularism, factionalism and the narcissism of small differences. This proved especially damaging for those not figuring as government supporters.

A vicious circle developed — the powerlessness of the opposition fostering *groupuscules*, whose internecine conflict then damaged the unity of the left. [90] On the other hand, the government itself attempted to substitute consultation for negotiation with the interest groups. But the creation of 500 councils, 1,200 committees and 3,000 commissions at the national level, was a device for taming the power of political intermediaries rather than an extension of the negotiating table. [91]

In consequence, where interests failed to get a response from government, their reaction to rejection was almost identical — a resort to direct action, displayed first by the small agriculturalists, then by students, left-wing factions and finally by the trade unions which were dragged into the May events. But their internal divisions prevented them from forming other than temporary alliances, cemented by the euphoria of revolt, never holding together long enough to consolidate the educational gains sought.

The absence of a cohesive opposition movement intensifies the tendency for educational demands to be expressed through extra-parliamentary action since it leads to continuous failures in political manipulation, above and beyond the legislative and constitutional bias towards government interests.

7 STRUCTURAL ELABORATION: PATTERNS AND PRODUCTS OF CHANGE

The final stage has now been reached, where the processes of interaction which have been examined in the last two chapters remain to be linked to patterns and products of change, thus bringing the analysis up to date. However, the present task is not to describe these historical changes or to assess the performance of modern educational systems, but to provide a sociological account of macroscopic changes in education in terms of the structural and cultural factors which produce and sustain them.[1]

Patterns of change

Different patterns of change are found in centralized and decentralized systems. In the centralized system, political manipulation, the process of interaction which accounts for the bulk of macroscopic changes, is also responsible for patterning them in a distinctive way. As we have seen, demands for change have to be accumulated, aggregated and articulated at the political centre, they have to be negotiated in the central political arena, and if they are successful, they are then transmitted downwards to educational institutions as polity-directed changes — evidenced and documented by laws, decrees and regulations. **The crucial point is that these represent a definite and often dramatic punctuation of educational stasis, for education can change very little in the centralized system between such bouts of legislative intervention. Patterns of change, therefore, follow a jerky sequence in which periods of stability (i.e., changelessness) are intermittently interrupted by polity-directed measures.** This has been termed the '*stop-go*' pattern, and its precise derivation from educational interaction in the centralized system will occupy the next sub-section.

It is contrasted with the pattern of change common to decentralized systems. In the latter we have seen that three processes of negotiation are of roughly equal importance for introducing educational change; hence demands do not have to be passed upwards to the political centre, some can be negotiated autonomously within educational institutions, others can be transacted independently by external interest groups. **Consequently, change is never-ending, it is constantly being initiated, imitated, modified, reversed and counteracted at the level of the school, the community and the nation. Equally, however, it is usually undramatic, frequently indefinite, and commonly specific and local in application. The three processes taking place simultaneously at the three levels, intertwine and influence one another, sometimes positively, sometimes negatively, to produce a seamless web of changes.** This has been termed the '*incremental*' pattern, signifying that macroscopic change is made up of small increments, of minor modifications introduced from different sources, whose sole significance may lie in their accretion. Once again, a separate sub-section will be devoted to the ways in which this pattern derives from interaction in the decentralized system.

In proceeding to make this connection between processes of interaction and patterns of change, it should perhaps be stressed for the last time that what is presented does not constitute a complete theory of educational change. What is being traced are the effects of structural conditioning on how social groups bring about educational changes and the imprint of this on the resulting patterns of change. Such a theory cannot itself explain the composition and characteristics of social groups at any time or their norms and values, for these require general theories about social structures and cultural systems.

(a) The centralized system and the stop-go pattern

As has already been seen, the centralized system in which unification and systematization are the predominant characteristics encourages the build-up of frustrated demands outside education and in the wider society. Instead of these demands being propitiated by direct negotiation at the local or institutional level, thus drawing off discontent on a day-to-day basis, dissatisfaction accumulates. To effect educational change all groups, including teachers, must move outside the educational field to engage in political interaction at the national level. As far as the successful negotiation of demands is concerned, the nature of the political structure and of elite relations influence *whose* requirements are met but have much less effect on the form of change which is introduced. **In fact, the polity-directed changes which are routinely negotiated through political manipulation are formally very alike in terms of their initiation, their legislation and their execution.** By examining these in turn, and discussing the mechanics involved in each of them, we can jointly describe how it is and explain why it is that centralized systems generate the same kind of pattern.

(i) The initiation of change
Basically, changes are slow and cumbersome to bring about in the centralized system: and this is the case regardless of the type of political structure or elite relations which prevail. It is not simply the problem of marshalling consensus which is responsible, since this is equally problematic for political manipulation in decentralized systems. Rather it is the commitment of every political elite to retaining the supreme responsiveness of education to government (inherited as part and parcel of centralization), which means that each governing elite monitors educational development in relation to its own goals and changing circumstances. For various reasons it hesitates to introduce a major change until there is pressing evidence that current policies are not working or are not appropriate.

First, since the change will be national, it entails detailed planning (even if not in its modern form), such as teacher retraining, building programmes, production of teaching materials, etc. Secondly, since this is costly, the inevitable competition of other priorities for public spending means that it will not be embarked upon lightly. Finally, the elite will hold back as long as possible because what is involved is a leap in the dark — a restraining feature generic to the centralized system. For these systems do not contain within themselves any fund of experimentation, they lack the local, private or autonomous institutions which provide concrete models of new ideas in action and thus furnish a practical basis for argument and a firm precedent for action.

Certainly, there appears to be a growing tendency for

governing elites themselves to initiate experiments (in a restricted area, a particular type or level of school, and for a limited duration) and we find increasing examples of this in twentieth-century France. Nevertheless, state experimentation carries with it many of the disadvantages common to legislation itself. After all, the decision to undertake an experiment is a political decision: and by and large this means that it will have to be promising, acceptable, responsible, justifiable and any number of other things which will distinguish it from the fund of spontaneous experiments in decentralized systems, which are both more diverse and more daring. State experimentation functions largely as a negative feedback loop, minimizing gross deviations from the status quo, by exercising a preliminary exclusion of radical, but possibly workable, alternatives. Thus, leaps in the dark are resisted, until pushed by political supporters or force of circumstances, and when they are taken they will be unadventurous, unless produced by a new group assuming power.

Because the political centre thinks long and hard before it legislates and because the intervening changes brought about through other processes are minimal in comparison, then long periods of relative educational stasis are typical in the centralized system.[2]

(ii) The legislation of change
Legislation in the centralized system always involves concession, compromise and a dilution of the goals pursued by those who help to pass it. This is most obvious, because witnessed at its most extreme in the accessible polity with a weak government. For if it succeeds in legislating at all, it produces the most innocuous compromise measures and the greatest discrepancies between the change introduced and the goals of any of the groups which participated — as the introduction of a few experimental *classes nouvelles* instead of the universal *école unique* illustrated in the last decades of the Third Republic. However, the same is also the case in the semi-penetrable polity, in which concessions have to be made to government supporters (like the loi Debré rewarding Gaullist Catholics despite the hostility evoked in most other quarters) and compromises with dangerous opponents (like the decré Berthoin intended to pacify the left-wing proponents of educational democratization without

alienating the right-wing defenders of educational elitism). Equally, the closed polity, with strong elite disunity, publicly betrays the same tendencies — the attempt to find formulae which give something to everybody who counts and take away as little as possible from any of them. The wranglings over modern, technical and professional instruction during the Second Empire revealed the design of two successive compromise policies (of bifurcation and then of special education), in a deliberate attempt to mobilize adequate support for limited modernization.

Finally, these tendencies also characterize the closed polity with highly superimposed and integrated elites, though they may not be worked out in public to the same extent. The reason is simply that, however harmonious their relations, different sub-sections of the governing elite want different services from education, and if none wishes to reduce educational responsiveness to the polity by relaxing unification, then all have to work doubly hard at a compromise which dovetails their requirements with one another.[3]

In other words, concession and compromise are general characteristics of legislative change in the centralized system, whatever the political structure or elite relations which go with it. Above all, this means that no polity-directed change is ever precisely what anyone wanted. Even if a group successfully pilots its demands through into legislation, the actual change introduced will be tempered by the requirements of powerful others: sometimes the compromise will be so gross that nobody really wants it. In brief, legislative change often fails to satisfy and never satisfies fully in the centralized system. The most successful use of political manipulation still means that demands are met without precision, and this lack of precision is inherent to legislation which is national in scope and at best meets the highest common denominator of those educational interests enjoying political expression. Because of this, each polity-directed change does not significantly reduce the pool of discontent. Interest groups continue to exact more or better and remain ready to extract it if political circumstances permit: they stay armed for further political manipulation and give the educational system no respite from the pressure of their demands. Typically, legislation has tepid supporters and brutally hostile critics in the centralized system.

(iii) The execution of change

Educational legislation is national and uniform both in conception and application in the centralized system. This is the concomitant of maintaining strong central control, in the interests of educational responsiveness to the polity, and a high level of co-ordination, to avoid conflict between the different services education is to provide. Its main implication is that change will be confined to measures which do not challenge unification and which dovetail with the current form of systematization.

This means that the logic of central control perpetuates the illogic of educational uniformity. Instead of allowing for variations to meet local conditions or for adaptation in response to changing circumstances, each legislative change imposes a standardized formula on the relevant part of the educational system. Usually this involves too gross a response to the variety of initial social conditions and proves inflexible towards social change. The obvious corrective which consists in allowing sufficient local and institutional autonomy for self-regulation is precluded by the fear of its abuse, i.e., fear that the parts will escape control, pursue their own ends or prove more responsive to groups other than the polity.[4] The alternative is polity-directed specialization, and this is what takes place, orchestrated from the centre and organized so as to fit in with other centrally approved goals for education. Unfortunately, it can swiftly be nullified by social action and social change — e.g., student failure rates or the decisions of pupils not to pursue their specialisms can wildly distort numerical targets, just as social, economic or technological changes can render them obsolete. These consequences are just as pronounced in imperative Soviet planning as in the indicative French plans, for they are not problems whose solution depends on the availability of sanctions.

In other words, **the uniformity with which change is applied and the tight co-ordination of specialist developments mean that changes both fail to satisfy and frequently fail to work. Once again they leave behind them a pool of discontent, the proportions of which increase as the dysfunctional consequences of change amplify over time.** This trend will continue as long as the polity refuses to cede some degree of unification and systematization, for the attempt to introduce more differentiation and specialization without weakening the predominance of the first pair of characteristics can only lead to further maladjustments and undesired consequences. However, given commitment to the centralized structure, such problems merely prompt the movement from one national and uniform plan to another — legislative inadequacy is met by more legislation in those 'over-controlled' systems. In this lies another part of the mechanism which' produces the 'stop-go' pattern of change.

It now remains to examine what happens if and when the political negotiation of educational demands proves impossible, for in Chapter 6 it was seen that every type of political structure was capable of frustrating a substantial volume of demands. **In general, if demands are consistently refused, the strains which produce them continue and grievances grow and aggregate. However, they do so outside the 'normal' political channels, whatever these may be, for the legitimate procedures have already failed to satisfy them repeatedly.** Whether this reservoir of discontent bursts depends partly on the political action taken and partly on the nature of the frustrated groups and the type of confrontation in which they are willing to engage.

That centralized systems can 'tolerate' considerable discontent there is no doubt, for they do so all the time, but the political centre can react in different ways if discontent reaches alarming proportions. Direct repression is most common in the closed polity. Here, a battery of threats, sanctions and punitive measures are used, the educational status quo is also buttressed by other social institutions (churches, youth organizations, the security forces) and widespread ideological indoctrination is disseminated through the media and education itself — all of these serve to keep the lid on by subtracting from the potential participants in disorderly outbursts. Indeed, when repression is supremely successful the collective character of discontent disappears, to be replaced (seemingly) by individual manifestations of 'dissidence' which can be dealt with on a personal basis. If these techniques work, discontent is contained, educational policy remains undisturbed from below, and the 'stop' phase continues — until the first hint of political instability.

Alternatively, and this is more typical of semi-penetrable and open polities, though it is not exclusive to them, concessions can be made when dissatisfaction appears to reach a dangerous level, the aim being to keep it within 'manageable' proportions and also if possible to break up any solidary groupings of dissatisfied parties. However, the assessment of danger levels and the estimation of the size of concession needed are both delicate matters of political judgement and they can be wildly wrong. Whether the polity is made to pay for such errors depends upon the extent to which the disgruntled groups can work together and recruit support from other parts of society for extra-parliamentary action. If they can, then the result is an explosion (like the May events in France in 1968), which is bigger when educational grievances are augmented by others, as they were then.[5] If dramatic, their participants may even envisage toppling the polity itself — for a month the Fifth Republic looked very insecure — and political change would then signal a new 'go' phase of educational reform.

The explosion of educational grievances may not reach this point, and obviously the governing elite will seek to put out the fire. In this context, panic legislation takes place to defuse the situation and restore order. Promises of unheard-of concessions are made, unprecedented shifts of principle take place, entrenched positions are yielded and a major reform is hurried on to the statute books. All of this is illustrated by the loi d'orientation, passed virtually unanimously in 1968, to solve the university crisis. If and when the furore dies down, and the government again feels secure, it may well try to renege on some of its more radical undertakings by administrative claw-back (as in this case)[6] and the disillusionment caused leads to the re-accumulation of discontent. Whether a new explosion takes place depends on the degree of unity retained (or forged anew) among the proponents of educational change, the sensitivity of government to signs of unrest, and its flexibility in propitiating them before flashpoint is reached again.

Thus, whether educational changes are polity-directed through peaceful political manipulation or are the products of explosion followed by panic legislation, they constitute a distinctive 'stop-go' pattern. Periods of stasis are punctuated by legislative reforms and change advances by jerks rather than the slow accretion of modifications. In all cases, universal reforms fail to satisfy, they are followed by a period in which grievances build up and finally result in another universal reform, the cycle repeating itself indefinitely.

**(b) The decentralized system
and the incremental pattern**
As was seen in Chapter 6, the presence and parity of the three
different processes for negotiating change in the decentralized
system means that although the educational status quo will
give rise to a variety of unsatisfied demands at any given time,
more of these can be fulfilled by direct transactions because
greater changes can be implemented internally or independently
and less of them depend upon central intervention.

**As all three processes of negotiation operate simultaneously
and successfully, educational change is ceaseless. There is no
period of stasis between educational acts and no sense in which
these represent the largest or most important changes,** except
that they are the most public — they are the most audible if
not the most visible. (This, of course, is why some are tempted
to assign a class character to educational interaction as a whole:
political manipulation is class based and it does command more
attention by definition because of the public character of
parliamentary proceedings.) Nevertheless, the changes introduced by sectional transactions can be just as far-reaching.

In the decentralized system, change is thus a combination
of small localized shifts, possibly concentrated on one level or
one establishment in a given area, the effect of which is
cumulative, and polity-directed changes, which are intended to
be larger in scope but in fact also bring about further increments
of change rather than root and branch reforms. **It is by following through the way in which the small localized shifts can accumulate to produce a significant scale of change as well as the
way in which central policy directives are systematically
reduced in scope that the overall pattern of incremental change
is understood. The 'incremental' pattern is the result of both
action sequences, in conjunction with one another.**

(i) The accumulation of small localized changes
Here we are concerned with the results of external transactions
and internal initiation, that is with the contribution which these
two processes of negotiation make to the overall pattern of
change. Both show a strong tendency to introduce unit changes
which fall far short of the macroscopic. Thus, external transactions usually involve localized changes negotiated between
interest groups and educational institutions. These may be

extremely small in scale (like one firm negotiating a research contract with its local university) and thus depend upon replication and aggregation if they are to influence educational development. (Alternatively, an institutional interest group can engineer a series of transactions, in different localities, which produce a network of changes simultaneously.) Similarly, the innovations introduced by internal initiation normally involve small changes in teaching materials and methods which take place in particular schools or classrooms. Again, only by their repetition in a large number of establishments, whether by spontaneous imitation or orchestrated by a professional organization, can these add up to large-scale educational developments. The rest of the argument is thus taken up with demonstrating two propositions: first, that the accumulation of large-scale change from both processes is a frequent and important occurrence, and secondly, that the kinds of change introduced in these ways have distinctive characteristics which in turn affect the central governance of education.

Quintessentially, external transactions provide services (to the interest groups involved) which are marked by their *specificity*. For negotiations are only successful when the buyer gets what he wants from a seller who is willing to supply him; dissatisfaction on the part of the former or reluctance on the part of the latter mean a breakdown in negotiations. [7] In turn, this specificity means that the new services which have been transacted represent a diversification of current educational practices. [8] Often these cannot be accommodated within the existing institutional, disciplinary and curricula frameworks. Consequently, external transactions foster the progressive segmentation of institutions, differentiation of courses, and specialization of knowledge, whether for teaching or research. But for such direct negotiations a whole range of educational establishments and activities would not have come into being in England — the development of civic universities, for example, represented the aggregate effect of hundreds, if not thousands, of independent transactions on the part of industry which continued to pump successive waves of differentiation throughout the tertiary level.

Certainly, many external transactions remain localized and without sequel: indeed, one of their purposes is to bring educational services in line with unique requirements or special circumstances. Equally, others which bid fair to introduce macroscopic change leave no lasting impression, like the repeated failure in England to make a form of *real* post-elementary instruction stick. However, the point here is not that all external transactions necessarily accumulate until they represent large-scale changes, only that they can produce macroscopic changes incrementally and that these increase the overall differentiation and specialization of the system.

Change introduced through internal initiation often involves nothing more than personal experiments on the part of individual teachers in the seclusion of their own classrooms — indeed this is its basic unit. However, these too can accumulate in a number of ways and result in macroscopic changes. First, concerted action orchestrated by a professional organization can co-ordinate changes which become national in scope. The transformation of English primary education along progressive lines was accomplished without legislative intervention and was solely due to an exceptionally high degree of pedagogical consensus among teachers at this level, encouraged and spread by the NUT. Second, there are various mechanisms of mutual influence within the profession. Often innovations are generalized through imitation — e.g. the copying of early prototypes of comprehensive schools by other LEAs. Similarly, the growing demand for a particular innovation can lead to the rapid diffusion of this service — like the spread of business education in English universities once this had attracted a market — through the creation of positive feedback loops.

Finally, a change which has prevailed at one level can acquire wider diffusion through the downward influence exerted by higher levels on lower ones, like the English universities increasingly reaching down to shape teacher training via the certification and BEd examinations. Furthermore, the conjunction between the two processes of direct negotiation will amplify some of these changes still further until they reach macroscopic proportions, as in university expansion.

The full range of changes which are brought about through internal initiation and external transactions is characterized by its untidiness. In institutional terms the changes are tacked on as unplanned extensions, they sprout out of the top of existing institutions, shoot up like a scaffolding against the mainstream schools, or sprawl out as new edifices built in their grounds. In terms of the definition of knowledge the changes are analagous; new disciplines are delineated, old ones are sub-divided, existing distinctions are blurred, prevailing categories are re-combined, the boundaries of educational knowledge are redrawn and status is redistributed. **Thus, because both external trans-actions and internal initiation intensify systemic differentiation and specialization, they threaten overall systematization. In other words, the changes they introduce jointly and separately result in anarchic structural elaboration.**

(ii) The modification of polity-directed changes
It is in their scope that polity-directed changes in the decentral-ized system are most sharply distinguished from those taking place in centralized systems. Here there are no grand reforms which radically transform national education and whose pas-sage marks a complete change of direction or a large stride forwards or backwards. Both the conception and application of polity-directed measures are modified by local and institu-tional forces whose general effect is to prevent legislation from introducing changes which are either uniform or universal. In-stead, such modifications mean that each polity-directed change is itself incremental in its effects. Its scope is reduced by resistance and its standardized provisions are distorted, re-defined and adapted at ground level. **In other words it has just been argued that there is no 'stop' phase in the decentralized system because internal initiation and external transactions maintain a ceaseless flow of small localized changes. Now it is being maintained that there is no distinctive 'go' phase, heral-ded by central legislation, because interaction at lower levels robs it of much of its impact.**
(a) Polity-directed changes are affected by existing developments.
Any projected legislation must necessarily take into account what is there — a truism, whatever the structure of the educa-tional system. However, at any given time the practices and provisions current in the decentralized system reflect the con-sequences of decentralization in the past. Their diversity and malintegration shape a practical context of considerable com-plexity which political intervention has always to confront. **In other words, the decentralized structure constantly produces and reproduces an untidy patchwork of educational activities which condition what legislation can do with or to them.** More-over, these engender vested interests in their maintenance:

defence of independence, autonomy, acquired rights, continued
services, established privileges and, most basically, of having
a say, all constitute constraints on political intervention and
fundamentally limit its scale. Thus, for example, the first two
Labour governments were limited to extending free places in
the grammar schools, to a slight democratization of what was
there and was well defended, rather than being able to replace
it by something altogether more egalitarian. In the same vein,
R. A. Butler reflected that his 1944 Education Act had merely
succeeded in 'recasting' the system, not transforming it.[9]

Equally, the ongoing practices and provisions have as much
effect on polity-directed change as does legislative intervention
on current educational activities. Such changes follow just as
much as they lead in the decentralized system. On the one hand,
legislation is often modelled on experiments which have been
conducted autonomously and have given concrete evidence of
their effectiveness, or at least provided a persuasive precedent.
In many ways, the fund of experimentation, made up from
private, local and professional innovations, constitutes the
research and development agency of the education industry.

On the other hand the impetus for central legislation itself
often comes from below. Because of their relative autonomy,
the local authorities, the schools, colleges and universities can
spearhead educational changes — which take shape at ground
level by a roll-on effect — from experimentation via imitation
and accumulation to substantial innovation. Often the centre
has to run to keep up, its legislative acts merely recognizing,
legitimating and extending what has already taken place. For
example, the English moves to found new universities were well
under way before the Robbins committee reported and the
government accepted its recommendations: similarly, it was the
LEAs which made the running with 'intermediate' instruction
between the wars, which began to drop 11 plus selection, and
to pioneer comprehensive reorganization. When polity direction
finally came, it no longer had a clean page on which to draw
a fresh design, but a set of burgeoning initiatives already in
operation, a new set of existing practices to take into account
and a new series of vested interests protecting them. Consequently, political action bent with the tide: it gave recognition
and it gave legitimation and what it sought to achieve in
addition was rationalization. Here both the Hadow proposals,
as accepted by the government, and Circular 10/65 are very

revealing, for both based their six recommended schemes on ones which were already in being. What was to be universalized was not a centrally determined plan but progressive local practice. Consequently, neither Hadow reorganization nor comprehensive reorganization could conceive or impose a specific kind of change establishing a particular type of school: they merely pointed to bundles of acceptable practices which were nothing more than the prior initiatives taken by local authorities.

(b) Polity-directed changes are mediated locally and institutionally

This dimension of interaction is almost entirely lacking in the centralized system. Here, local and institutional autonomy enables action to be taken at various levels which results in the modification of central directives. Because legislation is mediated by such forces it does not have a uniform effect wherever it is applied, and consequently it does not give rise to standardized changes in the institutions or processes involved.

On the one hand, the area or institutional authorities can be laggardly in their implementation of legislation or in their response to central directives. Without downright defiance they can be slow (pleading local difficulties), thus reducing the tempo of educational change; they can make ritual obeisance to the letter of the law while traducing its spirit, thus affecting the texture of educational change. History shows that local authorities have often been laggardly with impunity: Hadow reorganization was barely half finished by the outbreak of war; many areas never developed the technical schools which were an intrinsic element of the tripartite policy; schemes for comprehensive reorganization were not forthcoming from 50 per cent of authorities when they fell due in 1966.

On the other hand, mediation also operates in the other direction, pushing and stretching legal provisions as far as they will go, and often much further than was ever intended. Again this involves reinterpretation, the maximum use of enabling clauses, the exploitation of precedents and the pleading of 'special cases'; ducking restrictions, circumventing regulations and capitalizing on any ambiguity or vagueness in the central directive. Thus, between the wars a number of LEAs fostered a new outgrowth of post-elementary instruction, again blurring the official distinction between elementary and secondary

schooling; after 1944 certain areas pleaded population disper-
sal or bomb damage in order to establish multilateral schools,
against official policy; in 1958 Leicestershire initiated full
comprehensivization without official bye or leave, through re-
deploying its existing facilities.

The crucial fact to underline is that the two types of modifications — the positive and the negative, the amplifying and the
minimizing, those pushing forward and those holding back —
affect each polity-directed change simultaneously, for local and
institutional autonomy will be put to both ends by different
groups in different places. **Thus mediation means that a single
central directive leads to a plurality of practices, according to
the interpretations placed on it; practices which may be so
disparate that their common denominator is hard to detect.**
Furthermore, the balance of such modifications may represent
a substantial shift away from central policy — like the
predominantly bipartite organization of secondary schooling in
a supposedly tripartite system after the 1944 Act. In sum,
mediation prevents central policy directives from introducing
clear and uniform changes in national education.

(c) Polity-directed changes are rejected by parts of the system.
Any given polity-directed change can be resisted or rejected by
different parts of the educational system, but mainly those
which are most independent or those which determine to push
their relative autonomy to its very limits. Examples include the
recalcitrance of certain English LEAs vis-à-vis comprehensive
reorganization and the refusal of the majority of public and
direct grant schools to associate themselves with it. In other
words, not only do central policy directives fail to produce
uniform changes in education, they also fail to introduce universal changes.

Certainly the use of political sanctions can sometimes overcome resistance (and have already been used against the direct
grant schools) but the central polity is frequently impotent in
relation to the fully independent sector of education, whose
strength in decentralized systems enables it not only to limit
the scope of central policy but also to vitiate its workings —
public schools undermined both the notion of meritocratic
selection on which tripartism was based and the egalitarian
principles underpinning comprehensive reorganization.

Logically, of course, further political sanctions could
eliminate these sources of resistance and disruption. After all,

there is nothing inconceivable or unprecedented about the abolition of private schooling. In practice, however, we now come full circle back to the beginning of our discussion — to the ineluctable fact that polity-directed change in the decentralized system is limited by what is there and is well defended. **Ultimately, the polity has to resign itself to proceeding incrementally rather than radically towards the changes that it would like to introduce immediately and universally.** Hence, the results of political manipulation also contribute to the 'incremental pattern' of change, thus paralleling the effects of internal initiation and external transactions.

Products of change

(a) In centralized systems

So far, the importance of political manipulation in centralized systems has been examined exclusively in terms of the way in which it shapes the 'stop-go' pattern of change. Thus it remains to assess the cumulative result of changes introduced in this way over time. **In general, the effects of political manipulation have been consistently centripetal in nature: the substantive changes brought about through it have maintained and strengthened unification and systematization over time.** They have done so with extraordinary tenacity in the face of all kinds of counter-pressures from wider society and despite considerable political, social and economic change.

However, these formal continuities in educational control and co-ordination have consistently generated difficulties in the relationship between education and society. Thus, in the centralized system there is a continuous state of tension between education and its environment. Instead of educational inputs, processes and outputs being produced which corresponded to demands deemed politically acceptable, the strength of standardization and centripetalism militated against this harmony. In fact, the very tenacity with which the central authorities clung to unification and systematization, for purposes of control, produced an endless sequence of mis-matches with the environment. The inflexibility of such an educational system meant that any change of circumstances promptly threw it out of alignment and did so again and again, despite intermittent overhauls. Thus, while problems of integration are experienced in the decentralized system as tensions between the central authorities and the centrifugalism of other parts of the system, with centralization the problem of integration arises between the system as a whole and its social environment. It is a periodic problem of external maladaptation rather than an imminent threat of internal anarchy.

Why then were unification and systematization maintained with such tenacity if their concomitant inflexibility generated major problems at regular intervals? One suspicion it is important to remove is that educational centralization is nothing more than a reflection of authoritarian politics. This might well arise, given that France has undergone extensive periods of political closure, whether these involved monarchism, imperialism or bonapartism. Nevertheless, it is crucial to stress that the maintenance of these two characteristics was no less pronounced during the intervening periods when more open political structures prevailed, whether these took the form of bourgeois monarchy, republicanism, government by assembly, or a parliamentary presidential system. The fact that France has tried out most kinds of regime twice over, gives ample evidence that these educational characteristics are not narrowly associated with a particular kind of government. Indeed, the protestations of republicans like Jules Ferry[10] about the essential role of education in protecting the republican state and consolidating republican society, provide the key to this tenacious continuity. **For any incoming regime or government the inheritance of a highly responsive educational system was extremely advantageous: and the more the new regime differed from the old in structure and ideology, the more welcome was centralization since education could immediately be harnessed to legitimating and reinforcing the new polity.** Thus the basic structure of Napoleon's Université Impériale was passed unaltered from hand to hand through the whole spectrum of political organization, for each new regime hitched the educational system to the tasks of political socialization, political integration and political recruitment.

The course of change itself was moulded between the two factors just discussed: the intermittent need to re-establish harmony with the environment and the consistent defence of unification and systematization. But, necessarily, the first task had to be accomplished within the framework of the second,

otherwise a loss of control and of responsiveness would have been the result. It follows, therefore, that if the course of change was under-controlled in the decentralized system (being initiated from the periphery and barely rationalized or contained by the central authorities), it was over-controlled in the centralized system, where adjustments and adaptations were instrumented from the top down — once the need for such changes had been negotiated through political manipulation.

Thus, for example, the central authority in France continually acknowledged to the economic elite that a series of adjustments were needed to match the rapid changes in the industrial environment. But educational reforms always fell short of the moving target and did so because of their inflexible implementation and rigid co-ordination. Accepting the need for a shorter and more practical instruction, several formulae were tried out during the Second Empire (bifurcated secondary instruction, technical schools and finally special education), but only served to prove that the state's educational ideal could not be reconciled with vocational specialization. The Third Republic inherited the problem and made three different attempts at adaptive modernization. The policy of developing modern technical training failed largely because the centre would abandon no authority to local industrialists, enabling them to adjust it to their diverse requirements. The policy of updating secondary studies and diluting the hegemony of *culture générale* foundered because it was based on marrying special education to the *baccalauréat* in the *lycée* where modern education assumed an inferior status to classicism and special education lost its distinctive character.[11] Finally, the attempt to found real universities, as specialized centres of teaching and research, failed because all faculties were elevated in the same standardized fashion, spreading resources too thinly for specialization.

These examples serve to illustrate the basic fact that compatibility with the environment involves differentiation and specialization (since no aspect of it is ever uniform, it can only be matched by provisions which are adapted, or which can be adjusted, to local variations, special circumstances and unique configurations). Yet this kind of change has to be accommodated in an educational system whose unification and systematization are already strong and which the central authorities are determined not to relax. **Thus in the course of change the two pairs of characteristics, unification/systematization and** differentiation/specialization have to develop conjointly, but the latter remains the weaker pair as it was upon the emergence of the system. It is this pair which has to do the accommodating, has to take second place and has to accept the precedence of the first pair.

None the less, in its own interests the central authority cannot afford to let education slip grossly out of alignment with its environment, as this threatens its own goal attainment. Consequently, it has to make periodic efforts to introduce the requisite degree of differentiation and specialization in order to produce the services required. (Namely, those sought by the elite itself or negotiated by others through political manipulation.) What follows, therefore, is that progressive systematization and progressive segmentation develop simultaneously in a process of guided change — that is, within a context of strong unification. In modern terms this would simply be called planning, but it was practised in education long before it was conceptualized in this way.

Progressive segregation, through which diversification is accomplished, entails a successive division into sub-systems which is accompanied by a differentiation of their functions and a specialization of their activities. Progressive systematization consists in the strengthening of pre-existing relations between parts, the linking of parts previously unrelated, and the gradual addition of new components and relations to a system. The two take place simultaneously under the guidance of the centre and develop by a series of jerks during each 'go' phase. To call these 'progressive' is only to reflect on the overall tendency of the system to become more complex in both respects over time. The term carries no evaluative connotation nor does it preclude periods of structural inertia or of regression to simpler forms of organization. The history of the French system witnesses to the conjoint development of segregation and systematization, but also demonstrates the predominance of the latter, whatever the nature of the regime — **centralized systems have always been, and they remain, extremely neat in form compared with their decentralized counterparts.**

The heritage of the Napoleonic structure was a system subdivided into two levels unlinked to one another (the negative principle of hierarchical organization). The Third Republic retained and reinforced the basic segregation of the primary from the secondary level, such that these two sub-systems developed almost independently of one another — fulfilling totally different functions and enrolling very different social strata. However, within each sub-system, segregation and systematization both took a big step forward.

At the secondary level, the aim was to diversify, to introduce the degree of differentiation and specialization commensurate with modernization. Yet, as we have seen, the priority accorded to systematization meant that special education was the vehicle used for this and it soon lost its distinctiveness, disappearing altogether in 1902. Then a further assault was made on the same problem: a single secondary education now led to a *baccalauréat* with four specialized sections, intended to afford a greater variety of instruction. In other words, systematization and segmentation were to go hand in hand, but as usual there was no doubt which one led. Modern studies were confined to the fourth (inferior) option and lost their distinctive character between pressures to imitate the prestige branches and to prepare for university entry. In tackling the same problem yet again, an identical sequence was repeated in the twentieth century with the creation of the technical *baccalauréat* in 1946; [12] it again failed to attain parity and succumbed to academicism. **Thus, these attempts to achieve a higher level of reintegration, which included differentiated courses of modern subjects, made some progress but always suffered from the fact that systematization acted as a strait-jacket which denied distinctiveness, diluted specialization and thus demoted diversification.**

Exactly the same story was repeated at the primary level, with successive attempts to introduce more differentiated and specialized courses of vocational or pre-vocational instruction only really succeeding in rare cases when these institutions broke away from the Ministry of Education altogether. Otherwise, their practical orientation steadily gave way to general education the longer they remained part of the system — the fate not only of full-time institutions like the *écoles primaires supérieures*, but also of the part-time training courses for working youth, introduced immediately after the First World War. [13]

As the system entered the twentieth century, demands for more democratization bombarded the National Assembly, but produced grudging and tentative moves towards the fundamental structural change sought — the linking of the primary and secondary sub-systems. Slowly, progressive systematization and segregation again went forward together, but as usual the former predominated throughout. Even by the start of the Fifth Republic, all that had been introduced was a 'harmonization' of programmes at the end of the first *degré* and at the beginning of the second, the orientation, at least in principle, of pupils to different types of further instruction on the basis of their performance, and the establishment of *'classes passerelles'* allowing for the transfer later on of those who had taken the wrong route. Thus there was no audacious structural change and the differentiation of no new self-standing institution to combat social discrimination. [14]

Continued pressures led to the eventual segregation of the *Collège d'Enseignement Secondaire* but this was accomplished by the regrouping of existing components (the final class of primary, the first cycle of secondary and of the old *collèges*). To a large extent these elements resisted reintegration and refused to collaborate in a purposeful manner. [15] The introduction of the positive principle of hierarchical organization, the biggest rupture yet with the Napoleonic structure, needed to be articulated by a separate and forceful institution committed to overthrowing a century and a half of socio-educational discrimination, [16] like the original conception of the *école unique*: instead, the task was entrusted to this weak amalgam — the CES.

The composition of the Fifth Republic government made it considerably more sympathetic and creative in relation to modernization at secondary and higher levels. The same device was used to introduce greater diversification in both — the differentiation of cycles of studies, giving more chance for vocational and academic specialization. Each cycle which was segregated in this way was also systematized with those below and above it, although distinctiveness was protected by each cycle awarding a separate diploma. Thus, secondary education was divided into two cycles, a short and a long, while the historical influence of the *baccalauréat* as a force for standardization was reduced by its division into numerous sub-sections, related to different occupational outlets and higher educational inlets. At the higher level the differentiation of the *Instituts Universitaires de Technologie* replicated the segregation of short and long alternatives. University education was itself subdivided into three cycles, each with specialist options and a diploma at the end of it. Once again these changes betrayed the super-ordinate insistence on systematization — the reforms were imposed uniformly and universally from the centre, their rigidity defying local or institutional adaptation.[17] Only the outburst of the May events led to the concession of some university autonomy for differentiation and specialization to be defined *in situ* rather than at the centre — but even here the subordinate characteristics have not been grafted well on to the old tree.

(b) In decentralized systems

When the three processes for negotiating change are considered in relation to one another over time, certain long-term regularities become apparent in the types of changes which they have produced. In particular, external transactions and internal initiation have operated as forces for diversification, which have strengthened the *differentiation* and the *specialization* of the educational system over time. By contrast, political manipulation has represented a consistent force for standardization which has defended the *unification* and *systematization* of national education during the same period.

Thus, external transactions and internal initiation constituted *centrifugal* tendencies, whether considered alone or in conjunction with one another. The changes which stemmed from both processes constantly threatened to escape central governance and accountability and in turn often vitiated public policy by extending practices it sought to eliminate (e.g., private schooling) or developing ones hostile to it (e.g., the expansion of the social rather than the applied sciences in higher education). **Basically, such changes damage central policy because they involve differentiation and specialization in directions which are incompatible with it. They undermine central control and stress the absence of a leading part as well as preventing its emergence.**

Equally, direct transactions advance sectional interests but their particularism is often at variance with an integrated system. Thus, the transformation of the English primary school along progressive lines is held by some to have undermined integration between levels by not inculcating the skills or values needed later on, thus jeopardizing a high standard of secondary or vocational instruction.[18] These changes disrupt the system by failing to dovetail with other parts or activities. They serve to emphasize the fragility of co-ordination, as well as making this task more difficult.

In contradistinction, the changes introduced through political manipulation showed a strong tendency to reinforce unification and systematization over time, for the very determination to introduce centrally defined policies entailed their defence. In particular, the fact that the polity was increasingly preoccupied with the quest for educational democratization, especially after the Second World War, meant that it needed to defend a degree of unification sufficient to ensure the national implementation of a new form of systematization, based on the principle of the educational ladder. However, because the very introduction of *any* polity-directed change was predicated on buttressing the weaker pair of characteristics in the decentralized system, these were constantly reinforced by government in general, not just by the political representatives of labour. Consequently, polity-directed changes involved a consistent *centripetal* trend.

The basic effect of polity-directed change was thus to minimize developments which threatened to disrupt central policy. This involved the pruning and elimination of those institutions and activities which were not complementary, and a corresponding increase in standardization. In England there were three different phases in which such developments were pruned back hard to prevent their interference with a politically sponsored institution and to ensure the latter pride of place. Successively, the higher grade schools were cut down and replaced by the higher elementary schools at the incorporation stage; the outgrowth of a wide range of differentiated post-elementary institutions were weeded out in favour of the uniform Morant grammar school; and the senior, central and municipal schools proliferating between the wars were forced, root and branch, into the secondary modern format.

Training and containing are alternatives to pruning and eliminating, but have similar if weaker consequences in terms of loss of diversification. Thus, for example, adult education was trained along 'non-partisan' lines in England, the WEA being unified under the Board of Education and subordinated to university direction. Similarly, the burgeoning development of technical schools at intermediate levels was contained: in 1913, junior technical schools were reluctantly recognized providing they operated as terminal institutions, unintegrated with the secondary level. Again, after 1944, they were trained into line (by adjusting ages of entry, etc.) with the tripartite policy, then condemned to inertia through lack of positive official encouragement. The loss of a strong practical, real or technical definition of instruction was the price paid for the defence of central policies. In general, the centripetal drive stemming from political manipulation does everything it can to restrain practices which reinforce the predominance of differentiation and specialization, for from the start these were already too strong for government to exert effective governance over education.

Clearly, then, the products of internal initiation and external transactions on the one hand, and those of political manipulation on the other, are in a continuous state of tension. Centrifugalism is a perpetual threat to the integration of the system and the achievement of central goals: centripetalism barely contains these diverse developments and separatist tendencies. The changes which actually take place are shaped and reshaped between these pushes and pulls. They are woven by a ceaseless dialectic between the forces for diversification and the pressures towards standardization.

From the moment the decentralized system emerges, change fans out as both external transactions and internal initiation introduce an immediate increase in institutional differentiation and curricular specialization — thus threatening the weak unification and systematization which had been superimposed on the networks at the time of incorporation. The central response arising from political manipulation is to rationalize these disparate developments, pruning, containing and incorporating them — through a re-systematization and an increase in unification. But the central authorities, as we have seen, cannot proceed like a general, deploying and disposing at will in order to achieve a grand planned strategy, because the parts fight back to defend their autonomy. Instead, the centre more often has to work like a sheepdog patrolling the periphery, giving a nip here and a nip there, herding developments on the right trail. Moreover, although unification and systematization are mutually supportive when strong, the two here have frequently to be traded off against one another on the part of the centre. Thus, systematization was often bought at the price of unification, especially when the incorporation of independent elements meant the admission of new partners to control and therefore entailed educational power sharing. Equally, systematization sometimes had to be sacrificed as the only way in which to bring

about some important general change, such as the acceptance
of a plethora of local arrangements in order to achieve national
comprehensivization.

**Consequently, although unification and systematization were
periodically reinforced, they were never strong, and though they
held diversification back for a time, they themselves were
gradually sloughed off by the combined efforts of local initiative, external transactions and internal initiation. As they
gradually slipped, more and more changes would accumulate
and these would again accentuate systemic differentiation and
specialization. Another bout of central intervention would then
take place, confining and reordering these changes as unification and systematization were re-established. So the system
proceeded in undulating fashion, with changes swelling out and
then being squeezed in, only to bulge out again as the phases
of diversification and standardization alternated with one
another.** The phases, however, did allow for progression. They
involved no return to the status quo, and though they were
sometimes conservative in their effects, this represented no
structure-maintaining mechanism. Instead, it was much more
common for progressive segmentation and progressive
systematization to follow one another like successive waves. [19]

The major education Acts signalled the main phases in which
unification and systematization were reinforced: differentiation
and specialization expanded in the intervals between them, and
of course precipitated reintervention on the part of the centre.
Thus, in England, the 1902 Settlement was followed not just
by the spread of the higher elementary school and Morant grammar school which were officially approved, but by the growth
of diverse institutions (science schools, technical day schools,
pupil-teacher centres, trade schools, vocational schools, etc.).
The 1918 Act, which confirmed the structural and cultural
hegemony of the academic grammar school, intended to crowd
most of these other developments into the continuation schools,
which would be allowed some practical orientation but would
remain firmly elementary. Effectively, this Act was weaker than
usual as a concrete affirmation of unification and systematization because of the intervention of the Depression and the
suspension of many of its provisions. Consequently, despite
austerity, a variety of intermediary institutions again proliferated and these central, senior and technical schools
represented a real challenge since they enrolled two-thirds as

many pupils as the 'official' grammar schools. Thus, a chaotic array of provisions had accumulated by the outbreak of war, and the application of the 1944 Act again crammed them into the inferior part of the system, this time the secondary modern school. This Act, which had greatly strengthened unification, was also to produce an unprecedented degree of systematization, as the tripartite policy took root and achieved the closest integration between the primary and secondary levels. Almost immediately, however, local initiative began to push forward with multilateral developments which gathered speed with labour encouragement and became even less uniform with the conservative policy of co-existence. Once again, the minister threatened another round of legislative intervention in 1975 and made it clear that this would involve strengthening the powers of the centre. This final phase only serves to illustrate the endurance of a phenomenon which characterized the very inception of the decentralized system, namely that unification and systematization must always be superimposed on component elements which are already highly differentiated and specialized. [20]

Hence, systematization consistently trailed in the wake of segmentation and the central authorities often presented the picture of running behind and tidying up after the forces producing diversification. Even when the centre tried to take the initiative it could not do so imperatively and categorically but had itself to negotiate the implementation of such policies with the appropriate local authorities and institutions; and negotiation spelled concession, compromise, exception, exemption, reinterpretation, modification, dilution and every other antithesis of standardization. **Consequently, although progressive systematization has grown considerably, structural elaboration in the decentralized system remains an untidy jerry-rigged product. And this will always be the case as long as the three processes through which change is negotiated continue to operate alongside one another and to retain their rough parity of importance.**

8 CONCLUSION: PROSPECTS FOR CHANGE

The last problem to address is whether the accumulation of changes just discussed will alter the patterns of educational change to be expected in the immediate future. Specifically, this is to ask have the developments which have occurred in centralized and decentralized systems, since their inception, so transformed these systems that they no longer engender two distinctive patterns of change, because the structural differences generating them have been removed? The answer to this question thus hinges on the extent of convergence which has taken place between the two structures of educational systems, from their origins to the present day — as the product of intervening interaction.

Examination of the course of change in the centralized and decentralized systems led to the conclusion that in both a progressive segmentation and a progressive systematization had developed side by side since the initial emergence of these systems. Does this mean, then, that substantial structural convergence has taken place between them? To a certain degree this is undoubtedly the case. From their beginnings, the centralized systems have been subject to pressures to reduce their standardization and to meet a multiplicity of demands with greater precision, by introducing more differentiation and specialization. When such demands were successfully negotiated through political manipulation (and, of course, many were not) they were carefully co-ordinated by the central authorities into polity-directed changes which were transmitted to education from the top down. Sequentially these added up to a multipurpose system of much greater complexity, whose new subdivided parts permitted this differentiation of services. Subdivision was the key mechanism: through it levels could be broken down into cycles, cycles into differentiated branches, and branches into specialised courses — all without loss of control or co-ordination. Sub-division broke up the stark outlines of the original systems, whose simplicity reflected the

limited goals of their founders and the equally limited concessions they had been forced to make to get these systems off
the ground.

In the decentralized systems, the initial phase of incorporation which brought them into being did not finish there. The
processes of external transaction and internal initiation continued to generate new developments, in response to the
demands of professional and external interest groups, which
were characterized by their specificity. These took place with
scant attention to the central authorities beyond the need to
evade them and sometimes to propitiate them. Nevertheless,
the summativity of these developments did gradually give way
to wholeness. The integrative role of the central authorities
worked to contain, connect and co-ordinate these anarchic
changes. It reduced the internal chaos and contradiction
between parts in order to increase responsiveness to central
direction and to ensure complementarity between the great
variety of services provided. The move towards wholeness
increased the coherence of these systems, tidying up their
ragged outlines, streamlining their main components, and
simplifying the tangle of provisions which mirrored the diverse
goals which education had undertaken to service over time.

Thus, to stress convergence is to emphasize the growth of
progressive segmentation in the centralized system and of progressive systematization in the decentralized system. Both have
indeed taken place but they only represent one part of the story.
When discussing the products of change there was also cause to
accentuate the way in which the pair of characteristics which
dominated these two kinds of systems at their emergence has
retained its pre-eminence over time. In other words, it was
important to stress that the segmentation progressively introduced into the centralized system involved no diminution of
systematization or unification. On the contrary, the very introduction of these sub-divisions was planned, orchestrated and
monitored by the central authority, which thus strengthened
its position as the leading part. Equally, the systematization
progressively introduced into the decentralized system entailed
no loss of differentiation and specialization. On the contrary,
the coherence produced was an ordering of changes already
brought about autonomously by the parts which then retained
their capacity to instigate change independently of the centre.
In other words, **not only did the two kinds of system remain**

very different in these structural respects but the mechanisms which generated these differences remained largely intact.

Because of this, it appears that the structural conditions for a continuation of the 'stop-go' pattern of change in France remain largely unaltered and will continue to do so unless and until the polity manifests a thorough-going willingness to relax central controls over education. Otherwise, 'the more complex the system becomes, then if the present principles are retained, the more this form of administration runs the risk of losing itself in details at the expense of essential tasks, of draining itself in the effort to keep every situation, each of which has its own uniqueness, within a rigid framework and, ultimately, of paralysing the overall operation of the whole through its impotence. Decentralization is therefore a matter of urgency. It is at the level of the regional or local authorities, depending on the nature of the case, that the main problems concerning the practical organization and current operation of the public educational service can be resolved. It is at the level of each establishment, not only in higher education but in primary and secondary too, that from a clearly defined outline of aims, the contents and methods of instruction could be adapted to the concrete reality of the ill-served population.'[1] Yet, as the Fifth Republic has now survived three potential crises of presidential succession and the system has continued to stumble onwards despite repeated educational outbursts followed by propitiatory legislation, there is little ground for expecting any drastic move away from the 'stop-go' pattern of change. One of the best substantiated of comparative generalizations is that no governing elite voluntarily renunciates a centralized educational system.

If there are few signs that the leading part is abdicating any of its powers in the centralized systems, it is equally the case that decision-making powers remain dispersed in the decentralized systems. In England, the three processes of negotiation have maintained themselves over time and one has not continuously won out at the expense of the others. In particular, there is no consistent tendency for political manipulation to have increased in importance, relative to external transactions and internal initiation, thus spelling a drift towards centralization.

In decentralized systems, the relative importance of the three processes is always subject to temporal variations. The important point to stress, then, is that the rough parity between them has been preserved during the twentieth century as a whole. Certainly, it is true at the moment that the central authority would like to exert more control, especially over higher education. But there has probably never been a time at which the central authorities in a decentralized system have not wanted greater control over one level or another in order to redirect its activities.

Above all, we must resist the strong temptation to endow the most recent events with a greater significance than their predecessors. It is undoubtedly the case in England at the present time, that the centre seems poised to intervene more roughly at both secondary and higher levels, but this is better interpreted as one of the periodic reorderings conducted by the central authorities than as a dramatic change in the nature of educational control. After all, the 1944 Act seemed at the time to indicate a great lurch towards centralization, but it was in fact followed by the most active period of external transactions and internal innovations which effectively undermined any such convergence. Exactly the same is expected now, not only because a legislative act of that magnitude is not even on the horizon, and the central incursions which have been made depend upon the endurance of economic recession, but also because the rights acquired by professional and external interest groups have taken a number of additional steps forward in the intervening decades since the war.

In other words, both the centralized and the decentralized systems continue to exert different structural influences on educational interaction in their respective countries, despite the fact that some convergence has taken place between them. Does this mean, then, that they will continue to condition different patterns of educational change and to produce different kinds of systemic modifications? In answering this question in the affirmative, let it be absolutely clear that I am talking about structural conditioning and not about structural determinism.

There is no logical necessity about this, for neither in principle nor in practice is there any factor or force which ultimately prevents the appropriate decision-makers in both types of system from deciding to alter the structure of those systems. Thus, logically, there is nothing to stop a governing elite from passing an Act which would transform a centralized system into a decentralized one, hence destroying the conditional influences which have reproduced the 'stop-go' pattern of change over time and preserved structuration around a 'leading-part'. In reality, however, structures distribute vested interests in their maintenance and it is the fact that groups do defend these which makes patterns of interaction and change durable in the long-run. In our discussion of centralized systems we have examined numerous political elites with the most diverse ideological orientations and have found them unanimous in their support for and defence of the centralized structure. There is not a single counter-example in which centralization itself (rather than the purposes to which it was put) was thrown over by a governing elite, whether reactionary or revolutionary, which was willing to sacrifice the political advantages of educational control. It is because of the endurance of this vested interest that the centralized system is expected to condition its own maintenance in the foreseeable future.

Exactly the same is the case with the decentralized system. Again, logically, the appropriate decision-makers, here the profession and the external interest groups, could decide to terminate their independent initiatives and autonomous innovations. Indeed, in our empirical discussion we did encounter examples of groups which ceased such activities for reasons of financial hardship and others where these transactions were repressed or discouraged. However, this was never a systematic phenomenon, and at the very time that such examples occurred other groups were taking up these processes of negotiation for the first time. In other words, the initial structure again invites its own continuation. There is nothing deterministic about this, it is simply that, over time, the decentralized structure conditions small, localized changes which intensify the autonomy which allowed them to occur in the first place. This, in turn, distributes vested interests in educational control more and more widely through society and outside the central authorities. It is the defence of these interests from within and without the educational system which conditions the endurance of the 'incremental' pattern of change and will prevent the central authority from assuming the position of a 'leading-part' in the foreseeable future.

The lasting structural differences between the two kinds of system, which still allow them to be characterized as centralized or decentralized, mean that the present cycle is not yet over. In other words, structural conditioning continues to shape

interaction in different ways in the two systems; interaction itself still follows two distinctive patterns; and the structural elaboration which results reconfirms the differences between the two systems which caused one to distinguish between centralization and decentralization in the first place.

Thus, the prospects for change are that future educational interaction will continue to be patterned in dissimilar fashions in the two systems, and that the products of change will reproduce the main features of centralization or decentralization. The force of this argument rests on the endurance of differences in the structural conditioning of interaction and change between the centralized system and the decentralized system.

In opposition to this, it might be objected that such an argument neglects cultural factors whose contribution encourages educational convergence. The latter is incontestable. There is no doubt that the post-war period has witnessed a growing internationalization of student culture and of pedagogical approaches: nor is there any doubt that because students, teachers and academics read the same books, repeat the same arguments and respond to the same values the world over, they thus represent a force for convergence — a force which pushes national systems to address similar problems, to adopt similar methods and to accept similar solutions. Nevertheless, cultural forces, however international they may be, still have to contend with the established structures of the different national systems of education and the vested interests associated with their maintenance. In other words, the cultural forces for educational convergence are working against the structural forces which condition the endurance of different systems of education. The differences between the centralized and the decentralized systems of education may ultimately give way, but not yet, and not without tremendous resistance from those who benefit from these two different structures of educational system.

NOTES

In all the following notes, references to the unabridged version of *Social Origins of Educational Systems*, Sage, London and Beverly Hills, 1979, will be referred to as SOES.

1. Introduction: thinking and theorizing about educational systems

1. For a detailed discussion and defence of macro-sociology see SOES, pp. 5-45.

2. The main sociological works influencing the theoretical perspective used throughout this volume are:

P. M. Blau, *Exchange and Power in Social Life*, New York, 1964;

Walter Buckley, *Sociology and Modern Systems Theory*, New Jersey, 1967;

A. Etzioni, *The Active Society*, London, 1968;

D. Lockwood, 'Social Integration and System Integration', in G. K. Zollschan and H. W. Hirsch (eds), *Explorations in Social Change*, London, 1964;

A. W. Gouldner, 'Reciprocity and Autonomy in Functional Theory', in N. J. Demerath and R. A. Peterson (eds), *System, Change and Conflict*, New York, 1967;

S. N. Eisenstadt, 'Social Change, Differentiation and Evolution', in Demerath and Peterson, op. cit.

3. The main philosophical works informing the theoretical approach adopted here are:

Ernest Gellner, 'Holism versus Individualism', in May Brodbeck (ed.), *Readings in the Philosophy of the Social Sciences*, New York, 1971

Steven Lukes, 'Methodological Individualism Reconsidered', *British Journal of Sociology*, vol. XIX, no. 2, 1968

Leon J. Goldstein, 'The Inadequacy of the Principle of Methodological Individualism', *Journal of Philosophy*, vol. 53, 1956.

Alisdair MacIntyre, 'On the Relevance of the Philosophy of the Social Sciences', *British Journal of Sociology*, vol. XX, no. 2, 1969

H. R. Wagner, 'Displacement of Scope: A Problem of the Relationship between Small Scale and Large Scale Sociological Theories', *American Journal of Sociology*, vol. LXIX, no. 6, 1964

J. H. Goldthorpe, 'A Revolution in Sociology?', *Sociology*, vol. 7, no. 3, 1973.

4. P. S. Cohen, *Modern Social Theory*, London, 1968, p. 205.

5. Macro-sociologists reject the holistic assumptions that social structure dominates individual action in favour of a more moderate notion of emergent power, 'according to which social wholes influence individuals so that individual action is determined by a combination of two factors, social wholes and individual purposes'. J. O. Wisdom, 'Situational Individualism and the Emergent Group-Properties', in R. Borger and F. Cioffi (eds), *Explanations in the Behavioural Sciences*, Cambridge, 1970, p. 294.

6. For a clear example of the use of this cycle see S. N. Eisenstadt, op. cit.

7. A more detailed discussion of this theme is found in my 'Morphogenesis versus Structuration', *British Journal of Sociology*, vol. XXXIII, no. 4, 1982, especially pages 466-71.

8. For example, the position epitomized by J. W. N. Watkins: 'The central assumption of the individualistic position — an assumption which is admittedly counter-factual and metaphysical — is that no social tendency exists which could not be altered *if* the individuals concerned both wanted to alter it and possessed the appropriate information', 'Methodological Individualism and Social Tendencies', in Brodbeck, op. cit., p. 271.

9. Cohen, op. cit., p. 93.

10. Here the distinction drawn between 'system' and 'social' integration is the same as that outlined by D. Lockwood, op. cit.

11. 'Differentiation' is used by Eisenstadt as a classificatory concept which refers to the ways in which the main social functions of the major institutions of society become dissociated from one another, attached to a specialized collectivity and roles, and organized in relatively specific and autonomous symbolic and organizational frameworks within the confines of the same institutionalized system. Cf. Eisenstadt, op. cit. As far as education was concerned it was not dissociated organizationally, symbolically or in terms of roles and personnel, from various other parts of the historical empires or imperial civilizations. Educational activities intermingled with others which were themselves relatively indistinct — e.g., the position of the litterati in China and to a lesser extent the Brahmin in India witness to the intermingling of religious, political, educational and stratificational spheres.

12. It should be noted that the unabridged study involved a four-country comparison of England, France, Denmark and Russia. Thus, the range of variation was considerably greater than that presented in this textbook edition. The latter two case studies were omitted here for purposes of brevity and clarity. However, they are drawn upon at various times to supplement the cases employed. Their absence here should not be forgotten for the propositions advanced in the following chapters are not simply induced from the educational histories of England and France.

2. Structure: education as private enterprise

1. As Gouldner argues, reciprocity must not be assumed a priori, see A. W. Gouldner, 'Reciprocity and Autonomy in Functional Theory', in N. J. Demerath and R. A. Peterson (eds), *System, Change and Conflict*, New York, 1967, pp. 141-69.

2. P. M. Blau, *Exchange and Power in Social Life*, New York, 1964, ch. 5.

3. Patrick L. Alston, *Education and the State in Tsarist Russia*, Stanford, 1969, p. 5.

4. Michalina Vaughan and Margaret S. Archer, *Social Conflict and Educational Change in England and France, 1789-1848*, Cambridge, 1971, ch. 5.

5. R. Dahrendorf, *Class and Class Conflict in Industrial Society*, Stanford, 1959; 'Towards a Theory of Social Conflict', in Walter L. Wallace (ed.), *Sociological Theory*, London, 1969.

6. See Robert K. Merton, 'On Sociological Theories of the Middle-Range', in his *On Theoretical Sociology*, New York, 1967, p. 60.

7. For a more detailed discussion of this theme see my 'The Theoretical and Comparative Analysis of Social Structure', in Salvador Giner and Margaret S. Archer (eds), *Contemporary Europe: Social Structures and Cultural Patterns*, London, 1978, pp. 1-27.

3. Interaction: competition for educational control

1. The following discussion utilizes the theoretical framework developed in an earlier joint study of educational change in two countries before the advent of state systems. Cf. Michalina Vaughan and Margaret S. Archer, *Social Conflict and Educational Change in England and France, 1789-1848*, Cambridge, 1971, ch. 2. This earlier book gives a much more detailed analysis of educational conflict itself, especially at the ideational level, and should be consulted as an example of the expanded application of the theoretical framework. However, this book stops short of the final consolidation of state systems in the two countries.

2. Max Weber, *Basic Concepts in Sociology*, London, 1962, p. 117.

3. This is discussed in greater detail in Vaughan and Archer, op. cit., chs 7-10.

4. Ibid., p. 134. See also F. Vial, *Trois Siècles de l'enseignement secondaire*, Paris, 1936, pp. 48ff.

5. Cf. F. Ponteil, *Histoire de l'Enseignement, 1780-1964*, Paris, 1966, pp. 32ff., on Jesuit attempts to justify and strengthen their educational position.

6. For an estimate of their extensiveness at the beginning of the nineteenth century see H. B. Binns, *A Centenary of Education, being the Centenary History of the British and Foreign School Society (1808-1908)*, London, 1908.

7. Select Committee on the Education of the Lower Orders in the Metropolis appointed in 1816. (Its terms of reference subsequently included the whole country.)

8. W. R. Ward, *Victorian Oxford*, London, 1965.

9. Cf. J. Sparrow, *Mark Pattison and the Idea of a University*, Cambridge, 1967 ch. 3. During the period 1800-50, 25,000 matriculated from Oxford, over 10,000 of whom were later ordained.

10. A. O. J. Cockshut, *Anglican Attitudes*, London, 1959. See also D. Voll, *Catholic Evangelicalism*, London, 1963 and G. Faber, *Oxford Apostles*, London, 1954.

11. Mirabeau's condemnation of the Catholic definition of French education is equally applicable to the English one: 'There is no choice possible between courses in various subject-matters. A single one-way avenue is open to all types of intelligence. The homogeneity which is the result desired, is at the same time, the precondition of this result.' Quoted by F. Vial, op. cit., p. 48. See also G. de Mirabeau, *Travail sur l'Education Publique*, Paris, 1791.

12. 'The ancient tongues are only useful now to some specific sectors of society', D. Diderot, 'Plan d'une Université pour le gouvernement de Russie ou d'une éducation publique dans toutes les sciences' in *Oeuvres complètes* (Assezat-Tourneux ed.) Paris, 1875, p. 441. See also E. Caro, *La Fin du 18ᵉ siècle*, Paris, 1880, pp. 255-56.

13. President B. G. Rolland, *Compte-Rendu aux Chambres Assemblées des Différents Mémoires envoyés par les Universités sises dans le ressort de la Cour*, Paris, 1786, p. 60.

14. Cf. Vaughan and Archer, op. cit., pp. 60-79.

15. An admirable contemporary account of the links between clergy and nobility is found in the polemic by E. J. Sieyès, *Essai sur les Privilèges*, Paris, 1788.

16. A. O. J. Cockshut, op. cit.; T. W. Bamford, *Thomas Arnold*, London, 1960.

17. P. M. Blau, *Exchange and Power in Social Life*, New York, 1964, pp. 117-41. See also W. Buckley, *Sociology and Modern Systems Theory*, New Jersey, 1967, pp. 200-202.

To Blau a group can avoid imbalances of obligations from occurring, in one of four ways: (a) it can obtain benefits from X by providing services needed by X in return; (b) it can suppress the need for such benefits; (c) it can obtain these benefits from a source other than Group X; (d) it can secure such benefits by force.

In this study we have seen that (a) and (b) are not feasible strategies for assertive groups for they cannot negotiate the scale of educational changes required nor renounce the need for them because of the continuation of obstructions. Hence the present study concentrates on strategies which coincide with Blau's (c) and (d) for gaining the educational benefits needed. Alternative (c) 'leads to the study of competitive processes, of the exchange rates that become established in social structure and of monopolisation' (p. 140). These are in other words precisely the issues examined here for *substitutive* strategies. Alternative (d) calls attention to the differentiation of power in society, to organizations in which it is mobilized and to political processes and institutions. Again these are the crucial elements analyzed here for *restrictive* strategies.

18. Ponteil, op. cit., p. 46.

19. G. C. Hippeau, *La Révolution et l'éducation nationale*, Paris, 1883. M. Gontard, *L'Enseignement primaire en France de la Révolution à la Loi Guizot, 1789-1833*, Lyons, 1959. A. Duruy, *L'Instruction publique et la Révolution*, Paris, 1882. L. Liard, *L'Enseignement supérieur en France 1789-1889* (2 vols), Paris, 1888.

20. An apathy which led Engels to declare, 'So stupidly narrow-minded is the English bourgeoisie in its egotism, that it does not even take the trouble to impress upon the workers the morality of the day, which the Bourgeoisie has patched together in its own interests for its own protection'. F. Engels, *The Condition of the Working Class in England in 1844*, London, 1892, p. 114.

21. His most important work in this connection is his 'Plan d'une Université pour le gouvernement de Russie' (Diderot, op. cit.). Cf. Tourneux, *Diderot et Catherine II*, Paris, 1899; J. Oestreicher, *La Pensée politique et économique de Diderot*, Paris, 1936.

22. His most important work in this context is M. J. A. de Condorcet, *Sur l'Instruction publique*, Paris, 1792. Cf. F. Vial, *Condorcet et l'éducation démocratique*, Paris, n.d.; J. Bouissounouse, *Condorcet, le philosophe dans la Révolution*, Paris, 1962; F. Alengry, *Condorcet — Guide de la Révolution Française*, Paris, 1904. See also Condorcet, Sieyès, Duhamel, *Journal d'Instruction Sociale*, Paris, 1793.

23. The most important works dealing with education are: Sieyès, op. cit.

and *Qu'est-ce que le Tiers Etat?*, 3rd ed., Paris, 1789. Cf. P. Bastid, *Sieyès et sa pensée*, Paris, 1939.

24. Although Utilitarianism represented an attack of secular ethics on religious morals and appealed to an important section of the middle class, this ideological divide did not ultimately split the Dissenter-entrepreneurial alliance. Initially the reason for this was restraint on the part of the utilitarians themselves, who were cautious not to advance overt agnosticism and thus to antagonize the Dissenting sub-group.

25. 'Political economy, though its object be to ascertain the means of increasing the wealth of nations, cannot accomplish its design, without at the same time regarding their happiness, and as its largest ingredient the cultivation of religion and morality.' Thus Kay-Shuttleworth signalled the reincorporation of religion as a form of social control into middle-class thought. J. Kay-Shuttleworth, 'The Moral and Physical Condition of the Working Classes in Manchester in 1832' in *Four Periods of English Education*, London, 1862, p. 39.

26. B. Simon, *Studies in the History of Education, 1780-1870*, op. cit. See also E. Dolléans, *Le Chartisme (1830-1848)*, Paris, 1912; A. R. Schoyen, *The Chartist Challenge; a Portrait of George Julien Harney*, London, 1958; R. H. Tawney, *The Radical Tradition*, London, 1964; *The Life and Struggles of W. Lovett* (Tawney ed.) London, 1920.

27. The monitorial system was devised by A. Bell and described by him in *An Experiment in Education Made at the Male (Orphan) Asylum in Madras, Suggesting a System by which a School or Family may Teach Itself under the Superintendence of the Master or Parent*, 2nd ed., London, 1809. This system was used extensively during the early years of the British and Foreign School Society and thus played a part in middle-class substitution. It was used in France, experimentally towards the end of the empire and more extensively during the restoration. There it represented bourgeois anti-clericism and the attempt to replace the teaching Orders by the state as controller and supplier of elementary instruction. In Denmark after the Great Commission in 1814 the King introduced the Lancastrian system in an attempt to break the clerical monopoly of teaching staff and simultaneously to 'diminish the burdens that are necessary otherwise for the organisation of the common-school system' (Willis Dixon, *Education in Denmark*, Copenhagen, 1958, p. 56).

28. Cf. Vaughan and Archer, op. cit., pp. 89-92.

29. The main educational plans to come before the three revolutionary assemblies were those of Mirabeau, Talleyrand, Condorcet, Romme and Lanthenas, Lakanal, Sieyès, Daunou and finally that of Lepelletier. They differ considerably in their underlying principles and in the programmes of educational change advocated. Cf. R. Sevrin, *Histoire de l'enseignement primaire en France sous la Révolution, le Consulat et l'Empire*, Paris, 1932; see also H. C. Barnard, *Education and the French Revolution*, Cambridge, 1969.

30. This view was clearly expressed by Thomas Arnold and acted upon by his influential pupils. Cf. T. W. Bamford, op. cit.; J. Fitch, *Thomas and Matthew Arnold and Their Influence upon English Education*, London, 1897; J. J. Findlay, *Arnold of Rugby*, Cambridge, 1898; A. P. Stanley, *Life and Correspondence of Thomas Arnold*, London, 1846.

4. Structural elaboration:
the emergence of state educational systems

1. There is no assumption that the macroscopic changes discussed under Propositions (i) and (ii) are more adaptive, efficient, stable or legitimate than their antecedents. Such concepts can be used to describe or evaluate the consequences of educational change (which may or may not reveal greater adaptation, efficiency, stability or legitimacy), but they cannot be used as a substitute for analyzing the processes which produce change or examining the characteristics which are transformed.

2. Cf. E. Despois, *Le Vandalisme révolutionnaire*, Paris, 1868; R. Sevrin, *Histoire de l'enseignement primaire en France sous la Révolution, le Consulat et l'Empire*, Paris, 1932; C. Hippeau, *La Révolution et l'éducation nationale*, Paris, 1883; O. Gréard, *La Législation de l'instruction en France depuis 1789*, vol. 1, 1789-1833, Paris, 1887; and A. Duruy, *L'instruction publique et la Révolution*, Paris, 1882.

3. See C. Jourdain, *Le budget de l'instruction publique et des établissements scientifiques et litéraires depuis la fondation de l'université impériale jusqu'à nos jours*, Paris, 1857.

4. Quoted in L. Liard, *L'enseignement supérieur en France, 1789-1889*, 2 vols, Paris, 1888, p. 69.

5. Cf. M. Vaughan, 'The Grandes Ecoles', in R. Wilkinson (ed), *Governing Elites: Studies in Training and Selection*, Oxford, 1969.

6. M. d'Ocagne, *Les grandes écoles de France*, Paris, 1873.

7. Napoleon quoted by J. Simon, *Réforme de l'enseignement populaire*, Paris, 1874.

8. A. Delfau, *Napoléon 1er et l'instruction publique*, Paris, 1902.

9. A. Aulard, *Napoléon 1er et le monopole universitaire*, Paris, 1911, p. 242.

10. According to Guizot's aim these schools 'enabled the lower classes of society to increase their output, to improve their living standards and thus to create new sources of wealth for the State'. F. Guizot, *Essais sur l'histoire et sur l'état actuel de l'instruction publique en France*, Paris, 1816, p. 4. At the same time this new form of multiple integration was specifically designed by the political elite to introduce 'the degree of expansion in popular education which the evolution of the occupational structure demanded and a stable society could accommodate'. J. Simon, *Victor Cousin*, Paris, 1910, p. 107.

11. See M. T. Hodgen, *Workers' Education in England and the United States*, London, 1925; M. Tylecote, *The Mechanics' Institutes of Lancashire and Yorkshire, before 1851*, Manchester, 1957.

12. Eric E. Rich, *The Education Act, 1870*, London, 1970, p. 63.

13. The Chairman of the Educational League declared at its founding meeting in 1869 that 'what we are going to do is this; by means of this League and its branches, we are going to rouse the people — in whom now, happily, is placed political power — in order that we may say to Mr. Forster, "Be our leader and give us what we want; we'll support you".' Quoted by J. W. Adamson, *English Education, 1789-1902*, Cambridge, 1964, pp. 350-51.

14. The Report of the Newcastle Commission (1861) had shown that 76 per cent of children in school attended Church of England schools. *Report of the Royal Commission on the State of Popular Education in England and Wales.* See also M. Cruickshank, *Church and State in English Education, 1870 to the Present Day*, London, 1963.

15. See K. M. Hughes, 'A Political Party and Education: Reflections on the Liberal Party's Educational Policy, 1870-1902', *British Journal of Educational Studies* vol. VIII, no. 2.

16. Typical of this process was the Newcastle Commission's recommendation that the English voluntary system should continue: equally revealing are the reasons Robert Lowe gave for this decision in 1861. 'In making that recommendation, the commissioners, so far as I can understand the case, express, I will not say the opinion of the whole country, or of philosophers, or of persons of great powers of abstract thought, *but they express the opinion of those to whom education in this country owes almost its existence — of those who gave both time and money to promote education* before the present system was called into being. If we have spent £4,800,000 in educating the people, private liberality has spent double that sum ... *So long as it is the opinion of those who contribute to the maintenance of the schools that the present system is the right and the best one, so long will the present system continue* ... it is not the intention of Government to infringe on the organic principles of the present system.' (My italics.) Quoted by D. Sylvester, *Robert Lowe and Education*, Cambridge, 1974, p. 59.

17. Thus, a radical like John Bright held that 'The fault of the Bill, in my mind, is that it has extended and confirmed the system which it ought in point of fact to have superseded . . . it was a Bill to encourage Denominational education, and where that was impossible, to establish Board Schools. It ought, in my opinion, to have been a Bill to establish Board Schools, and to offer inducements to those who were connected with Denominational schools to bring them under the control of that Privy Council.' John Bright, *Public Addresses*, London, 1879, pp. 201-202.

18. Eric Eaglesham, *From School Board to Local Authority*, London, 1956, p. 52.

19. Brian Simon, *Education and the Labour Movement 1870-1920*, London, 1965, p. 158f. The unpopularity of the School Boards with the Tory Party was exacerbated by the number which, like the London School Board, were captured by a socialist majority.

20. See E. C. Mack, *Public Schools and Political Opinion Since 1860*, New York, 1941.

21. Divide and rule appeared to be the tory strategy throughout the last decade of the century when it furthered the aims of the National Association for the Promotion of Technical Education (largely inspired by industrialists) as a weapon against the school boards. The Technical Instruction Act of 1889 and the whisky money encouraged this network at post-elementary level, that is outside the aegis of the boards. The technical definition of instruction was thus incorporated into the system and came under control of the local authorities in 1902.

22. See R. D. Roberts, *Eighteen Years of University Extension*, Cambridge, 1891.

23. V. A. McClelland, *English Roman Catholics and Higher Education, 1830-1903*, Oxford, 1973.

24. A. D. Hall and R. E. Hagen, 'Definition of a System', in Joseph A. Litterer (ed.), *Organizations, Systems, Control and Adaptation*, New York, 1969, vol. II, p. 36.

25. P. S. Cohen, *Modern Social Theory*, London, 1968, p. 229.

26. Hall and Hagen, loc. cit.

27. All to varying degrees lose something of their distinctiveness and autonomy upon incorporation. At the very least they have to concede things like school inspection, financial accountability and teacher certification. But the development of central agencies to undertake such tasks is jealously monitored by the networks and their political sponsors to ensure that their composition is as favourable as possible.

28. Napoleon quoted by L. Liard, op. cit., vol. II, p. 35.

29. Cf. M. Vaughan and M. S. Archer, *Social Conflict and Educational Change in England and France, 1789-1848*, Cambridge, 1971. See Chapters 8 and 10.

30. Cited in Antoine Prost, *L'Enseignement en France, 1800-1967*, Paris, 1968, p. 338.

31. Delfau, op. cit., p. 16.

32. A. Aulard, op. cit., p. 305f.

33. Eaglesham, op. cit., pp. 12-16.

34. The Taunton Commission had witnessed 'innumerable bodies of trustees continued in perpetuity, whose schools were submitted to no public test of an official kind, whose actions were virtually uncontrolled save by the terms of statutes'. Liberal attempts to undermine these predominantly Anglican strongholds, to rationalize their statutes and financing, and to exchange public support for central inspection and examination, met with severe opposition.

35. *Report from the Select Committee on Education, Science and Art (Administration)*, 1884, p. 399.

36. *Report of the Royal Commission on Secondary Education*, 1895, vol. I, p. 324.

37. A. S. Bishop, *The Rise of a Central Authority for English Education*, Cambridge, 1971, p. 262.

38. Ibid., p. 263, quoted from *The Times*, 16 February 1899.

39. Adamson, op. cit., p. 469.

40. Bishop, op. cit., p. 276.

41. Simon, op. cit., p. 103.

5. Structure:
state systems and new processes of change

1. Cf. A. Etzioni, *The Active Society*, London, 1968.

2. See Margaret S. Archer, 'Theorizing about the Expansion of Educational Systems', in her (ed.), *The Sociology of Educational Expansion: Take-off, Growth and Inflation in Educational Systems*, London and Beverly Hills, 1982. Especially note diagram on p. 16.

3. Cf. A. Gouldner, 'Reciprocity and Autonomy in Functionalist Theory', in N. J. Demerath and R. A. Peterson (eds), *System, Change and Conflict*, New York, 1967.

4. For example, concentration on technical subjects in a *realschool* can prevent its pupils from being qualified for higher education, early confessional schooling can lead to clashes in the definition of knowledge if pupils later transfer to secular establishments, and all higher levels of activities can be impeded by the pupils' preparation at lower ones.

5. In particular they treat all three groups — governing elites, external interest groups, and professional interest groups — as *undifferentiated* entities, when in reality each always displays a high level of sub-division (into parties, factions, associations, unions, confederations, institutes, etc.) and a good deal of internal conflict between them, which is also ignored here, although it is taken up in detail in the next two chapters. Secondly, the three types of groups have been presented as *distinct*, whereas in fact there is usually a substantial overlap between their members (e.g., teachers in politics, academics in industry, business representatives in Parliament, politicians with industrial interests, and company directors on governing bodies of universities), which is of considerable importance for educational change. Thirdly, the social environment has literally been reduced to these three kinds of groups and the broader influences of wider society have temporarily been neglected, in the sense that they are presumed to work through these agencies.

6. Interaction: educational negotiations

1. See P. M. Blau, *Exchange and Power in Social Life*, New York, 1964, especially ch. 4, 'Social Exchange'.

2. Ibid., ch. 5, 'Differentiation of Power'.

3. Margaret S. Archer and Salvador Giner, 'Social Stratification in Europe', in Archer and Giner (eds), *Contemporary Europe: Class, Status and Power*, London, 1971.

4. Power is conceptualized throughout this chapter in line with Steven Lukes, *Power: A Radical View*, London 1974. This finds the simple concentration on 'decision-making' (e.g., R. Dahl, *Who Governs? Democracy and Power in an American City*, New Haven, 1961), even when supplemented by the inclusion of 'non-decision-making' (e.g., P. Bachrach and M. S. Baratz, *Power and Poverty; Theory and Practice*, New York, 1970) essentially incomplete because they omit the structural bias exerted by the political system itself, which favours certain objective interests and represses others.

5. In fact, underlying *any* discussion of power is a recognition of the existence of some kind of political framework. Thus Dahl refers to the 'openness' and 'diversity' of pluralistic government (Dahl, op. cit., p. 93f.); Bacharach and Baratz talk variously of a 'decision-making arena', of covert conflict being 'outside the political arena', and of certain grievances being denied 'access to political processes (Bacharach and Baratz, op. cit., pp. 25-50); Lukes discusses how 'political systems' prevent demands from becoming political issues, or even being made. In other words, despite their completely different theoretical perspectives on power, all acknowledge the existence of an area which is distinctly 'political' (where issues, decisions, processes occur), and which has distinctive characteristics (like being open, or of restricted access or organized so as to repulse demands).

6. For *in practice* (alone) Dahl is right in asserting that where *change* is concerned, 'a political issue can hardly be said to exist unless it commands the attention of a significant segment of the political stratum', Dahl, op. cit., p. 92.

7. On the one hand, the constitutional framework of government can remain constant while elite relations vary — elites either increasing in solidarity or undergoing fragmentation as different issues become salient: on the other, unity between elites can remain unchanged while constitutional arrangements

are transformed. Not only does conceptual confusion arise if the two elements are conflated but also theoretical deficiencies result which weaken explanatory power. First, the individualistic error of reducing all statements about political structures to statements about political groups (A. F. Bentley, *The Process of Government*, Cambridge, Mass., 1967, p. 257, coined the phrase that where politics are concerned 'when the groups are adequately stated everything is stated') leads to a complementary neglect of the structural bias exerted by the political system itself, whose extensiveness, openness or hierarchical nature are essential to account for why 'some issues are organized into politics, while others are organized out', E. E. Schattschneider, *The Semi-Sovereign People*, New York, 1960, p. 71. Secondly, elite relations and activities cannot themselves be understood without reference to the framework of government (David Nicholls, *Three Varieties of Pluralism*, London, 1974, p. 24, said, 'group structure and activity in a particular State can be understood only in the context of the whole "political system" '). Factors like the method of attaining elite positions, the scope of elite action, the machinery at their disposal, the checks limiting their freedom of decision-making, all depend on the prior existence of a state framework which cannot itself be explained in terms of interaction among contemporary elites. Conflating the two usually constitutes a denial of the independent influence of the political structure and always precludes analysis of the interplay between structures and elites which is essential to an adequate theory of political manipulation.

8. More detail has been sacrificed in abridging this chapter than in most others. For interaction in twentieth-century England see SOES, pp. 472-612.

9. For a more detailed discussion see SOES, pp. 472-78.

10. See David Butler and Donald Stokes, *Political Change in Britain: the Evolution of Electoral Choice*, London, 1974; Samuel H. Beer, *Modern British Politics: A Study of Parties and Pressure Groups*, London, 1965; and George Sayer Bain, Robert Bacon and John Pimlott, 'The Labour Force', in A. H. Halsey (ed.), *Trends in British Society since 1900*, London, 1972; Henry Pelling, *A Short History of the Labour Party*, London, 1968, p. 11f.

11. See Guy Routh, *Occupation and Pay in Great Britain: 1906-60*, Cambridge, 1965, p. 106f.; A. L. Bowley, *Wages and Income in the United Kingdom since 1860*, Cambridge, 1937, ch. 4.

12. Asher Tropp, *The School Teachers*, London, 1957, esp. pp. 114-71; P. H. J. H. Gosden, *The Development of Educational Administration in England and Wales*, Oxford, 1966, p. 181f.; Harold Perkin, *Key Profession: The History of the Association of University Teachers*, London, 1969, p. 15f.; Graeme C. Moodie and Rowland Eustace, *Power and Authority in British Universities*, London, 1974; A. H. Halsey and M. A. Trow, *The British Academics*, London, 1971.

13. R. J. W. Selleck, *English Primary Education and the Progressives, 1914-1939*, London, 1972.

14. Michael Sanderson, *The Universities and British Industry, 1850-1970*, London, 1972.

15. Brian Simon, *Education and the Labour Movement, 1870-1920*, London, 1965, p. 309f.; W. W. Craik, *The Central Labour College*, London, 1964.

16. Tropp, op. cit., pp. 117-18.

17. H. A. L. Fisher, *The Place of the University in National Life*, Oxford, 1919, p. 6.

18. Thus averting the threat of state 'dirigism' which had formed part of Haldane's approach, see Eric Ashby and Mary Anderson, *Portrait of Haldane at Work on Education*, London, 1974, pp. 78, 100.

19. Lawrence Andrews, *The Education Act, 1918*, London, 1976.

20. R. H. Tawney, *Secondary Education for All*, London, 1922, pp. 83-84.

21. See SOES, pp. 478-83.

22. Maurice Cowling, *The Impact of Labour, 1920-24*, Cambridge, 1971; Ralph Miliband, *Parliamentary Socialism*, London, 1961, p. 148f.; Robert McKenzie and Alan Silver, *Angels in Marble*, London, 1968, p. 13f.; V. L. Allen, *Trade Unions and the Government*, London, 1960, p. 29f.; Henry Pelling, *A Short History of the Labour Party*, London, 1968, p. 140f.

23. Routh, op. cit., pp. 106-32; Bentley B. Gilbert, *British Social Policy 1914-1939*, London, 1970, chs 3, 5 and 6; Bowley, op. cit., pp. xviii-xix; Beer, op. cit., p. 333f.

24. William Taylor, *Society and the Education of Teachers*, London, 1969, p. 69f.; Tropp, op. cit., pp. 243-46; Norman Morris, 'England' in Albert A. Blum (ed.), *Teacher Unions and Associations, a Comparative Study*, Illinois, 1969.

25. James Murphy, *Church, State and Schools in Britain, 1800-1870*, London, 1971, p. 106.

26. Cf. W. A. C. Stewart, *The Educational Innovators*, London, 1968, vol. 2.

27. Simon, op. cit., pp. 141-42.

28. Sanderson, op. cit., pp. 250-53.

29. John Vaizey and John Sheehan, *Resources for Education*, London, 1968, p. 122.

30. Cf. Maurice Kogan and Tim Packwood, *Advisory Committees in Education*, London, 1974.

31. R. J. W. Selleck, *English Primary Education and the Progressives, 1914-1939*, op. cit., pp. 46-47.

32. Brian Simon, *The Politics of Educational Reform*, London, 1974, p. 63f.

33. Ibid., pp. 266-69.

34. David Rubinstein and Brian Simon, *The Evolution of the Comprehensive School, 1926-1966*, London, 1969, pp. 23-24.

35. The key phrase made it the duty of local authorities to offer 'such variety of instruction and training as may be desirable in view of their different ages, abilities and aptitudes, and of the different periods for which they may be expected to remain at school'. See H. C. Dent, *The Education Act 1944*, London, 1969, p. 13.

36. Ibid., p. 47.

37. SOES, pp. 483-87.

38. S. M. Miller, 'Comparative Social Mobility' in C. S. Heller (ed.), *Structured Social Inequality*, New York, 1969, pp. 325-40; Butler and Stokes, op. cit., pp. 177-82; Nigel Harris, *Competition and the Corporate Society: British Conservatives the State and Industry 1945-64*, London, 1972; S. E. Finer, 'The Political Power of Private Capital', pt 2, *Sociological Review*, vol. IV, no. 1, 1956.

39. H. F. Lydall, *British Incomes and Savings*, Oxford, 1955 and his 'The Long Term Trend in the Size of Distribution of Income', *Journal of the Royal Statistical Society*, series A, vol. 122, pt 1, 1959; F. W. Paish 'The Real Incidence of Personal Taxation', *Lloyds Bank Review*, 1957; H. F. Lydall and D. G. Tipping, 'The Distribution of Personal Wealth in Britain', *Bulletin of Oxford University Institute of Economics and Statistics, 1961*; Routh, op. cit., p. 106; Richard M. Titmuss, *Income Distribution and Social Change*, London, 1963.

40. Tropp, op. cit., pp. 252-61; Sanderson, op. cit., pp. 347-58.

41. Vaizey and Sheehan, op. cit., p. 107, also pp. 116-20. Half the pupils still at school, aged sixteen, were in independent establishments. In general, parental investment was plumped at transition points in the school career where it yielded the highest return.

42. It should be noted that the personal transactions just discussed did not serve individual class interests alone. The Industrial Fund for the Advancement of Scientific Education provided large grants in the mid 1950s for laboratories and equipment in direct grant and independent schools to increase the throughput of those enrolling for science degrees. Some firms also sponsored schoolboys through university to secure them afterwards.

43. B. Tipton, *Conflict and Change in a Technical College*, London, 1973, p. 19f.

44. P. E. P., *Graduates in Industry*, 1957, p. 43.

45. Audrey Collin, Anthony M. Rees and John Utting, *The Arts Graduate in Industry* (Acton Society Trust), London, 1962.

46. 'There has been a strong tendency through most of the present century to leave more and more of the question concerning the content of education to local authorities, schools, training colleges, area training organizations and the like. The amount of devolution of authority from the centre that has taken place here is not fully recognized.' Gosden, op. cit., p. 220.

47. Maurice Kogan, *The Government of Education*, London, 1971, p. 31. However, the establishment of a body equivalent to the General Medical Council was politically vetoed.

48. Maurice Kogan, *Education Policy Making: A Study of Interest Groups and Parliament*, London, 1975, p. 111; R. D. Coates, *Teachers Unions and Interest Group Politics*, Cambridge, 1972; R. A. Manzer, *Teachers and Politics: The Role of the National Union of Teachers in the Making of National Educational Policy in England and Wales since 1944*, Manchester, 1970.

49. Sanderson, op. cit., p. 358.

50. Harold Perkin, op. cit., p. 132.

51. Michael Locke, *Power and Politics in the School System*, London, 1974, p. 86f; Rodney Barker, *Education and Politics 1900-1951: A Study of the Labour Party*, London, 1972.

52. Rubinstein and Simon, op. cit., p. 73.

53. Caroline Benn and Brian Simon, *Half Way There*, Harmondsworth, 1972, p. 70.

54. Cumulatively their effects constitute and reconstitute the environments of one another over time. (E.g., the general rise in expertise, transmitted through instruction, steadily pushed the loci of external transactions up the educational system. This process gradually deserted the primary level, as it became essentially 'preparatory', and clustered around the new, later, terminal points: correspondingly internal initiation at the lower levels became much more untrammelled.) Conjointly their interplay shapes the contemporary context in which each takes place. (E.g., the increased volume of external transactions with the universities enabled much greater internal initiation within them.)

55. SOES, pp. 487-91.

56. Andrew Shonfield, *Modern Capitalism*, Oxford, 1965, p. 368f; Harris, op. cit., pp. 270-72; Butler and Stokes, op. cit., pp. 193-207.

57. S. Pollard and D. W. Crossley, *The Wealth of Britain*, London,

1968, ch. 9; Routh, op. cit., p. 133f.

58. Taylor, op. cit., pp. 83-92; Halsey and Trow, op. cit., p. 64f.

59. Murphy, op. cit., p. 124.

60. Sanderson, op. cit. Logically there is nothing mutually exclusive about internal initiation and external transactions, indeed 'the 60s also saw an unprecedented creation of administrative arrangements as linking mechanisms binding the Universities and industry more formally and more closely together than ever before' (p. 378).

61. Manzer, op. cit.

62. Perkin, op. cit., p. 223.

63. Benn and Simon, op. cit., p. 56.

64. The following section dealing with France has also undergone substantial abridging. For more detailed discussion of interaction see SOES, pp. 306-91.

65. For an extended discussion see SOES, pp. 312-16.

66. David Thomson, *Democracy in France since 1870*, London, 1964, p. 14.

67. Cf. J. Maurain, *La Politique Ecclésiatique du Second Empire de 1852-1869*, Paris, 1930.

68. Basically, the loi Falloux allowed any Frenchman over twenty-five to open a school providing he had five years teaching experience and possessed the *baccalauréat* or a diploma given by a departmental jury on which the bishop was influential. No qualifications were demanded of teachers and previous prohibitions on teaching orders were lifted.

69. Cf. R. D. Anderson, *Education in France 1848-70*, Oxford, 1975.

70. See SOES, pp. 284-306.

71. Paul Gerbod, *La Condition Universitaire en France au XIXᵉ Siècle*, Paris, 1965.

72. Cf. Georges Weill, *Histoire du Catholicisme en France 1828-1908*, Paris, 1925.

73. J. B. Piobetta, *Le Baccalauréat*, Paris, 1937.

74. For a more extended discussion see SOES, pp. 333-44.

75. Louis Legrand, *L'influence du positivisme dans l'oeuvre scolaire de Jules Ferry*, Paris, 1961.

76. John E. Talbott, *The Politics of Educational Reform in France 1918-40*, Princeton, 1969, p. 160.

77. See Luc Decaunes and M. L. Cavalier, *Réformes et Projets de Réforme de l'enseignement Français de la Révolution à nos jours (1789-1960)*, Paris, 1962, p. 125f.

78. Eckstein argues that pressure groups take on the same structure as the organizations they seek to influence. Harry Eckstein, *Pressure Group Politics*, Stanford, 1960.

79. James M. Clark, *Teachers and Politics in France*, Syracuse, N.Y., 1967.

80. 'Under the IVth Republic the summit of party ambition was to win a share of power rather than to exercise it outright. One way to achieve this was to outbid one's rivals for the support of a clientèle — Gaullists against Conservatives against MRP over the Catholic Schools, Communists against Socialists against Radicals on behalf of secular education — and each against all for the favours of home-distillers, ex-service men, peasants or small shopkeepers.' P. H. Williams and M. Harrison, *Politics and Society in de Gaulle's Republic*, London, 1971, p. 144.

81. Lipset has tried to show how, in parallel, the overlapping of these

cleavages produced such a complex configuration of political parties. S. M. Lipset, *The First New Nation*, London, 1964.

82. Henry W. Ehrman, 'French Bureaucracy and Organized Interests', *Administrative Science Quarterly*, vol. V, 1961, p. 547.

83. See SOES, pp. 360-70.

84. M. Prélot, *Pour Comprendre la nouvelle Constitution*, Paris, 1958; Maurice Duverger, *La Vᵉ République*, Paris, 1959 and *Institutions Politiques et Droit Constitutionnel*, Paris, 1970; Jean Blondel, *Contemporary France; Politics, Society and Institutions*, London, 1972. On the growth of the Gaullist Party organization see Jean Charlot, *L'UNR. Etude du Pouvoir au sein d'un Parti Politique*, Paris, 1967.

85. Catholic support continued: De Gaulle received four times the number of votes from practising Catholics in the 1965 presidential elections than from those with no religious affiliations, while Mitterrand gained nine times more votes from agnostics and aetheists than from Catholics. Pierre Avril, *Politics in France*, 1969, p. 261.

86. 'La réforme de M. Berthoin . . . réalise en effet ce qui peut l'être des écoles moyennes, si l'on veut ménager les corporatismes rivaux.' Antoine Prost, *L'Enseignement en France, 1800-1967*, Paris, 1968, p. 422.

87. For an analysis of the participants in the May events see Margaret S. Archer, 'France' in Archer (ed.), *Students, University and Society*, London, 1972.

88. Jacques Fournier, *Politique de l'Education*, Paris, 1971, p. 61.

89. Jean Maynaud, *Les Groupes de Pression en France*, Paris, 1957.

90. Dorothy Pickles, *The Government and Politics of France*, vol. I, London, 1972, p. 262.

91. Gordon Smith, *Politics in Western Europe*, London, 1972, p. 71.

7. Structural elaboration:
patterns and products of change

1. Space precludes any detailed discussion of substantive changes here. See SOES, pp. 639-69 for France and pp. 704-75 for England.

2. Bearing in mind the universal deterrents to speedy political redirection of education which have just been discussed, the circumstances leading to protracted stasis can be specified more closely. Given an accessible polity, the quicker the alternation of majority governments, the shorter the period between polity-directed educational changes. Conversely, if the same governing elite remains in office, if parliamentary parties lock in immobilism or produce weak centrist coalitions, stasis will be prolonged (the latter being the story of the Fourth Republic). Given an inaccessible polity the quicker the succession of elite factions dominating decision-making or the more dramatic the changes in domestic or foreign circumstances, the faster polity-directed changes will succeed one another in education. Conversely, a durable elite and a stable political environment will foster educational continuity.

3. The clearest example of this is found in the post-Stalinist period in the USSR where Soviet leadership hunted for a compromise formula to resolve the tension between the use of education to produce socialist society and to service the planned economy. Elite composition meant that polity has leaned first

towards the one, then the other — with the oscillation of compromise being the dominant theme of the last three decades.

4. Often this straightforward dread of losing control is not confessed but is concealed behind an *étatist* ideology which stresses the positive connections between uniformity and social justice, standardization and national integration, or identity and geographical mobility.

5. For a detailed analysis of the May events see Margaret S. Archer, 'France' in Archer (ed.), *Students, University and Society*, London, 1972.

6. This has become rather a common pattern in contemporary France. See Margaret S. Archer, 'Education' in John Flower (ed.), *France Today*, London, 1983, 5th revised ed.

7. Obviously, as in any sort of dealing, there is some room for manoeuvre — for vendors to oversell their products and to try to tell the buyer what he wants, and for purchasers to be blinded by status considerations rather than guided by their practical requirements. Both were true of relations between industry and the English universities at different times in the twentieth century.

8. Incidentally this also works in reverse, when a particular kind of external transaction stops, either through lack of money or political embargo, the system loses one source of diversity. Thus, for example, the worsening finances of the established church and most other denominations has meant a gross diminution of a religious definition of instruction in England, with the exception of Catholic schooling.

9. 'The unco-ordinated development of primary and secondary, further and university education, and of different categories of schools and colleges has always tended to make the pattern of English Education complicated and overlapping.' H. C. Dent, *1870-1970 Century of Growth in English Education*, London, 1970, p. 125.

10. To Jules Ferry, 'quand nous parlons d'une action de l'état dans l'éducation, tendant à maintenir l'unité, nous attribuons à l'état le seule rôle qu'il puisse avoir en matière d'enseignement et d'éducation. Il s'en occupe pour maintenir une certaine morale d'état, certaines doctrines d'état qui importent à sa conservation', cited by M. Reclus, *Jules Ferry, 1832-1893*, Paris, 1946, p. 174. Equally, 'L'unité d'éducation est essentiellement conçue comme un instrument de fusion morale et affective et comme le moyen de vulgariser l'idéal republicain', cited by Louis Legrand, *L'influence de Positivism dans l'oeuvre scolaire de Jules Ferry*, Paris, 1961, p. 188.

11. Special education ,'écartait . . . l'élément veritablement professionnel, en d'autres termes la préparation à un métier, l'apprentissage d'un état agricole, industriel et commercial', F. Buisson, *L'Enseignement Primaire Supérieure et Professionnel*, Paris, 1887, p. 11.

12. 'The logic of the French Educational System seemed to have no room for an education which was secondary in spirit but too short and practical to fit into the traditional secondary pattern', R. D. Anderson, *Education in France 1848-1870*, Oxford, 1975, p. 218.

13. 'Former le producteur, l'enseignement française y repugne. Son rationalisme tourne à l'intellectualisme', Antoine Prost, *L'Enseignement en France 1800-1967*, Paris, 1968, p. 340.

14. 'Ces mésures restent fragmentaire et ne modifient pas la physionomie générale de l'enseignement public. Aucune d'entre elles n'annonce la refonte d'ensemble que les circonstances et l'évolution technique et sociale réclament

impérieusement depuis des années.' Luc Decaunes and M. L. Cavalier, *Réformes et Projets de Réformes, de l'enseignement Français de la Révolution à nos jours (1789-1960)*, Paris, 1962, p. 154.

15. W. R. Frazer, *Reforms and Restraints in Modern French Education*, London, 1971, p. 131f.

16. See P. Bourdieu and J-C. Passeron, *Les Héritiers*, Paris, 1964 and *La Reproduction*, Paris, 1970.

17. University reform was 'dans la forme comme au fond, d'essence technocratique: dans la forme car il s'agit d'imposer plus que d'inciter, et la centralization demeure la règle', Jacques Fournier, *Politique de l'Education*, op. cit., p. 184.

18. The 'freedom of the individual school makes it difficult for a national policy of education to be formulated and carried through', Maurice Kogan, *The Government of Education*, London, 1971, p. 32.

19. Although this was the dominant tendency, morphogenesis must not be elevated to the status of an automatic or inevitable process; for in the course of development some elements were killed and remained permanently excluded from twentieth-century education.

20. Where comprehensive reorganization was concerned, 'the total approach was uneven and unsystematic and suffered from the lack of any real "central guidance" ', Caroline Benn and Brian Simon, *Half Way There*, Harmondsworth, 1972, p. 72.

8. Conclusion: prospects for change

1. Jacques Fournier, *Politique de l'Education*, Paris, 1971.

APPENDICES

APPENDIX 1

Extended diagrams of interaction in centralized and decentralized systems

The two diagrams which follow represent expanded versions of Figures 4 and 5 (Chapter 5) and form the basis of the patterns of interaction discussed in Chapter 6. The expanded diagrams break up each of the three basic categories (governing elites, professional and external interest groups) into sub-divisions and show the kind of interplay which can take place between them in the course of educational interaction (see Chapter 5, note 5). The sub-units (I-1, I-2, I-3'/P-1'/E-1') which figure in them do not represent specific social institutions, actual political parties, or particular professional associations. Similarly, the relationships depicted do not portray current events in any given society. Each such relationship is illustrated once only, for clarity of presentation, and then only if it is a fairly common occurrence.

Neither of the diagrams approximates to models of empirical reality. The latter would be numerous and varied in their actual patterning of relationships over time: in any society at any given point in time, some relationships may be found in greater profusion than shown here, while others may be lacking altogether. Instead of modelling empirical reality, the two diagrams are intended to be of heuristic and theoretical utility in understanding the patterns of interaction common to all instances of centralized and decentralized systems respectively. Without stylization and abstraction there would be little possibility of generalization and theory formation. However, a few practical examples of the relations depicted follow the first diagram in order to show the kind of flesh which covers its bones.

DIAGRAM 1
Educational interaction in a centralized system

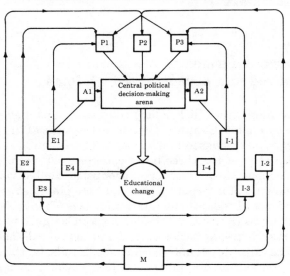

KEY

P = Political party or faction
I = External interest group
A = Advisory committee or council
E = Professional interest group
M = General public

Patterns of interaction — illustration

E1 — P1	A teachers' union affiliated to a political party.
E1 — A1	Educational advisory committees to government with strong professional representation.
E3 — I3 — P3	The alliance between denominational teachers, their church and a sectarian political party.
E4	Internal initiation to advance professional interests.
I1 — P3	A trade union or business federation affiliated to a political party.
I2 — M — E2 — P1	A pressure group of an agricultural organization, farming parents, rural school-teachers, and a political party sponsoring agricultural interests.
I4	External transactions between industry and the private sector of education.
M — P1, P2, P3	The general public voting, mandating or otherwise influencing political parties or factions.

DIAGRAM 2
Educational interaction in a decentralized system

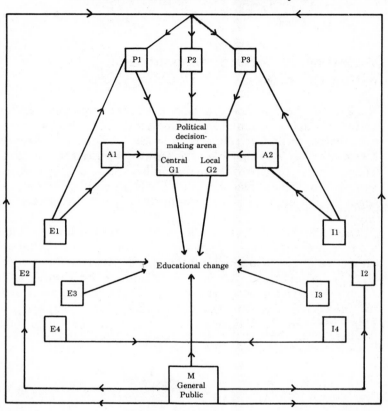

KEY

P = Political party or faction
G = Government body or authority
I = External institutional interest
    group

A = Advisory council or committee
E = Professional educational
    interest group
M = General public

APPENDIX 2

Variations in political manipulation within centralized educational systems

Neither of the two factors held principally responsible for variability in political manipulation within centralized systems manifested *their* full range of possible variation in French history, which was the sole case study presented in the text. These two factors are (i) the penetrability of the political centre *and* elite relations inside it, and (ii) the superimposition *and* organization of supportive or oppositional interest groups in education.

Together these represent the parallelogram of forces which are responsible for specific patterns of interaction and different outcomes of political manipulation in all centralized systems. Hence the following diagram supplements the French case study with further permutations of the above factors, drawn from the Soviet and Japanese experiences, in an attempt to provide a more complete (though very schematic) picture of their interplay and effects.

DIAGRAM 3
Variations in political manipulation within centralized systems

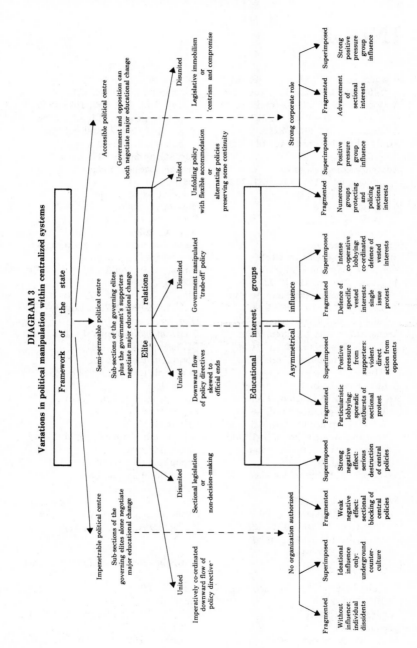

INDEX